AF084540

FRUIT FOR LIFE

A friendly guide
to growing fruit organically

by
Tim Foster

eco-logic books

Tim Foster

timfostergardener@gmail.com

First published in 2019
Fourth Reprint 2023

Copyright © text and illustrations: Tim Foster 2019

ISBN 978-1-899233-26-7

All rights reserved. No part of this publication may be reproduced or transmitted in any form or by any means, electronic or mechanical, including photocopy, recording or any information storage and retrieval system, without permission in writing from the copyright holder.

Further copies of Fruit for Life can be ordered from
www.eco-logicbooks.com

Cover illustration: 'Fruits Tree'

" The daubing of trees with lime, sulphur, tar, or caustic mixtures, proclaims to all visitors that there is something wrong, and it is more frequently in the gardener than in the trees. "

George Glenny (1878)

in

'The Culture of Fruits and Vegetables'

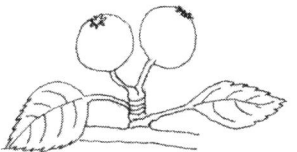

CONTENTS

Introduction 6

Layout of Chapters 7

Apples 15

Apricots 39

Blackberries 45

Blackcurrants 52

Blueberries 63

Cherries 69

Damsons 77

Figs 81

Gooseberries 88

Grapes 96

Hybrid Berries 105

Kiwis 109

Medlars 115

Mulberries 119

Peaches 123

Pears 130

Plums 138

Quinces 147

Raspberries	153
Redcurrants	164
Rhubarb	169
Strawberries	176
Other Fruit	187
Growing Systems	193
Tools	199
Planting	206
Feeding	211
Pruning	219
Pollination	238
Thinning	247
Storage of Fresh Fruit	250
Propagation	254
Weeding	262
Pests and Diseases Lists	263
Glossary	266
Bibliography	269
Index	271
Acknowledgements and Thanks	279

INTRODUCTION

Somehow, after all these years, a few things appear to be falling into place. How plants react to my gardening efforts is not one of them: plants seem determined to defy my intentions especially when pruning.

What seems to be a little clearer is a feeling for the soil – an understanding might be going too far. This has developed from learning, albeit a tiny amount, about the web of creatures in the soil and its effect on plants. And it is a feeling about what is right and decent.

When we want to grow our own food it now seems to me only right that we respect these organisms by not killing them, via chemicals and cultivations, and by letting them help us. It makes the clearest sense to use a system that enables food production which is non-destructive and self-sustaining, not our current agricultural policy which supports soil exploitation and intensive chemical use, with knock-on effects to us and the environment. This all translates into the simple term **no-dig, organic**.

The easiest way of achieving this is to grow plants which don't need replacing each year – no soil cultivation is required with perennial plants. There are some perennial vegetables, but the vast majority of food perennials are fruit plants. On top of that, there is little in this world to surpass the joy and exhilaration of eating fresh, clean, nutritious, delicious, ripe fruit straight from the plant. So there.

Fruit breeders have, over the millennia, provided us with a wide selection of impressively large fruits, accounting for their popularity over most native and unselected species. That doesn't mean we shouldn't tuck in to appropriate plants in the countryside or chosen to be part of a forest garden, for example – quite the opposite: these provide us with an even wider selection of unusual and tasty fruits in a 'natural' setting. It is just that, in terms of productivity and the range of variants, it is hard to beat the bred versions of the fruits discussed in this book.

'Fruit' is a technical term. It should mean 'a structure developed from particular flower parts; a structure that houses, protects and helps distribute the seed'. There might be a certain number of liberties that have been taken. Sorry.

LAYOUT OF CHAPTERS

This book is divided into two sections: fruit chapters and important fruit-related topics. In most cases, the latter are there because there needed to be plenty of explanation which couldn't be fitted into individual fruit chapters. As it is, 'Apples' went a bit out of control. Each fruit chapter starts with the essentials and is really quite serious. Then, as we continue, there are more useful parts but it also starts to fall apart into frivolous nonsense. Splendid.

The Name
Chapters are in alphabetical order of common name. It seemed most sensible at the time.

The family name (written in capitals) indicates the general grouping of the fruit in question, and plants in a particular family are related, often with similar features such as flower parts. Interestingly, many of the fruits covered are in the same family, the rose family, ROSACEAE.

The 'genus' is the part of a plant name which denotes a particular group of plants within the family. For example, *Malus* is all of the apples including wild, crab and cultivated types. The second part of a name, the species name or specific epithet, is a narrowing down of a genus, so one species of apple is *Malus domestica*.

Why we should grow……?
Hopefully this paragraph, at the beginning of each fruit chapter, will help you decide whether it is worth bothering or not. There are lots of reasons: the appearance, the flavour, the nutritional content, the challenge.

Explanation of Fruit Essentials
'Essentials' is an attempt to give a condensed version of everything you need to know. Inevitably, it fails and there has to be further elaboration (found later in the chapter or, if so much information is required, in a separate chapter altogether).

Varieties
The word 'variety' actually means a naturally occurring variation of a particular species. The word 'cultivar' (**culti**vated **var**iety) means a variation which has been found, encouraged, propagated or generated in a garden or

nursery or similar non-natural situation, such as the apple 'Cox's Orange Pippin'. So you can see that throughout this book we should be using the word 'cultivar'. Guess which word we are going to use (yes, 'variety', simply because that's what everyone else does and I wouldn't want to upset anyone – much).

The varieties (told you) that are listed under each particular fruit can never be complete, either because of the sheer number of them out there – this is a modest volume – and the constant arrival of new varieties. Still, those selected are proven or promising or have some extremely fascinating feature.

Size

The size of fruit trees is dictated by the rootstock onto which they are attached, so there is enlightening discussion of the properties of some of the various rootstocks available. See also 'Propagation' to (try to) understand why this is necessary. The size of soft fruit bushes is dependent on the particular species and varieties.

Spacing

This is strongly related to size. If plants are put in too closely they will compete and yields will be reduced. Too widely spaced and yields per plant will be good but might not be the best yield per unit area: that translates as a waste of space. However, there are reasons for going for those wider spacings, notably an improved air movement and resulting health benefits, and even growing other (low) plants in between.

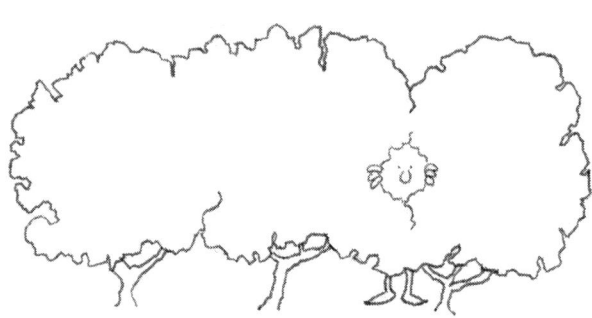

Pollination

Most plants in nature won't self pollinate – they cross pollinate. They try to mix genetic material by exchanging pollen with different plants of the same species.

If this is already sounding complicated prepare to be baffled further by reading the chapter on pollination. Suffice it to say that, here, all we need to know is if the plant in question actually needs a second plant for cross pollination in order to get fruit. If it says 'self fertile' it doesn't, and you can have just one plant all by itself, cropping happily. To contradict that slightly, you will often get better yields if there is actually more than one plant – different varieties, of course.

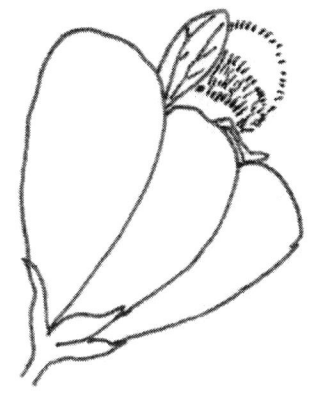

Position

Some species of fruit must be given certain positions, normally relating to aspect (north, south, east or west facing), which dictates not only the amount of sun they get but shelter too. It can also relate to soil but, for virtually all of the fruits in this book the recommendation for soil is 'moisture-retentive, free-draining'. If the pH of the soil isn't mentioned then it will be around the optimum for many plants, 6.5. There are notable exceptions.

Plants which tolerate a range of conditions can be used to your advantage to, perhaps, stagger ripening times: a fruit bush in a shady place will fruit slightly later than it will in a warm, sunny place.

Feeding

Plants lose nutrients if we take fruit from them. They will also lose them if we prune, pinch out or generally muck about with them. It is worthwhile emphasising that we feed plants not only to keep them healthy but, in the case of the plants in this book, to feed ourselves with the maximum levels of minerals, vitamins and a range of other beneficial compounds such as antioxidants: fruit plants that are deficient will produce lower yields and fruit of lower nutrition for us.

On a regular basis, applications of bulky organic matter, especially compost, will be the ideal since it does much more than supply nutrients. However, depleted soils may benefit from a source of concentrated nutrients, popularly known as 'fertilisers' and they can be homemade or bought in. The latter, for organic growers, will have come from living organisms, with a range suitable for those with a conscience about the exploitation of animals, as well as some for meat-eaters. There is a lot more information in the chapter 'Feeding'.

Pruning

Unless something exceptional has happened, this will just be a summary and the detail will come later in the chapter. There is a whole separate chapter looking at the pruning of fruit trees.

Most pruning depends on when a plant initiates its flowers: for example, if flowers (and hence fruit) are initiated in spring / early summer for the following year then none of the new growth that follows in that summer will have flowers next spring – it wasn't around at the right time. That initiation is purely setting up the potential to have flowers and fruit and will be taking place at the same time as the current season's fruits are forming. The 'potential' means that there are lot of other things that can stop us getting fruit. This could include not having a chilling requirement satisfied during the following winter: most fruit plants need a certain number of 'cold hours', hours below 7°C, before the flowers that have been initiated can continue to develop. Once they have developed and actually open then brace yourself for a whole cloud of flies trying to get into the ointment: frost, wet and windy weather, pests and diseases.

If initiation has taken place as early as spring / early summer then theoretically any of the new growth that follows can be pruned off with no ill effects on next years crop, such as most apples (this is actually the case with espaliers and cordons).

Initiation later in the year means that fruit could potentially form on the new growth so that its removal would be inadvisable, such as blackcurrants.

Weeding

It stands to reason that if you stick two plants closely together, there will be competition for water, nutrients and light. This can be overcome by providing lots of water and nutrients (perhaps not light) or by removing one of the plants. In some respects, if the plants are the same species (in other words, we've planted our fruit bushes too closely) then it is worse because they are after exactly the same resources. Weeds, though, are often not productive, certainly not in the way we would like (in actual fact, there is barely a weed that doesn't have a use: culinary, medicinal, even physical). The extent of the effect of weeds depends on many factors, not least the age of the fruit plant, the kind of fruit plant, the species of weed, the proximity of the plants, the soil type, and so on. In the end it often just boils down to 'Weeds? – bad, get rid of them'.

Harvesting

When and how, basically. This is where we have the upper hand by growing our own – we can harvest when the fruit is fully ripe and at its most scintillating, unlike the supermarket stuff often picked under-ripe to last longer and survive the transporting. Exceptions include some apples and pears which have to be picked early to then gradually ripen in store.

Propagation

Often this is given purely out of interest since it is at the limits of most of our capabilities, not in skill but tools and material. In other words, budding and grafting is perfectly achievable but where do we get appropriate rootstocks etc. and a bit of instruction? Most fruit trees are started this way. Fruit bushes and strawberries, on the other hand, are really quite easy – and successful.

More detail is given in a separate chapter with extra handy bits hidden away in 'Discussion' of individual fruits.

Origins

The only reason for including this is out of mild curiosity. It does also give us a bit of an idea what sort of conditions / climate a fruit has adapted to.

If a country of origin is tropical it is unlikely that a fruit will grow well outside on an allotment in Wolverhampton, hence the remit of this book is to look only at fruit from which there is a chance of getting some produce outdoors. In some cases, in some parts of the UK, it may be necessary to provide some shelter.

Nutrition

Most of the fruits in this book have similar quantities of protein (low) at around 1g/100g (e.g. apples); pears and plum relatives are lower, around 0.5g/100g. Strangely, raspberries are highest at 1.4g/100g.

Fat is very low, in the range 0.1-0.2g/100g. Almost all carbohydrate is present in these fruits as sugars, with compound berries such as loganberries, blackberries and raspberries at the lower end (around 4g/100g) up to grapes at the higher end (over 15g/100g) – now you know the reason for the popularity of the latter for winemaking.

BLUEBERRY MAN

The biggest variations between fruits tend to be with vitamins such as vitamin C: blackcurrants have splendid levels (up to 200mg/100g) unparalleled by any other temperate fruit, followed by kiwi fruit (over 100mg/100g) and strawberries (70mg/100g). Something we don't often think about is the variation within a species; apples have an average of 6mg/100g but some varieties can be as high as 30mg/100g.

Minerals also vary a bit. Iron, for example, is (surprisingly?) 1.6mg/100g for mulberries - about the same as curly kale – and a pitiful 0.2mg/100g for apples. But then we'll eat a lot more apples than mulberries. Occasionally a fruit will have other notable properties such as antioxidant levels.

Botany
The technical definition of a fruit is a structure that has developed to house the seeds and has originated from the ovary in the flower.

A minor problem we have is that some fruits don't quite fit that (apples, strawberries, etc.) and one or two that don't *remotely* fit that (rhubarb). On top of that there are plants that produce botanically-correct fruits that are not included simply because we regard them as 'vegetables' – tomatoes, peas and beans, squash, etcetera. Blimey.

Discussion / rambling / elaboration
This is a shambling compost-heap of nonsense hiding some useful information, some vaguely related stimulating facts and an expansion of some of the points already begun in the essentials section. Read this when it is too miserable outside to do any gardening and there is no decent novel to hand.

It does include, usually towards the end:
Plant Problems
It is not an aim of this book to concentrate too much on the negative, and a section on Problems is going to be a bit of a downer. However, it is important to know what is happening to our plants even if we don't want to do anything about it. How these problems are dealt with is a major feature of organic growing – clearly, none of us want to ingest toxins (a.k.a. pesticide sprays) but some of us are happy to ignore that in order to try to solve issues with fruit-growing. Personally, I think it is worth the sacrifice of potentially reduced yields, or of the extra effort required, to avoid this. We already have dozens of artificial chemicals in our bodies simply from trying to exist in the modern world and I'd prefer not to add to them if possible.

In addition to us, there should be the equal consideration of the effect on our fellow creatures of using chemicals to control pests and diseases. In many cases, pesticides begin a vicious circle: predators of pests are killed in the attempt to wipe out a pest, meaning that there is no natural control when it is required to deal with a further infestation.

In the separate chapter 'Pests and Diseases', for those of you with that kind of mind, the scientific names of the ailments noted in the fruit chapters are provided. For the rest of us, avoid this section like the plague (*Yersinia pestis*).

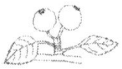

APPLES *Malus domestica*
(*Malus*, L. for apple, *domestica*, domesticated)
Family: ROSACEAE

Why we should grow apples
Maybe the question should be 'what possible reason can you give for not growing apples?'

Apple Essentials
Varieties: There are estimated to be over 6,000 varieties of cultivated / named apples worldwide, about half of which are in the UK's national collection at Brogdale. A separate section in this chapter is devoted to descriptions of a range of apples selected entirely with prejudice and bias, based on their flavour and the ability to grow them easily organically.

Size: Extremely variable depending on the rootstock to which they have been grafted. Choice of rootstocks is usually from the following (in increasing size): M27 (1.2-1.8m/4-6'), M9 (1.8-2.4m/6-8'), M26 (2.4-3.5m/8-12'), MM106 (4.5-5m/15-18'), MM111 or M25 (both above 6m/20').

Spacing: Depends again on the rootstock and the pruning system. For example, if the tree was developed into a lollipop shape, the spacings would be about the same as the height of the tree for each rootstock. Cordons and Spindlebush shapes would be a lot closer: 75cm/2 1/2' and 1.8-2.2m/6-7' respectively.

Position : Half a day's sun would be nice. Not as fussy as pears but too shady a spot will affect yield and fruit quality. The other side of that is that if too sheltered a position is used, a tree may not receive enough cold in the winter to promote flowers.

Feeding: The smallest trees ironically need the most attention. Feed with compost annually as well as liquid feeds high in potassium, in the spring.

Pruning: Remove whole branches to keep the framework open and well-spaced.

Pollination: In most cases, a single tree should have a mate nearby which is a different variety and flowers at the same time. For more details (lots) see the chapter on 'Pollination'.

Apple Origins

According to Roger Deakin in 'Wildwood', possibly the best book ever written (even better than this one), apples originated in Kyrgystan and adjacent countries. An adjacent country is Kazahkstan which is also attributed by many as being the source. Apple source. How and when they made it to this country is also subject to some conjecture. The main hindrance to the easy spread of apples is the fact that to capture and reproduce a particular variety requires vegetative propagation, specifically grafting: saving and sowing seeds gives too much variation.

Apple Nutrition

Apples have a water content around the average for most fruit at about 84% and of the remainder about 11% is sugar (sucrose and fructose). The 5% left covers protein, fibre, fat, vitamins and minerals (none of them spectacular in quantity but still there nonetheless) plus tannins and in the region of 250 different alcohols, aromatics and volatile compounds that contribute to each variety's particular flavour. When one tastes some modern varieties, one wonders where the other 249 have gone to.

Vitamin C average for apples is about 6mg/100g but with considerable variation: 'Ribston Pippin', for example, exceeds 30mg/100g and the miserable 'Golden Delicious' contains 3mg/100g. In comparison, blackcurrants contain around 200mg/100g.

Botany

The apple is technically a false fruit called a 'pome': the core, containing the seeds, has developed from the ovary in a flower, yet the majority of the fruit has developed from a part of the flower called the receptacle. As with most flowers of the plants in this book, the apple flower is bisexual (male and female parts in one structure).

Discussion / rambling / elaboration
Introduction to Apples

I have a strong affinity with apples, mainly through assorted female ancestry. One grandmother's maiden name was Bramley. My other grandmother married Albert Smith who was my fearsome (when I was young) grandfather, so eventually she became Granny Smith. Her daughter, my mother, was named Alma, a relatively unusual name which most people will have instantly spotted as being Hungarian for apple (there is also a variety called 'Mother'). With that kind of pedigree, her daughter, my sister, should've at least been called Cox's Orange Pippin. You were dashed lucky there, Braeburn, I mean Lindsay.

The effect of weather on a crop

We're probably aware of the problems of poor weather at blossom time but what comes afterwards can also have a considerable impact. To investigate this it is worthwhile knowing that an apple consists of about 85% water. It is exceptionally useful to also know that the 'structure' of an apple is formed in the first six weeks following pollination / fertilisation. From then onwards most growth is made by the cells taking up water and expanding. That doesn't mean that the products of photosynthesis aren't required – the fruit gets sweeter as they mature – but water supply is very important later in the growing season. Therefore the ideal weather conditions for a good apple crop are as follows:

April and May: Calm, warm, dry (for pollination)

(May) June (July):   Hot, plenty of sunshine (for apple building: photosynthesis)

July - August: Warm, plenty of rain (for apple inflating)

August - September: Sunshine (for skin colouring / ripening) and calm (to reduce windfalls)

October - March: Some cold weather. This is to promote development of flowers that were initiated the previous spring/summer: apples need over 900 hours below 7°C. That is why apples don't thrive in the tropics.

If nothing else, this programme might suggest why things weren't perfect in any given year and you can then blame it on the weather. It does also give you one small opportunity to influence things: you may not be able to increase outside temperatures and light levels but it is possible to irrigate in prolonged very dry weather especially in July and August.

Choosing Apple Cultivars / Varieties

There are many issues surrounding the choosing of a variety to the point that, after reading this, you'll throw your hands in the air and shout 'I only wanted an (expletive) apple!' Well, I can't accommodate your tantrums so here's a list regardless:

1) Local or national or international
2) Yield
3) Pest and disease resistance
4) Flavour
5) Biennial (see 'Pollination')
6) Texture
7) Size of fruit
8) Keeping potential / storage
9) Shape of tree
10) Interesting names
11) Time of ripening
12) Usage: dessert / cooker / cider
13) Shape and uniformity of fruit
14) Ornamental value especially blossom
15) Pollination compatibility

This modest volume should be impartial when it comes to such things as this and I shall stand steadfast as an open-minded, unbiased commentator (though I would quite like to say that 'Pink Lady' is one of the most execrable fruits ever foisted on the public purely, it seems, to satisfy supermarket demands). All it takes is a modicum of restraint.

Any single variety will encompass a number of these points but only you can prioritise them. For example, at the top of my personal preferences is flavour – there seems to be little point growing a fruit unless you really enjoy the taste. My favourite apples are those which are juicy and sweet but they must also have the complex aromatic flavours typified by 'Cox's Orange Pippin'. There are wonderful varieties with hints of other fruits such as 'Pitmaston Pine Apple' with distinct, yes, pineapple flavours.

Anyway, it is the richness of flavour that is missing in most of our modern varieties. These have been chosen for reasons other than flavour, specifically uniformity, yield, transport and ease of cropping.

Uniformity is important to growers who have to supply supermarkets which reject produce at the drop of a hat: they want everything in a display to look identical. For us growing our own, this has to be pretty near the bottom of the list. Yield is, however, important to us – there is little point choosing a splendidly-flavoured apple if you hardly get any fruit. Though perhaps yield doesn't have to be above everything else.

So breeders, growers and supermarkets have colluded to produce and sell the 'perfect apple' which many people enjoy, partly, it is sad to say, because they've never tried anything else. They are crisp, juicy and sweet (or are supposed to be – there are some dire specimens of 'Gala' out there) but they miss any flavour that could be described as 'interesting'. If you enjoy boiled sweets you'll probably be very happy with 'Pink Lady'. Another reason to be a bit grumpy about modern commercial varieties is that you can't grow them even if you wanted to: 'Golden Delicious' and 'Granny Smith' are not grown in the UK because conditions aren't good enough, whereas you are not allowed to grow 'Pink Lady' (phew) by the holders of the patent – they reckon it would get a bad name (!) if it was grown in the 'inferior conditions' of a UK climate. 'Braeburn' and 'Gala' can be grown in the UK but huge numbers of them are grown cheaply abroad.

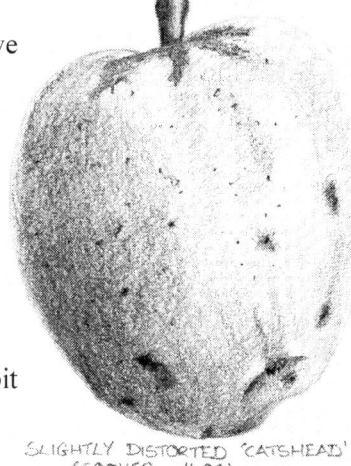
SLIGHTLY DISTORTED 'CATSHEAD' (COOKER c1600)

The only ways you can get to know whether a particular variety will be the best flavour for you is by reading a description (and taking a chance) or, preferably, by tasting them. Some wholefood shops have small batches of unusual varieties – organic growers tend to veer away from the high-input commercial varieties. Then there is the Apple Day: orchards, community groups and fruit collections in increasing numbers have open days in October to celebrate Apple Day, frequently with tasting sessions. Give it a go.

Also near the top of my list when choosing a variety is pest and disease resistance. When planting a new tree it is an opportunity to save yourself plenty of angst later on by choosing a variety that is able to thrive without attacks from pests and diseases, particularly the latter.

The three main diseases (see in more detail later) are all fungal. Scab (affecting leaves and fruit) and canker (affecting bark and branches) are more likely in wet parts of the country whereas powdery mildew (leaves and shoot tips) appears in drier areas. In a way, this links up with whether to choose local / national varieties since varieties local to you are still in existence because they cope with the climate near you and should be resistant. There is an apple local to you, from 'Clydesdale' to 'Cornish Gilliflower'.

Having said all of that, certain varieties are so wonderful that it might still be worth trying them especially if you can provide the optimum soil conditions and best aspect. 'Cox's Orange Pippin' is a good example: apparently, if it wasn't for the fact that a good proportion of the population still knows of and requests 'Cox's Orange Pippin', commercial growers would never grow it again. However, many excellent, resistant varieties have 'Cox's Orange Pippin' as a parent to provide the terrific flavour, the other parent providing the robustness e.g. the offspring 'Winston' and 'Laxton's Superb'. Incidentally, 'Cox's Orange Pippin' was grown from a pip by a brewer from Bermondsey called Richard Cox around 1830. That pip came from a 'Ribston Pippin' – the other parent, providing the pollen, is unknown. 'Ribston Pippin' was itself grown from a pip around 1680.

Here is a selection of varieties with good flavour and mostly good disease resistance (scab, canker and mildew) arranged according to the time they are ready to eat. Note that the later varieties are all picked before they are ready to eat (usually October) and kept in store until the time they are ripe – for the very latest dates the storage conditions have to be pretty good. There are many more lovely apples than in this list.

The number after each name refers to the flowering group – see 'Pollination'.

Late Summer Apples (Ripe: August – possibly as early as July and maybe into September)
Beauty of Bath (3)
Fruit: when ripe sweet and tasty, small-medium. **Skin**: lots of red over green-yellow. Good if possibly irregular yields. Spreading, vigorous tree. Fruit drops when ripe, often starting in July – one of the earliest apples. Perhaps grow as a cordon or a branch in a family tree. **Negative**: such a short time when it is perfect – beforehand it is sharp; too late and it is soft and pretty unpleasant.
Discovery (3)
Fruit: flat-round, medium size, crisp and juicy with strawberry flavour and occasional pink-stained flesh. **Skin**: pale with bright red flush. Tolerant of late frosts. Good yields. Fruit remains attached unlike many early apples. **Negative**: fruit can crack.

Early Autumn Apples (Ripe: September)
Charles Ross (3)
Fruit: Sweet, firm, juicy, slightly aromatic, medium-large. **Skin**: green-yellow with orange-red flush and stripes. Spreading habit. Good yields. Unusually for a September ripening variety, can keep until December. 'Cox's O.P.' is a parent. **Negative**: not especially resistant (or susceptible) to canker and mildew.
Ellison's Orange (4)
Fruit: small to medium, rich and aromatic with hints of pear, some say aniseed. **Skin**: green-yellow with strong red flush. Heavy crops. Blossom frost tolerant and ornamental. **Negatives**: some susceptibility to canker though very resistant to scab and mildew. Can become biennial. Aniseed?
Saint Edmund's Pippin (3)
Fruit: medium size, firm and juicy, 'pear-flavoured vanilla ice cream' (Joan Morgan). **Skin**: thin, golden with light russetting. Upright growth. Good cropper. **Negative**: has to be fully ripe to get the wonderful flavour. Thin skin means prone to bruising.

Late Autumn Apples (Ripe: October to December)
Christmas Pippin (3)
Fruit: juicy, melting flesh with 'Cox's' flavour, medium size. **Skin**: green-yellow with lots of red and a little shoulder russetting. Heavy crops and reliable. Found as a chance seedling by the side of the M5 in Somerset and propagated by F. Matthews Nursery. Average disease resistance. **Negative**: very new – long term prospects?
Egremont Russet (2)
Fruit: medium size, slightly flat, nutty and firm. **Skin**: orange, mostly covered in russetting. Good cropper. Tolerant of late frosts. Upright growth. **Negative**: gets drier with storage. Russetting, for some.
Falstaff (3)
Fruit: medium-sized, crisp, 'fruity'. **Skin**: yellow-green with red stripes. Heavy cropper. Tolerant of late frosts. **Negative**: maybe not the strongest flavoured. Also colour may be poor in less sunny areas – perhaps choose 'Red Falstaff'.
Lord Lambourne (3)
Fruit: medium size, crisp, refreshing and juicy with a certain strawberriness. **Skin**: green-yellow with red stripes. Good crops. **Negative**: not spectacularly disease resistant.

Mid Winter Apples
(Ripe: November to February but pick in October and store until ripe)
D'Arcy Spice (4)
Fruit: small-medium, juicy, firm, nutty and aromatic – rather lovely. **Skin**: green

with some russet. Can keep from November to May. Tolerant of late frosts. **Negatives**: not the heaviest cropper and can be tannic in poor autumns apparently. Sometimes biennial.

Pitmaston Pine Apple (4)
Fruit: small, conical shape, strong flavour of pineapple. **Skin**: golden yellow. Heavy crops. Upright growth. Ornamental growth. **Negative**: small size of fruit. Potential to become biennial. Resistant to canker and mildew?

Jupiter (4)
Fruit: large, sweet and juicy, rich flavour. **Skin**: yellow-green with stripes of red. Triploid. Heavy cropper. Vigorous tree. Late 20th century. **Negative**: can be biennial. Crisp enough?

Rosemary Russet (3)
Fruit: firm, intensely flavoured fruit, medium size, conical shape. **Skin**: yellow-green flushed orange-red with russet patches. Upright habit. Attractive pink blossom. **Negative**: russetting is not universally liked.

New Year Apples (Ripe: December to early March)

Adam's Pearmain (3)
Fruit: nutty, rich flavour, crisp and juicy, medium-sized conical shape. **Skin**: yellow with red stripes / flush. Good cropper. Spreading habit. **Negative**: can become biennial cropping. Resistant to canker and mildew?

Ashmead's Kernal (4)
Fruit: the best flavoured apple? Strong, sweet flavour. Juicy and firm. Medium size. **Skin**: green-yellow with occasional russetting. Good crops on upright branches. Over 300 years old. **Negative**: affected by cold springs leading to a reduced yield. Not the prettiest of fruit.

John Standish (3)
Fruit: small, crisp and juicy with intense fruit flavour. **Skin**: bright crimson flush. Upright tree. Heavy crops. **Negative**: small size of fruit

Tydeman's Late Orange (4)
Fruit: small-medium, intensely rich and aromatic, crisp. **Skin**: green-yellow with purple-red flush. Heavy cropper. Vigorous tree with long, bendy new growth. Parents are 'Laxton's Superb' x 'Cox's Orange Pippin' which is interesting since one of 'Laxton's Superb's' parents is also 'Cox's'. Tolerates late frosts. **Negative**: resistant to canker?

Winston (4)
Fruit: rich flavour, juicy and crisp, small to medium size. **Skin**: green-yellow with dark red flush. Good crops. Upright growth, medium vigour. Tolerant of late frosts. Very resistant and late-keeping. **Negative**: smaller size.

Spring Apples (Ripe: December to possibly May)
Sturmer Pippin (3)
Fruit: medium size, crisp and juicy, strong flavour. **Skin**: becomes yellow with a pink-brown flush as it ages. Very long keeper. Good crops. Ornamental flowers. **Negative**: needs warm, sunny conditions especially in autumn.

Court Pendu Plat (6)
Fruit: juicy and crisp, intensely fruity, slightly flat. **Skin**: green-yellow with red stripes / flush. Good crops. Upright growth. Late flowering so avoids frosts. Historical variety – from before C15. **Negative**: late flowering can miss cross pollination.

Winter Gem (3)
Fruit: strong aromatic flavour, crisp, medium size. **Skin**: orange flush on a green-yellow background. Usually good cropping. Resistance to canker. Good flavour before December, stores to April. **Negative**: can have occasional poor years – can't we all?

COURT PENDU PLAT

Cooking Apples
Cooking apples are characterised by their size (they are nearly all medium or large) and they are sharper in flavour, caused by higher levels of acids. There are some interesting people who enjoy eating such sharp fruit fresh, but most of us stew or bake them. Some of the best cooking apples retain their shape after baking yet the flesh is beautifully soft. Many dessert apples don't soften when they are cooked but those that do are often described as 'dual-purpose'. This short list of, again, resistant varieties are in order of ripening.

Grenadier (2-4)
Pick in August to eat until October. **Fruit**: large, sharp and crisp. **Skin**: green-yellow. **Cooked**: puree texture but not frothy, with a good, sharp flavour. Flowers for a long time. Heavy cropper.

Tom Putt (3)
Pick in September to use into November, maybe longer. **Fruit**: medium-large, quite sharp. **Skin**: greasy, bright red flush with stripes. **Cooked**: light flavour, sweet. Spreading tree. Good crops. Also used for cider. **Negative**: no reports on resistance to canker and mildew.

Annie Elizabeth (5)
Pick in October and start eating in November (through 'til at least the following April if stored well). **Fruit**: large, sharp, dry and soft. **Skin**: flush of orange-red with short stripes, on green-yellow background, plus tough and greasy. **Cooked**:

sweet with a light flavour, holding its shape but still good for stewing. Good cropper. Upright growth. Tolerates late frosts. Attractive dark pink blossom. **Negative**: tends to fall as it ripens so prompt picking is necessary.

Bramley's Seedling (4)
Pick in October to eat from then onwards, possibly until late spring next year. **Fruit**: sharp, juicy and firm, very large, acidity drops with storage. **Skin**: yellow-green with brownish flush and possibly red stripes. **Cooked**: forms a puree with a strong acidic flavour. Triploid (so won't pollinate other apples). Vigorous and spreading. Heavy cropper. The original tree is currently on its last legs in Southwell, Notts, approximately 210 years old. **Negative**: slightly susceptible to scab. Can be biennial and susceptible to late frosts.

Howgate Wonder (4)
Pick in October to use from November to March. **Fruit**: large, sharp and juicy with a pleasant flavour – can be eaten fresh. **Skin**: greasy, pale green with brown-red flush. **Cooked**: keeps shape, light flavour. Heavy cropper. Vigorous spreading tree. **Negative**: not renowned for scab and canker resistance. May be considered insipid compared to 'Bramley's Seedling'.

Lane's Prince Albert (3-5)
Pick in October to use from November to March. **Fruit**: medium size, sharp, soft and juicy. **Skin**: green-yellow with small amount of a red flush. **Cooked**: forms a puree, fresh flavour, not strong. Long flowering period. Good crops. Spreading tree. **Negative**: some susceptibility to mildew. Bruises easily.

Newton Wonder (4)
Pick in October to use from November to March. **Fruit**: large, slightly flat, sharp, crisp and juicy. **Skin**: green-yellow with orange flush and red stripes. **Cooked**: juicy puree produced, with a good fresh flavour, again quite mild. Tolerant of late frosts. Heavy cropper. Spreading tree. **Negative**: some susceptibility to mildew. Biennial.

Pruning
There is a whole, separate chapter on this for you to peruse, but it is worth noting one or two related facts here.

Apples have their flowers initiated the previous early summer. It means that any new shoots produced last year will come after that and be too late to have flowers initiated upon them. It also means that the new growth is clothed entirely with vegetative buds which will respond by growing into new (flower-less) shoots if that growth is pruned. This is why, if we spend each winter snipping off hundreds of bits of new growth, we are just encouraging them to grow again, though usually multiplied. The result is a thicket of new growth with no flowers (and consequently no fruit) plus a lot of energy going into that shoot production that perhaps should

be going towards the production of fruit elsewhere on the tree. The maximum to cut from a tree in one season is a quarter to one third.

Biennial Cropping

Biennial cropping, or bearing, means that a tree develops a routine of one year producing lots of fruit and the next year there are no flowers or fruit. One reason why this happens is, as above, flower initiation normally occurs in early summer and, if a heavy crop of young fruitlets are forming nearby at the same time, this floral initiation can be inhibited. Result? Nothing next year. This can be a flaw with particular varieties such as 'Jupiter' and 'Newton Wonder' and is a natural occurrence. One way of attempting to even things up is to remove lots of young apples in the 'on' year as soon as possible in June.

We can, however, push a tree into biennial cropping by injudicious pruning: too much encourages lots of new growth at the expense of that year's crop and the following year (if there is no more pruning) there can be a bumper crop. This is the beginnings of one year on / one year off and is an excellent reason not to employ a tree surgeon to sort out a tree in a single pruning session. If 'sorting out' is indeed the request it should be carried out over two, preferably three years.

Tree Names

One of the most popular things to do after buying and planting an apple tree (or pear or plum etc.) is to forget its name. I have reached a stage in life now where I am constantly forgetting names, so the usual answer is to make a note of them. I've written down lots of things in order to remember them – the problem is I can't remember where I've written them.
We need a system and if you haven't got a kitchen drawer full of plant labels to give you a fighting chance of re-identifying a tree, then you should at least have a plan of the plot. Even with such sound advice as this, it is extremely common for an apple tree owner not to know the variety – many anonymous trees are inherited. How does one go about discovering its identity?

Identifying Varieties

The most common way of identifying an apple variety is to say "It looks like a 'Cox's Orange Pippin'" and since many 'Cox's Orange Pippins' have been planted that stands a good chance of being right. The old, less frivolous method would be to look at a number of specimens of fruit (there is always a certain amount of variation) and make a series of measurements and observations. 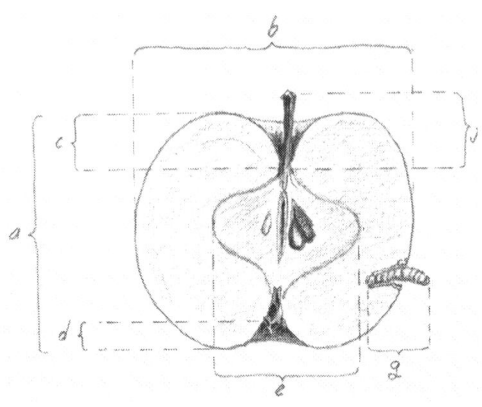 For example, the diameter in relation to the depth, the width of the core, the colour of the flesh as well as the skin, the depth of the dimple at the top (the stalk end) and the dimple at the bottom (the flower end) and so on. You can see that this is a fairly complicated affair and apart from needing the experience, you also need a reference with which to compare your findings. And wouldn't you just know it if it turns out to be a 'Cox's Orange Pippin'.

A more recent alternative has been genetic fingerprinting. I haven't attempted this but I'm guessing it's not something many of us can try out in the evening after work on an occasional table in the lounge. You need to send it off, for a fee. One of the best known sites that can help you here is the National Fruit Collection at Brogdale in Kent. There they have a database of apple varieties with which to compare your specimen. If they can't come up with an answer it will almost certainly be because you have an unrecognised variety, also known as a seedling. There are plenty of them around – either by accident (think of the cores chucked out of train windows) or deliberately planted (it is enormous fun sowing pips and the like). Just be aware that you would be extremely lucky to grow anything that is superior to existing selected varieties – and it can take 12 years for a tree raised from a pip to fruit.

Incidentally, the word 'Pippin' is from the French, *pepin*, meaning seedling. A name including 'Pippin' is effectively a waste of time because all new varieties have originally come from a pip so it isn't really giving us any new information. Still, it provides fun for particular pedants to point it out, as well as giving us the name for a Hobbit.

Picking / Harvesting

This is probably the main reason for the way our orchards have changed over the years, from wonderful craggy huge individuals to rows of tiny, trained disposable trees. You can inspect the fruit on a small tree, even selectively harvest (pick just a number of fruits from a tree at any one time). But for a lot of us we still want a tree to look like a tree even if it makes the picking (and pruning) more complicated

The physical act of removing fruit is one of the great pleasures in the autumn, especially if you haven't got a whole orchard to do. Part of the fun, for me, is clambering around in the branches and chucking the apples down to a willing accomplice. You need to choose someone who has reasonable hand-eye co-ordination and won't, at the end, present you with a mound of bruised fruit. The best quality fruit on an apple tree is usually to be found on the outside of the canopy where it is sunniest. Inevitably, this is the hardest to reach. A ladder is the usual answer but the periphery of a tree is pretty flimsy and unlean on-able. So then we switch to a step ladder and wobble around precariously
at the top trying to reach that last superb specimen.

Another answer is to purchase a cloth bag on the end of a (telescopic) stick, cleverly called an 'apple picker'. The rim of the bag usually has little metal fingers to help detach the fruit, and the bag itself should hold up to half a dozen apples. Just remember that the more apples at the end of a long pole the more unstable you become – it's physics, you know. If you happen to be using it in conjunction with the stepladder, arrange several mattresses around you to make the fall less catastrophic.

LES POMMES DE TERRE

Incidentally, the little apples that remain on a tree (presumably either missed or rejected) are known in the South West as 'gribbles' – thanks to Robert Macfarlane's splendid 'Landmarks' for that gem – and thanks to Somerset County Council for the definition of 'gribble' as a young tree that has grown from a pip from the cider apple pulp thrown out after pressing (the pomace). Two gribbles for the price of one.

Time of Harvest and Storage
This is pretty dependent on the variety. Actual dates vary with the season but the sequence will be the same. A simple rule is: the earlier the variety ripens, the shorter the storage time. The earliest varieties don't keep at all and for that reason alone it might be best to avoid a very early variety if you only have room

for a single tree: you may get lots of fruits but unless you can eat or process them rapidly it will be a brief glut then nothing for the rest of the autumn and winter. There's a whole chapter on storage.

Apple Problems

Deficiency and Disorders

Bitter pit

The skin and flesh is speckled with little clusters of dead cells giving the appearance of brown spots no more than 1mm across. The flesh can be pretty unpleasant, as the name suggests, bitter. It is caused by lack of calcium which, like blossom end rot in tomatoes, can in turn be caused by lack of water or something else interfering with calcium uptake. The solution lies in the causes: lime acidic soils and water well in dry situations.

Splitting

Splits appear in the skin and deeper into the flesh with possible secondary rots arriving. They are often found at the stalk end of the apple. Lots of water following a dry spell can lead to a rapid increase in growth, almost taking the skin by surprise – it can't expand quickly enough. Steady, even watering is important especially on light soils, as is mulching in the spring to buffer changes in water content of the soil.

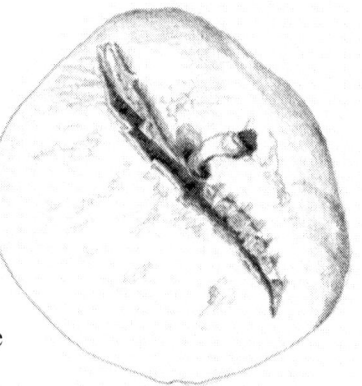

AN UNFORTUNATELY, BUT NOT DISASTROUSLY SPLIT 'ASHMEADS KERNAL'

Water core / Glassiness

A fascinating disorder with any number of possible causes. The flesh of the apple, especially that closest to the core, develops a transparent appearance. The apple is still edible if damage is minor. The finger is pointed at the following: high temperatures, too much light, damage to the bark, too much thinning, over-pruning. If you look at that lot closely, you'll find it makes our care of apples a lot harder: high temperatures generally give an enhanced rate of growth; high light levels are supposed to be encouraged to give the fruit a 'good colour'; thinning normally gives larger, higher quality fruit and over-pruning would normally result in the absence of fruit (by promoting vegetative growth). Perhaps heatwaves are the issue here. If the glassiness is minimal in area, it may actually disappear during storage. Severe 'attacks' can however lead to rotting.

Pests
Aphids

There is a fine range of aphids lining up to satisfy their hunger at Café Apple, such as the rosy apple aphid and apple-grass aphid. We shouldn't really call them greenfly since there is such a lovely range of colours apart from regular green. There are variations on timings of egg-laying, alternate hosts and appearance but they all have in common a desire to reproduce rapidly and colonise young growth in spring into summer. Leaves can curl or discolour and severe attacks can result in stunted growth and reduced cropping. The main symptom of an attack of aphids is the shoots coated in the little blighters themselves.

There is probably no better example of how well a balanced ecosystem works than with aphids. In a well-designed and maintained plot, all the appropriate predators should be there so that when an outbreak occurs (as we hope it does to maintain the food web) then it never becomes a serious issue. There should be ladybirds, lacewings, hoverflies, parasitic wasps, blue tits and so on, all ready and waiting. Failing that, brush them off.

Woolly aphis

A special kind of aphid, imported from the States, just in case we didn't have enough pests already here. It is a pink-brown sort of greenfly which you only tend to notice when they are squashed because they are hidden under a snuggly white blanket of waxy fluff. They distort growth and create wounds for fungi such as canker to enter. In the winter through to the summer this cotton wool masquerading as a strange fungus is found in cracks in the bark and even around roots of trees in pots. Later in the summer the aphids may move to younger shoots and fruiting spurs and can disappear to neighbouring trees when winged versions are produced: new aphids that have wings are produced in response to changing conditions. Which is amazing. It is called polymorphism and is almost as interesting as the fact that all offspring of woolly aphis are parthenogenetic – there is no sexual / egg stage, so they are all clones. Perhaps they are too busy producing their woolly blanket for any of that nonsense. They don't seem to have worked out yet that this is not a good approach and that genetic variation will help in long term survival. It is probably so because this is not its country of origin and in the USA other factors will enable it to complete a sexual stage.

The best method of control, especially on smaller trees, is to use a stiff brush possibly with methylated spirits at the junctions and cracks. Inevitably not all aphids will be removed, but, if repeated, it will keep them in check. Another interesting bit: back in the 1920 s a parasitic wasp was introduced from North America, to control woolly aphid. It lays eggs in the aphids and the resulting larvae eat the insides of the aphids. Well, shipping in predators from one country to another is a particularly dodgy thing to do without massive investigations into the effect on the rest of the adoptive ecosystem. Witness the debacle of the cane toad in Australia. It appears that 'we' have got away with it: *Aphelinus* is now happily ensconced throughout England and Wales and parasitized woolly aphis aphids are common; nothing else seems to be affected. Letting them do their work as well as that of hoverflies is the best advert for not using chemicals of any kind. Hoverfly larvae sneak under the white fluff and will consume 800-900 aphids each in their lives. Let them get on with it.

Birds

Most of the time birds are welcome, rummaging around amongst the foliage and stems for insects, many of them pests. Only later in the season, when the fruit is ripe can they become a nuisance when they have this unfortunate tendency to sample lots of different apples on the tree. It wouldn't be so bad if they finished off an apple before moving on, but it is almost as though they want to check if the next one is any better.

Pecked apples don't keep. For this reason, it is wise to pick all apples in October, including those not ripe and / or still firmly attached. They can then be stored safely to finish ripening if necessary. Leaving some windfalls is a pleasant thing to do since fieldfares and redwings will feast on these later in the winter, though it may allow some pests to escape the fruit and hibernate in the soil.

PECKING

There is one bird which is an exception to the above and that is the bullfinch. These beautiful little birds have an unfortunate knack of pecking buds in the winter and early spring and, as a result, have been strongly persecuted. Nowadays, their numbers are not great enough to be a concern though should they return to their mob mentality and naughty ways it would be a hard-hearted grower who recommences killing them.

Codling Moth

The principal despoiler of apples. Not a threat to the integrity of the tree itself like the fungi below, but still a wretched nuisance. In summer, a fertilised female moth lays eggs individually, one per young fruit. After about two weeks the eggs hatch and a tiny grub wriggles off to enter the fruit via the bottom, flower end (the calyx). It spends a good time – up to six weeks – rummaging around the core of the apple before departing, no longer tiny, through the side. The exit hole is accompanied by plenty of dark, dry frass (caterpillar poop). It then seeks a hidey place, something like a crevice in the bark, in which to pupate and hibernate until the following year.

This pest alone warrants putting up a nest box. A family of blue tits will despatch thousands of insects and you can enjoy the sight of adults pecking and probing the bark for just these little stinkers. Another possible way of reducing the population is to collect any prematurely ripened fruits and use or dispose of them: the tree gets rid of damaged or infested apples early. If using them, just beware of the possibility of a resident still residing, or a mouthful of frass to contend with.

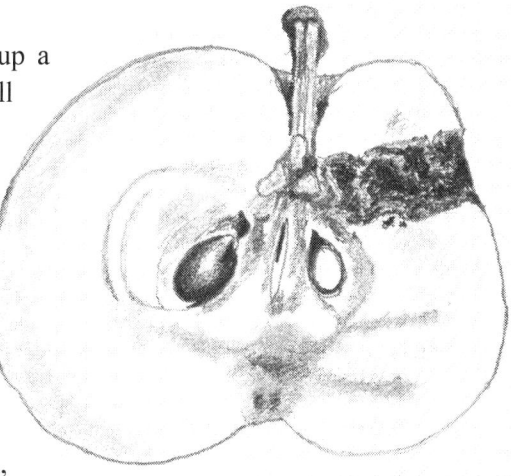

CODLING MOTH

Pheromone traps, loaded with the scent of female codling moths, attract the males which stick to the inside of the trap, wishing they'd had the idea of celibacy. This reduces the population of males (and hopefully the number of fertilised females) but could of course draw more moths into the area.

A final suggestion has a distinct echo of a stable door being bolted with the horse disappearing over the horizon: the damage has already been done. Sacking or corrugated cardboard is tied around the trunk in late July effectively with a neon hotel sign flashing away: come hither and pupate here. The sacking is removed in October and 'disposed of'.

Red Spider mite
This is possibly the first pest to be created by pesticides. Red spider mite feeds on mosses on trees and is controlled by natural predators such as the rarely mentioned acorid bug. With chemicals applied, including tar oil winter wash to kill pest eggs, the mosses and predators were wiped out (as well as, initially, many mites). When the mites returned, as they inevitably did, they fed on the leaves in the absence of moss, with no opposition. Result? They are now a pest. The simple answer is don't use toxic chemicals and let a natural balance re-develop.

Sawfly

A bit like codling moth but earlier. Eggs are laid in the flowers in April/May so that the resulting grubs (larvae) can enter developing fruitlets two weeks later. At first it tunnels just below the skin before heading deeper to the core to eat the seeds forming there. The tree is understandably fed up about this and gets rid of the fruitlet. If the sawfly has already left (its frass is noticeable, being wet and red-brown, unlike the dark, dry poop of the codling moth) it may have another snack in a neighbouring fruitlet or two. Eventually, the grub drops within its final fruitlet before exiting and pupating in the soil.

Occasionally, for some reason, the larva can die before heading to the core in which case the fruit may develop to maturity bearing the trademark russet ribbon damage. This fruit is perfectly okay to eat. Prompt collecting of fallen fruitlets (or any showing signs of damage while still on the tree) before any grubs have a chance to move on or leap out into the sanctuary of the soil, can reduce the population. Employing predators is again a useful technique: ground and rove beetles (e.g. violet ground beetle and devil's coach horse respectively), encouraged by organic matter in and on the soil, will happily chew through a sawfly larva or pupa. Birds will scratch and peck so you could possibly rent a chicken.

Winter moth

A pest that probably does more damage than we realise: but then gardeners often control it without realising they are doing so. Adult moths emerge from pupae in the soil in late autumn until mid winter. The males fly, the wingless females crawl, the latter doing so up fruit tree trunks to lay eggs on the branches. The eggs are usually dotted around the tree where they remain for the rest (worst?) of the winter. The green, looper caterpillars, emerging from the eggs in March, sport three eat-faster longitudinal yellow stripes. They feed on anything they can get their teeth into: young leaves and shoots, buds, flowers and fruitlets (which grow to become distorted and disturbing). Their accommodation is to camp in little tents of leaves stitched together and when they reach their full size of 25mm/1" they abseil down out of the tree on long silk threads. This is in May to June and their aim is to get to the soil, not stuck in your hair, so they can pupate and remain until the whole adventure starts again later in the year.

For control, we can look for the damage and remove the caterpillars by hand or find the tents and pinch them in the middle until some goo squeezes out of the end (bleugh). Using birds to scratch around in pupa-land is possible but applying fruit tree grease or a sticky grease band to prevent the females climbing is very common. Except many gardeners erroneously think they are doing it to trap codling moth. Attach your chosen stickiness early in October.

Look up the scientific name of winter moth under the chapter 'Pests and Diseases' if only to have fun trying to pronounce it.

Diseases

Blossom wilt

Wind-borne spores, more prevalent in wet weather, infect blossom which wilts and dies. The infection can then spread back to kill the fruit spur and even cause dieback of the shoot bearing the affected blossom. Prune away any dying blossom (the petals will be brown, shrivelled and still attached unlike healthy old blossom which drops).

Brown rot

With apples this disease is closely related to blossom wilt. Spores infect fruit via damage (caused by birds, insects, other diseases, cracking) and a soft, brown patch develops which gradually enlarges until the whole fruit is subsumed. White rings of pustules may be seen. Remove the affected fruit as soon as the damage is seen or at least the dry, mummified apples along with part of the spur later in the season.

Canker

Possibly the worst problem to be encountered by apple trees. It rarely kills a tree but keeps it in suspended animation, neither able to crop nor look good. It is a fungus that enters branches via a natural opening (a lenticel), a bud or a wound. As it grows, the bark is killed and shrinks, often becoming flaky. The tree tries to fight back by growing around the edge of the damage, so giving a nobbly appearance. If the fungus wins, the shoot can be girdled and everything above the infection dies so that the tree may later re-shoot below the girdling. As a silhouette, the badly-cankered tree can therefore have the nightmarish appearance of a thicket of young shoots, dead branches and lumpy, nobbly bits. Trees affected as badly as this are a lost cause and should be removed especially if no crop is being produced. If the tree is affected but not in as extreme a way as this, plus it regularly produces fruit, then try to ignore the damage and prune / look after it as you would a healthy tree. There is the issue of it being a source of more spores for infecting other trees but, frankly, they're all over the shop anyway.

Only if a tree has a small amount of damage is it worthwhile pruning out the cankers (remember, one way that the fungus gets into a branch in the first place is though pruning wounds). If canker is in the trunk or large branches, obviously it can't be pruned out – it should be pared out. This means using a knife to cut away the infected tissue around the edge of the patch: this is where the fungus lives, not in the dead, middle part. Cut away until fresh, live, greenish-white tissue is reached. George Glenny (1878) in 'The Culture of Fruits and Vegetables' comments: "After paring away the canker and… everything is clean, the part will heal and do well; but so sure as any canker remains, there will be mischief." It is fairly universally recognised that we don't want mischief in our apple trees.

Things *not* to bother doing:
Spray with fungicides including so-called 'organic' ones – it is too messy, toxic and ineffective.
Treat wounds with a proprietary wound paint – many of these simply seal in a moist, rot-inducing environment: Let the cut tissue dry as much as possible. Plant susceptible varieties, especially in wetter areas of the country where canker is encouraged.

Powdery Mildew
Young leaves and new growth are stunted, distorted and coated in a white, powdery fungal growth. New shoots can wither and die in severe attacks. Whereas scab and canker thrive in wet areas, powdery mildew is more common in drier parts. The ideal conditions for infection are when the soil is dry yet there is some moisture in the air, a surprisingly common combination. Imagine, in a dry spell, a dew or a light shower, known as 'nuisance rain' since all it does is wet the foliage and us and doesn't get into the soil. Wet leaves encourage spores which have over-wintered on buds and shoots to germinate and the dry soil serves to stress the tree and reduce resistance.
The remedy, if it attacks, is to cut out the worst pieces but, far better, is to prevent it in the first place: resistant varieties, judicious watering, plenty of organic matter in the soil and thick mulching.

Scab
If canker is The Penguin then scab is The Joker in the orchard of Gotham City, pitted against Batman apple and Robin pear. I wish I hadn't started that now.

Both are encouraged by wet, warm conditions, typically found in Wales, the far west of England and Scotland and in Northern Ireland. Probably for this reason alone, these areas are not major apple-growing regions. Scab is another fungus, one that affects leaves and fruit. Dark patches appear on the fruit and, if severe, they can join up, the fruit can crack and other rots can get in. Generally, small infections are superficial and the apple is perfectly edible, though storage may be affected. Possibly more of a problem is when scab attacks the leaves: the grey spots can coalesce and leaves then go yellow and fall. If this happens very prematurely then the tree can be weakened so that, next year, it may leaf-up and flower as usual but cropping will be poor.

Answers include, again, resistant varieties and hygiene. The latter involves either collecting up the fallen infected leaves or mulching on top of them. If the tree is in a lawn, these leaves can be run over with a mower to collect them along with the clippings or left for the worms to take away.

SCABBY LEAF

Virus

Like virtually any other plant, viruses can get into an apple tree. We probably wouldn't notice it as such but just see a decline in cropping and possibly a yellowing of the leaves. Neither of these improve year on year despite extra watering and feeding leaving us with the only solution of stacking a large heap of apple firewood.

Apple Histories

One of the best known apple characters is from the USA – 'Johnny Appleseed'. He was an evangelist who moved from farm to farm dressed, allegedly, in a coffee sack shirt and a saucepan hat. As he went he distributed apple pips from a cider mill and so, instead of being a hero of the pioneering days, was (perhaps unkindly) responsible for more alcoholism than a reputable dealer in fruit trees: trees from pips generally gave fruit only fit for making cider. Maybe Johnny could be described as a gribble-monger.

Apple Pressing

There will hopefully be a time when you stand before boxes of your own produce and wonder what on earth you're going to do with it all. One answer is to make juice followed by another question, how? Domestic kitchen appliances can extract juice but will do so in disappointingly small quantities so the decision has to be made whether to invest in 'proper' equipment. The first item is something to reduce the fruit to small pieces: scratter, crusher, basher – basically make up your own name. Homemade devices include a length of timber (say, 4'x2"x2"), a clean bucket and some energy. The apples are bashed until crushed. Marginally more sophisticated is the scratter, a hopper at the bottom of which are reciprocating blades / projections. These are rotated by using a handle on the side and quartered apples are reduced to pulp which drops out of the bottom.

There are various construction recipes for making a press, usually involving a bottle jack (the kind of thing you need, but forgot to put back in the car after cleaning it, to lift the vehicle in order to change the tyre). I'm a great fan of making our own equipment but I have yet to see a homemade press that a) works well or b) doesn't disintegrate during its first use. A little barrel press may be worth buying if you think you'll get enough of a crop on a regular basis to make the expense worthwhile. The pulp is squeezed to great excitement and tasting is essential, particularly if you're using a single variety: sometimes it works, sometimes it really doesn't. It may be best to use a mix of apples or to blend juices at the end.

The juice itself can become a problem. Drinking some fresh is fine and it keeps in the fridge for, well, it depends if you like sparkling apple juice. With several litres, you may need to find another method of preservation: if it ferments too much then it's not so nice unless you want to go the whole hog and let it ferment into cider in which case it ought to be in a demi-john (gallon glass jar with airlock). Even then, I have found that it is exceptionally easy to make a particularly foul brew, possibly indicating the need to use cider varieties of apple.

Pasteurising is another option requiring even more equipment. Freezing is probably an easier answer – if you have the freezer space: don't quite fill plastic bottles and squeeze them a bit as you fill them. As the juice freezes and expands the squozen bottle can return to normal shape and not split.

Wassailing

(Wassail – from Anglo-Saxon *waes hael* meaning 'good health' – refers to the drink and wassailing refers to the fun including drinking the drink).

Usually on January the 6th, twelfth night, or, if using the old calendar, the 17th. This is an opportunity to stand around in an orchard wishing you'd put on that thermal underwear, trying to sing songs you don't quite know and drinking cider until underwear and songs don't matter any more.

It is a kind of combination celebration: a thank you of sorts with offerings made to the orchard spirits. It is a wakening of the same spirits, typified by beating the tree trunks with sticks, an activity with debatable success since nothing seems to happen with the trees for another three and a half months. And, of course, it is an excuse to simply have a good time with some friends, new and old.

Other typical activities include decorating the trees (ribbons, clouties [more ribbons], toast soaked in cider), firing shotguns (using blanks I'm relieved to say) over the orchard and pouring cider around the trees. The latter slightly puzzles me in that the cider-maker presumably would have preferred to drink the stuff, and almost certainly the trees would have preferred a good soaking of seaweed solution rather than alcohol, but perhaps it is best not to look at some things too closely. You could even squeeze in a little morris dancing.

Apple Games

At the end of October, before 'trick or treat' and pumpkins infested this land, Hallowe'en was celebrated with apples and root vegetables. Groups of local juveniles were herded into sheds or garages and encouraged to bite or even eat an apple that is suspended from a rafter by a piece of hairy string. This obviously

APPLE GAMES

had to be done without using the hands and, because of the ages of most of the children, the loss of front teeth in the process wasn't a major catastrophe.

Bobbing for apples, still I gather an occasional activity, is similar in that children gathered around a large receptacle filled with water and apples, and had to extract the fruit again without using hands. Added excitement accompanied this in the form of potential drownings and the inadvertent consumption of earwigs, dead leaves and woodlice in the process.

I remember the cartoonist Gary Larson's take on this game. He received an 'irate mailbag' following his picture of a roomful of wolves and the title 'Bobbing for Sheep'.

APRICOTS *Prunus armeniaca*

(*Prunus*, L. for plum, *armeniaca*, from Armenia)

Family: ROSACEAE

Why we should grow apricots

Because you'll never buy an apricot as good as one you can grow yourself. The blossom alone makes apricots worth growing.

Apricot Essentials

Varieties

Many of the more long-established varieties have been superseded by a range of new developments, some ending in the syllable 'cot' just in case we hadn't connected them. For example '**New Large Early**' and '**Moorpark**' have been around for ages. There is also '**Hongaarse**' which is hard to find but I've included it simply for a schoolboy giggle.

Then come '**Goldcot**', '**Flavorcot**' and '**Tomcot**', all from the USA: 'Goldcot' may be worth considering because of its good disease resistance and tolerance of more variable weather. However, its mid season (August) fruit have only 'average' flavour. 'Flavorcot' produces fruit earlier (late July) and has a good flavour. It is recommended for growing in the UK but then most of these are. 'Tomcot' has large fruit also around late July.

Then comes the French contingent. '**Bergeval**', bred from the classic 'Bergeron', is sweet, orange-red and early. The recent '**Kioto**' is a late variety but is not too vigorous (= smaller tree) and flowers a bit later.

'**Golden Glow**' is, surprisingly, a UK variety having been found as a chance seedling in the Malvern Hills. This makes it more likely to cope with UK conditions. It is early and the fruit is smaller than most but it has an excellent true apricot flavour.

Amongst the many other varieties is a little oddity: '**Compacta**' is a genetic dwarf, meaning that it is very small (about 1.25m in 10 years) without the help of a dwarfing rootstock. The website Orange Pippin recommends that 'Compacta' is best planted in the ground not a container.

Size: Rootstocks, in ascending size, 'Wavit' at 3m / 10' is the smallest – it is a plum rootstock but works for apricots. 'Torinel' and 'Apricor' are larger (4m / 14') so can be used for half standard trees – 'Torinel' has good disease resistance and copes with wet soils and 'Apricor' is an apricot seedling so compatibility is excellent (that is only interesting if you are into grafting your own trees). 'St. Julien A' is a long established rootstock at 5m / 16' or more.

Spacing: Plant apricot trees the same as or marginally less apart than the height dictated by your chosen rootstock.

Position: South-facing site; free-draining soil of neutral pH.

Feeding: Well-composted soil surface in the spring.

Pruning: Apricots fruit on spurs on the older wood as well as one year old growth (= growth produced the previous year). This suggests that it is impossible to prune a tree without reducing the sites of fruit production and this is actually the case. Therefore, after formative pruning (getting a young tree in shape with a strong framework) pruning can be pretty minimal. It doesn't mean you can get away with doing nothing, however. See below for more details.

Pollination: Apricots are self fertile which is terrific if we only have room for one tree. However, early blossoming means the flowers are susceptible to frost damage and also that pollinating insects (the pollen still has to be moved around even on self fertile trees) may be in short supply. Consider doing a little light hand-pollination with a soft brush.

Harvesting: The joy of having your own apricots is focused at the harvesting stage in that the maximum flavour, unachievable in commercial orchards for export, is found when the fruit is fully ripe on the tree. Pick the fruit when it has some 'give': too firm and it is under-ripe, too squishy and you've missed it.

Propagation : Grafting in late winter or budding in mid to late summer.

Weeding: Keep clear for the first three years. Avoid major plantings in the root zone of the smaller growing trees.

Apricot Origins
This is a Chinese plant (and East Tibet) and has trundled its way westwards over the millennia via, one presumes from the name, Armenia.

Apricot Nutrition
Good levels of most minerals and vitamins though probably the best for Carotene (precursor to vitamin A) at 400µg/100g and good for potassium at 270mg/100g.

Apricot Botany
An apricot is a true fruit meaning that most of it has developed from the ovary in the flower. It is also called a 'drupe' – part of the definition of a drupe is that it has a single seed, housed in a stone. That means that other Prunus species produce drupes, too, giving them all the collective name of 'stone fruit'.

Discussion / rambling / elaboration
Extra Pruning Information
As noted in 'Apricot Essentials', regular pruning of a free-standing tree is fairly minimal and the reason why is reasonably fascinating.
Fruit is produced on one year old growth (the most recent growth) and on little fruiting spurs (knobbly buds) on older branches. Removing a lot of stems / branches will therefore remove potential production sites. The flowers for the year's crop are actually initiated the previous year but, unlike apples where this happens in early summer of the previous year before much new growth has occurred, for apricots it occurs in late summer, hence all of the new growth so far that year could have flowers initiated upon it.

Some pruning could or should still be done, not least the three D's – dead, diseased and damaged. Occasional branches can be removed to maintain good spacing for air and light. Fruiting can decline on the very oldest wood so it makes sense to have a certain amount of turnover, albeit very slow: occasionally remove an older branch and tie in a younger replacement. This is perhaps more important with a fan-trained tree.
To avoid too many young shoots, they can be rubbed off as they form, again particularly with a fan; not really pruning, more infanticide.

Apricot Crosses
Not only are there lots of new varieties coming through, there are a range of crosses between plum (the Japanese plum *P. salicina*) and apricot, almost

inevitably called plumcot, which are more reliable. Cross a plumcot with apricot again and you get an aprium (groan) which is, if you have being paying attention, three quarters apricot and one quarter plum. An example of an aprium is 'Aprisali'. This is easier to grow than the pure apricot and produces fruit in July, but is undermined by having a plum flavour. I like plum flavours which is why I grow plums, but if I want an apricot I want an apricot flavour. Sorry.

Apricots and Weather
Perhaps because of their origins, apricots have a reputation for being difficult to grow in temperate climates. This is partly true. The trees themselves should be fully hardy and in that respect pose no problem in the UK. The bluebottle in the apricot conserve is the flowering time: it is usually quite early in the spring, earlier than peaches. This invites damage to the blossom from, particularly, night-time frosts.

Spring frosts are not the only reason for erratic fruiting however. Imagine the conditions in Armenia (I'm sure this is something you do regularly): in the winter it can get cold but it will be fairly dry and in the summer it will be hot and dry. In both seasons the weather will be steady and reliable (a.k.a. boring). All we need to do in this country for maximum, regular production is replicate these conditions. Instead we come up with mild wet winters interspersed with occasional cold spells and summers that are as reliable as a 1980s Mini Metro.

The amount of winter cold actually required by the apricot is not huge (around 500-700 hours below 5°C) and a lot more than this, as mentioned, isn't a problem. The difficulties we have are finding dryness and steady non-fluctuating weather (plus a good helping of summer heat). If it isn't cold enough soon enough in the winter then the tree isn't dormant. Then, if this is followed by a classic UK cold snap, then the young growth can be killed. Diseases can get into this and dieback results.

Two possible answers that help to iron out these issues: grow under cover (almost impossible for most of us due to the size of the structure required – try 'Compacta'?) or grow against a south-facing wall. The latter is distinctly possible and helps in all of the following ways: it is usually drier next to a wall because at least some rain doesn't make it to the base and the foundations of the wall aid drainage. The bricks act as a storage heater, radiating out heat during a frosty night following a sunny day. Temperatures are higher because of the shelter of the wall from northerly winds. Material (polythene, fleece, sacking) can be hung over the tree down from the top of the wall to protect blossom, keep off rain and warm up the tree.

It doesn't mean free-standing apricots in the open won't produce fruit, just that they will be less reliable at doing so.

Almost apologetically, the apricot compensates for its temperamental nature by producing at some point we hope one of the most sublime fruits that we can grow. Too often the imported fresh apricot is a disappointment, resembling a cross between a tennis ball and a wad of cotton wool. Home-grown fruit, picked at just the right stage, bursts with juice and flavour such that it might be best to eat it in the bath.

It is a reasonable question to ask why this is the case and perhaps there are a number of factors at play. The imported fruit is not always as fresh as it could be, has been picked early as is the curse with much produce from abroad or it has desiccated. UK apricots, on the other hand, develop slowly and are potentially fresher so producing a superior product. A supermarket or two have recognised this difference and have sponsored the planting of UK apricot orchards.

Another extra is that home-grown fruit has a rather lovely red blush to the standard beige-orange background.

Dried apricots are splendid – rich and succulent, especially unsulphured ones – but they don't have the same unique flavour and texture as the fresh version. The answer to this is to make sure there are no fresh specimens needing preserving in the first place.

Apricot problems
Apricots are often lumped in with peaches and nectarines when it comes to pests and diseases, but in fact even if an apricot gets them they tend to be milder. Peach leaf curl has no effect at all, for example. Brown rot and die-back are the main issues.

Brown rot
The fungus *Sclerotinia laxa* infects fruit via wounds caused by birds or insects. It develops into a soft brown rot and can spread easily to neighbouring touching fruits. Infected fruits rot and can eventually dry and mummify, becoming a source of infection the following year. Unfortunately, the same fungus can infect blossom (and occasionally leaves) which shrivels giving the name blossom wilt: two diseases for the price of one. It doesn't stop there. The strands (mycelia) can spread down into the branches which may die back or wither.

Die-back
This is often attributed to the weather, when freezing temperatures kill non-dormant shoots, and to fungal diseases such as the aforementioned *Sclerotinia*. There is also bacterial canker which can cause shoots to die but is usually less of an issue with apricots than cherries.

Silver leaf
If bacterial canker is fonder of cherries, silver leaf has a penchant for plums; have a look at that chapter.

Frost-damage to the flowers
Avoid low-lying sites (frost pockets). Also, exposed sites will discourage the early pollinating insects. Consider growing in a way that gives the opportunity to protect the blossom, such as training on a south-facing wall.

BLACKBERRIES *Rubus fruticosus*
(*Rubus*, L. red, *fruticosus*, shrubby)
Family: ROSACEAE

Why we should grow blackberries
A range of flavours covering several months. Blackberries make one of the best fruit wines, perhaps together with elderberries to make a port type.

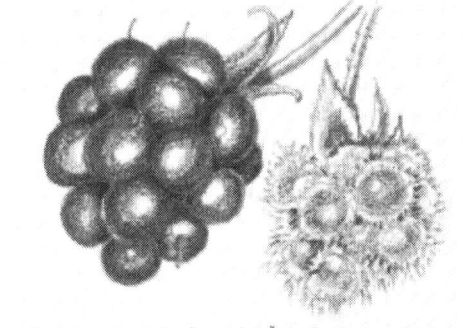

ONE CLEAN-SHAVEN BLACKBERRY AND ONE WITH BOTRYTIS

Blackberry Essentials
Varieties
Loch Ness. Positives: shorter growing, thornless, long-fruiting (August to November), fruit is large and easy to pick, good yields. Negatives: sweetness is a bit low.
Oregon Thornless. Positives: thornless, attractive fern-like leaves, shorter growing. Negatives: low yielding, flavour?
Chester. From Maryland, USA. Positives: thornless, disease resistant, long-fruiting (Late August to October), variable sweetness, high yields, attractive pink flowers. Negatives: vigorous so needs plenty of space, flavour perhaps not the best.
Black Butte. Positives: huge (double normal berry size), early (mid July onwards). Negatives: less sweet, poor flavour, yields below average, pest and disease resistance questionable, the name.
Reuben. A late-fruiting 'primocane' type (see below). Positives: easy to prune, less support required. Negatives: thorny, not very sweet or flavoursome, poor yields in UK (bred in Kansas, USA).

Size and Spacing: 3.5m / 12' between plants, 2.5m / 8' between rows (!). Closer spacings for a few particular varieties.

Feeding: Good, basic complete nutrition from compost (for example) with a top up of potassium.

Pruning: Most varieties, in winter, will have old fruited canes removed leaving young canes still to fruit.

Pollination: Not an issue.

Harvesting: When the fruit comes away cleanly and without effort. Choose dry conditions.

Propagation: Layering: bury the tip of one-year-old canes at the end of summer, in prepared ground or a sunken pot. Detach from the parent plant the following spring and transplant.

Weeding: Keep cultivated blackberries as weed-free for as long as possible – it simply maximises production. Clumps of volunteer / wild plants – leave them alone; they'll cope and probably shade out the competition quite comfortably.

Blackberry Origins
Blackberries (if you want to eat the fruit) or brambles (if they are where you don't want them) are one of the few ice age survivors in this country – a true native.

Blackberry Nutrition
Nothing exceptional but blackberries have reasonable levels of calcium and iron (41 and 0.7mg/100g respectively) whilst vitamins E (2.4mg/100g) and Folate (34µg/100g) are excellent. Being coloured black-purple too, it is reasonable to expect good levels of antioxidants just like blueberries and blackcurrants. The sweetness of blackberries, as measured in 'Brix', is seemingly not terrific – Brix 5 to 11.

Blackberry Botany
As for raspberries except that blackberries re-shoot annually from a central point and the turnover of stems is two years or more.

Discussion / rambling / elaboration
Varieties, Cultivars and Species
'Grow blackberries? Are you serious? These things are all over the place and half the time they're a wretched nuisance.' And this is true. However, despite being the same species, it is worthwhile having wild and cultivated blackberries as different propositions. In other words, they're not quite the same thing. There are reckoned to be 'hundreds of species' of blackberry in our hedgerows (and covering our allotments). This is a fairly lazy way (it is actually one species only, *Rubus fruticosus*) of saying there is lots of variation, which is what you would expect from a plant that has no difficulty spreading itself around by seed. One of the delights of foraging wild blackberries is that one minute you're picking small, pippy fruits, the next you've found huge, watery things and then again

on to wonderfully sweet specimens, probably with maggots in them. Where there are specimens which have been bred, selected or cultivated then, correctly, they should be referred to as 'cultivars' (or cultivated variety). And this has been done, as with *Rubus fruticosus* 'Fantasia' (found on a London allotment) or R. fruticosus 'Loch Ness' (bred in Scotland). There are other, genuine, species of *Rubus* that are very like the native blackberry, such as the parsley-leaved blackberry *Rubus laciniata* (some suggest that *R. fruticosus* 'Oregon Thornless' is the same plant) and dewberries *Rubus caesius*. Complicated, isn't it?

Here are some jolly good reasons why we should grow blackberries on our plots:

- We can control them (?)
- They will have been selected for reliability.
- Some will be thorn-free.
- Possibility of primocane varieties (see later).
- Potentially long production period (July to November).
- Very hardy and resistant.
- Wildlife plant: as with many native plants, there is a strong relationship with wildlife still evident in cultivated varieties.

There are some reasonable reasons not to have them in our fruit garden:
- Most have thorns.
- There are wild, free versions available on any country walk or unused allotment.
- If space is short, is it perhaps a waste?
- Need support and training.
- 'They cause scalp conditions resulting from excessive consumption' by children and so were called bumblekites and scaldheads. This is clearly very accurate 19th (?) century information.

BUMBLEKITES, SCALDHEADS

We are not supposed to pick blackberries after the end of September since the devil will have spat on them. Spitting is one of the friendlier things he is said to do on the fruit – just use your imagination. This may be a country way of saying that fruit quality is 'not as it was' and this may be true but 'inferior' doesn't mean they shouldn't be picked at all. Unless they are particularly foul they can still be used in pies etc. Of course, in some years, when there are early autumn frosts, this wouldn't be an issue.

Pruning

When it comes to pruning and training, most blackberries are treated the same as summer fruiting raspberries which, if you're reading this book front to back (a fairly popular direction with most books) isn't much help. It means this: each bramble shoot is kept for two years. The first year it grows vigorously and needs tying in, the second year it produces flowers and fruit. After that it is removed. It differs from raspberries by producing new shoots from the same point each year whereas raspberries grow from below ground (sucker) some distance from the parent.

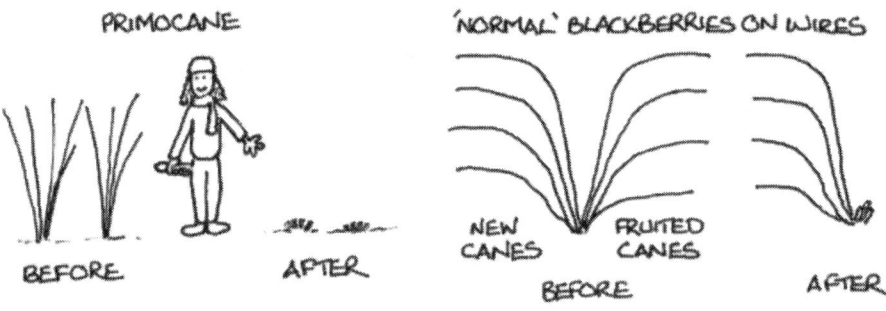

There are new varieties on the horizon called 'primocane' and these compare to autumn raspberries. The most notable so far is the variety 'Reuben'. Basically, fruit is produced on shorter canes in the same (first) year that they have grown. The advantage of that is the pruning and training. Pruning of primocanes is the easiest pruning in the fruit-growing world (apart, perhaps, from mulberries where you might not do any). All canes are cut off in the dormant season. That's it.

New canes emerge in the spring and go on to fruit late in the year. To do well with primocane blackberries you need a long growing season and a variety that fruits quickly – as quickly as autumn raspberries do. 'Reuben' has all of the publicity as the first variety but unfortunately being a primocane blackberry is just about its only selling point.

Conventional blackberries should be trained so that the two ages of canes are kept separate, simply for ease of management. For example, when training against a wall or on a post-and-wire system, the new canes can be trained in one direction while the fruiting canes are tied-in in the other direction. At the end of the year, the old (fruited) canes are removed, leaving space for the next year's canes to be trained in as they grow.

Planting

For bare root plants, November into December is ideal: cut back the canes to about 30cm (1'). Anytime of year is fine for container raised plants, with the caveats of frozen / droughted / saturated conditions, and they don't need cutting back. Plant container-grown specimens at the same depth as the compost in the pot or slightly deeper. Use the soil mark on the stem to judge the planting depth of bare-root specimens. Spacing of plants is wider for the cultivated blackberries at 3.5m (12') except for 'Reuben' – follow as for autumn raspberries – or 'Oregon Thornless' for which the same spacing as for hybrid berries should be used: 2.5m (8').

If you are fortunate enough to have space for more than one row then the row spacing is wide at 2.5m (8'), but narrower for 'Oregon Thornless' at 1.8m (6').

Feeding

It is worth providing some sustenance to your blackberries and hybrids, particularly the latter which need good levels of potassium. The best answer is, as ever, a good mulch of compost. Some nitrogen is required for the re-growth of canes and potassium for the stimulation of fruit production and also, though in lower quantities, every other essential plant nutrient, basically because we are feeding plants. Never apply a particular nutrient in isolation so, if some wood ash is to be used to provide potassium then include it with some compost or other organic matter.

Harvesting

Nobody really needs to be told how to pick blackberries, do they? Oh all right then. Avoid the thorns. Also, pick on a dry day and, when the fruit easily detaches with the plug, it will be at its sweetest.

Don't put too many in a container otherwise the bottom ones get squished (not a problem if jam or wine is your aim). Fruit is overripe if it smears when you try picking it. If harvesting 'in the wild' get a good selection from a range of plants to even out any variations in flavour, sweetness, etc.

Propagation

This is as easy as it gets. Most of the time it is an effort to stop them multiplying (training should stop it). Both blackberries and the hybrids would love to spread all over your plot by rooting in at the tip of any branches low enough to the ground. They start doing this naturally in late summer so if you direct them to a particular area of ground, or even a pot, they will easily root into it. Separate it from the parent plant the following spring or wait until a stronger plant has developed and move it in the autumn

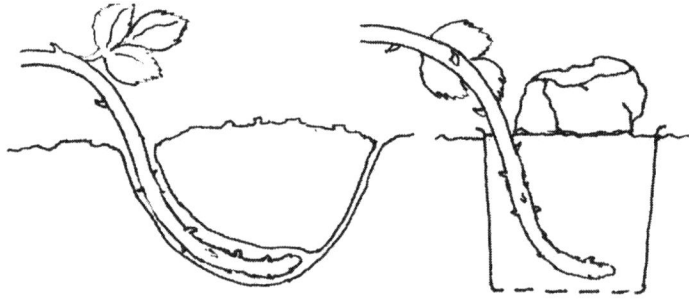

TIP LAYERING: IN THE GROUND OR SUNKEN POT

Blackberry Problems
Raspberry beetle
The grub that hatches from eggs laid in the flower will start by feeding at the base of the fruit, later moving into the core, making it perhaps harder to spot with blackberries because they are picked with that core / plug. They over-winter in the soil. For more exciting details, see 'Raspberries'.

Aphids
A wild bramble patch may have aphids but you'll probably not notice them before they are predated. A cultivated blackberry however may have an outbreak which could slow down growth. If greenfly annoy you that much then try brushing them off.

Cane Spot
This is a fungal disease that produces oval-shaped grey spots on the canes. Severe attacks can cause canes to dieback, so hygiene in the form of removal of affected canes is the first port of call. It can also be minimised in two ways:
 1) good spacing of the canes so that they, and the leaves, can dry out after rain.
 2) training of the new canes so that they are held in the centre of the plant, they

are tied in to one side or that they are on wires above the old canes, all so that the spores of cane spot don't drop from the old on to the new. Clever, eh?

Capsid bugs / shield bugs / stink bugs
These are sap-sucking insects which occasionally feed on the ripening fruit, which results in a damaged / partially collapsed berry. Not really a major problem, just make sure this visitor isn't still attached when consuming.

Red Berry Mite
This is an extremely under-studied little chap which, apart from being tiny, sucks the sap throughout a blackberry plant. Its presence only registers when it feeds on the fruit itself which fails to ripen fully with a proportion of the drupelets remaining hard and red (hence the name). More berries are affected as the season progresses.

You'll be pleased to hear, especially if you have just sampled one, that the non-ripening is caused by the mite's saliva. Control, to a certain degree, is by the regular pruning out of the older, fruited parts, which is what you should be doing anyway.

Virus
Compared to many other fruits, blackberries seem less afflicted by viruses. This is partly because of the wider genetic variation found with wild specimens and also aphids, the main vector for most viruses, seem to be less attracted to blackberries.

Any yellowing of leaves, especially unusual markings, could indicate a virus and would be accompanied by reduced cropping. Regardless of the cause, perhaps once we have had two or three successive years of poor yields, we should think about removal.

BLACKCURRANTS *Ribes nigrum*
(*Ribes*, from Arabic, acidic, *nigrum*, black)
Family: GROSSULARIACEAE

Why we should grow blackcurrants
Ease of maintenance, heavy yielding, reliable, vitamin C.

A SOMEWHAT SPARSE STRIG

Blackcurrant Essentials
Varieties
Big Ben: Recent (2013), mildew and leaf spot resistant, early, good flavour and sweet fruit double average size.
Ben Connan: Resistant to mildew, large berries, full flavour with good sweetness levels, highest yielding?, compact 1.2m / 4', good disease resistance but not to virus or mite.
Ben Gairn: Early flowering (first week of April) and fruiting, the only variety resistant to reversion virus, a cross between 'Ben Alder' and the Russian 'Golubka'. Rich flavour and reasonably sweet, medium-sized fruit; neat, compact bush 1.5m / 5' across, yields variable.
Ben Hope: The most popular / widely planted variety, resistant to big bud mite and mildew, vigorous 2.1m/7' wide 1.8m / 6' high, high yields, fruit is small to medium sized.
Ebony: Sweet (comparatively), large fruit, resistant to mildew though not much else, spreading habit, below average yields.

Size: Usually 1.2-1.5m / 4-5 feet.

Spacing: 1.2-1.5m / 4 to 5 feet apart (closer with compact varieties). 1.8m / 6 feet between rows.

Position: A minimum of half a day's sun. West, east or south facing aspect.

Feeding: Pre-season wood ash and mulch of good compost / manure. Dilute urine and / or comfrey liquid throughout the season.

Pruning: Dormant season, preferably February. Old growth where possible, about one third. See below.

Pollination: Self-fertile, requiring insect pollination, subject to frost damage.

Harvesting: July is blackcurrant month but this can vary depending on the season and the variety. For the process of harvesting, see below.

Propagation: Hardwood cuttings in November.

Weeding: This is important because blackcurrants are shallow-rooted. It is best achieved by starting with a clean bed (which is what my mother always said) and by regular mulching. Weeds are hard to control once established in that crown of suckering shoots.

Blackcurrant Origins
Blackcurrants appear to be from quite a wide area, Northern Europe to North and Central Asia, possibly even being native to the UK. Having said that, they weren't that popular here until the nineteenth century. Earlier references describe it as a medicine. This was presumably on the principle that if you dislike eating it, it must be good for you.

Blackcurrant Nutrition
High levels of Vitamin C and good levels of potassium, magnesium, iron, calcium and vitamins A and B. Probably the best fresh fruit for a range of vitamins and minerals.

Blackcurrant Botany
A true fruit, technically called a 'berry': a fruit consisting of a thin skin, flesh and a number of seeds. So's a tomato.

Discussion / rambling / elaboration
A wonderful plant, easy to grow and look after, with the one substantial skeleton lurking in the closet – reversion virus. It is exceptionally difficult to keep plants clean on an allotment (marginally easier in back gardens) because of the ever-present infected bushes on someone else's plot.

Propagation
This is best from hardwood cuttings taken from the current year's growth in November. Shoots should be about 20-25cm / 8-10" long and ideally from a young, clean plant. The material for such cuttings is therefore crying out to come from newly-planted, certified virus-free bushes that are cut back to 2-3 buds when they are first planted. Remove the tips of the cuttings and cut just below a bud at the bottom. It is not necessary to remove the buds as with many

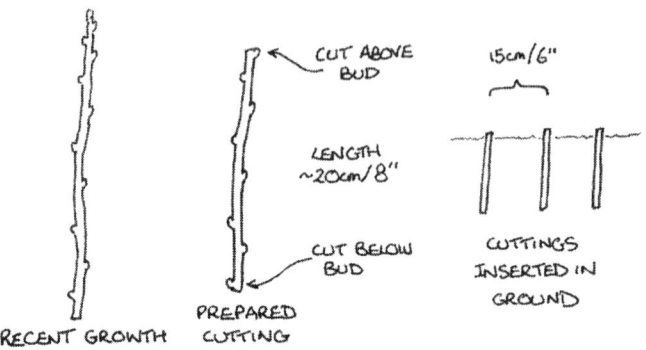

hardwood cuttings. They can be inserted directly in the ground up to their necks or in deep pots (it's easier in the ground – choose good, free-draining soil in a sheltered place). If the soil is a little heavier than desired, pour grit or sharp sand into the bottom of a slit made with a spade before popping in the cuttings at about 15cm / 6" apart.

The cuttings are inserted relatively deeply compared to other currants because blackcurrants sucker readily (new shoots are formed at the base of the plant to produce a clump) so there is no point trying to produce a plant on a single, short stem. They will root very readily and before you know it, there will be blackcurrant bushes all over the place. Lift them the following November when the leaves have dropped off and transplant to their final positions.

Planting

Using the spacings above, dig holes that easily accommodate the roots. Unlike almost all other plants, it doesn't matter if they go in a little deeper than they were propagated – they sucker from below ground anyway. Immediately after planting, whether they are home-propagated transplants or bought plants, all of the top is removed down to a couple of buds. If planting has taken place in November (the best time of year, to make the most of warm moist soil) then the shoots removed, all being new growth, will make excellent cuttings. Those from a bought (certified) plant should be clean of diseases, too.

Pruning

This is not quite as easy as, say, raspberries but not as problematic as gooseberries. That kind of information is not especially helpful if you don't have a clue how to deal with either of those in the first place.
Blackcurrants produce fruit only on the growth produced the previous year. It is almost colour-coded: the young growth, limbering up to flower and fruit, is an unexciting grey-buff colour whereas the curmudgeonly old growth is a darker purple-brown. All we have to do is satisfy the following three directions:

1) Remove one third of the whole plant.
2) Select only the old growth if possible.
3) Select growth that opens up the plant to give an airy, open-centred goblet shape.

Number one means it is helpful to have a heap of prunings next to the plant so

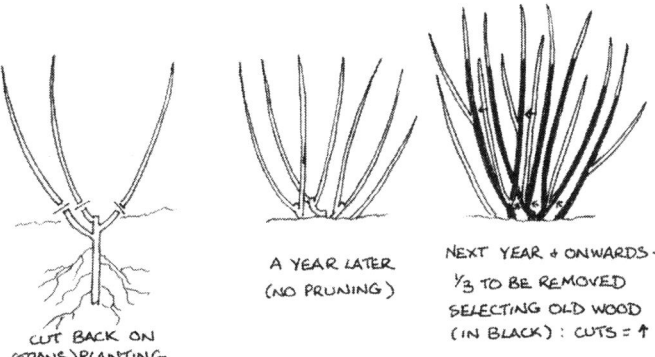

you can assess when a third has been removed. Number two is obvious when you know where the fruit is to be produced but is trickier in practice.

Ideally, we should aim to remove big old branches by cutting out at the base so stimulating new growth to appear there. However, some young growth is on the end, or off the side, of old growth – you can't remove the one without removing the other. We can prune part way down an old shoot to where there is a particularly handsome, strong new shoot – it is not set in stone that we have to remove entire old shoots. But let's not get overly upset if we lose a bit of new growth in the process; it is almost inevitable.

Number three is the most hopeful of the lot: the old branches all seem to be around the edge of the plant and the new growth still to fruit has appeared in a thicket smack in the middle. Do what you can. It might be that you remove a few of the weaker new shoots to keep it more open in the middle and leave it at that. Old plants can be coppiced – everything cut off. The new growth that appears will produce no fruit that year ('Fruit is produced on the growth that appeared the *previous* year'). However, it will have rejuvenated the plant and got rid of a lot of congestion and missing one year's fruiting is perhaps worth enduring. An approach to regular pruning is to coppice half the plants one year and coppice the other half the next, so that you are never without fruit, the plants are stimulated and maybe diseases are less likely to get a hold. Occasionally (it has been stated) such a radical approach as coppicing can upset or shock a plant and it never really recovers. Still, the alternative is to go through the tortuous process of trying to bring a huge gnarled old bush back into production when there is hardly a bit of new growth to produce fruit.

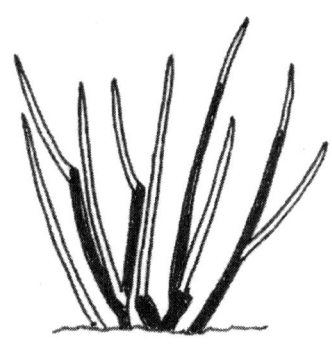

... AFTER PRUNING. ONLY THE NEW GROWTH WILL FRUIT (IN WHITE)

What happens if you don't prune a blackcurrant bush? It gets bigger and denser. Less of the new growth comes from the base and more on the ends and sides of old shoots. The berries tend to be smaller and there can be a build up of diseases, more so than if a proportion of the plant is taken away each year, plus the reduced air movement can encourage diseases like mildew. Verdict: probably worth pruning.

Harvesting

You could just get on with it and pick the berries when and how you fancy, but the tips below might save a little time (and fruit).

1. It might sound a trifle stupid but wait until most of the fruit is black: being called blackcurrants, if you pick them green or red there is the Trades Descriptions Act to consider.

2. You may decide to harvest in two goes. Just one picking is possible but there will be some wastage of unripe fruit if you don't return. Three pickings might be over-doing it – just how much time have you got?

3. Firstly, gently shake a branch, preferably the one you're about to pick. This will hopefully dislodge the prematurely ripened fruit (i.e. squishy ones) and other debris.

4. Position a tub, plastic box or, optimistically, a bucket beneath the branch so that as you pick the fruit it can drop either accidentally or by design and be caught.

5. Use 'soft fingers' to gently run through the fruit. This doesn't refer to digits that have been immersed in washing up water excessively. It means that the berries are not gripped tightly but 'eased' off the stalks. With blackcurrants for home use, picking is usually done as single berries not on the strigs (a cluster of fruits attached together and connected to the branch by a single stalk). It is a little like combing.

6. Periodically, stand up and pick through the fruit. Despite the pre-picking shaking process, the container will have an assortment of dead and yellow leaves, berries still on the strigs and strange, long-legged, yellowish spider-like things which only seem to hide in blackcurrant plants. This could, of course, be done in the comfort of an armchair, down the sides of which squashed berries will be found for decades to come. However, by sorting through during the picking process, it gives you the opportunity to straighten up: roll the shoulders, arch the back, extract the insects, leaves and stalks then on with the picking.

My grandfather developed a neat technique for harvesting, based on the fact that he found it tiresome to bend over and pick fruit. He harvested and pruned in one operation. When the fruit was ripe he would cut out the wood bearing fruit, effectively the old wood, then take it back to the kitchen table where he could remove the berries whilst sitting in comfort with a cup of tea and with Test Match Special on the radio. The plants would continue to grow that year and produce new wood which would fruit the following year. The plants were growing in quite a fertile soil which will have helped. The downsides to this approach are surprisingly few. It is a single harvest meaning that, depending exactly when he did it, he would be wasting some fruit because a proportion of it would be either under ripe or overripe. Also, it would probably involve removing more of the bush than is desirable which inevitably meant a lower yield. He would also get those spider-like things in his tea.

Blackcurrant Problems
Aphids
Sap-sucking stinkers of the highest order. More problematic on blackcurrants because not only do they deplete the plant's resources but one of the main species of pest aphid on currants, the currant blister aphid, also distorts leaves. Here, the leaves towards the ends of shoots (where aphids naturally aim for – it is where a lot of plant resources are being focused) are puckered or, yes, blistered with a yellow and / or red discoloration. Underneath, hidden in the puckering, are these small, pale aphids. The distortion makes it hard to brush out the blighters but hoverflies and ladybirds can easily find them. The infestation is in the spring and early summer, so it is a temporary thing and the effect on the plant is fairly minimal. After that they migrate to their summer

hosts, including hedge woundwort (*Stachys sylvatica*) to return again in the autumn.

Blackcurrant Leaf Midge

This pest simply doesn't get the same press as big bud mite, below, which is fair enough but it can still be a nuisance. Emerging from over-wintering pupae in the soil, the adult flies mate and the females lay eggs in the shoot tips. The eggs hatch in a week and the tiny grubs, usually an unexciting white, feed on the opening leaves for a month. As a result, those leaves fail to open fully, staying small and crumpled and eventually going brown and dying. The larvae return to the soil and further generations ensue, effectively ensuring that the midge can be around from April to August. Healthy leaves can form at intervals. A difficult one to control. If affected tips are noticed relatively early on they can be removed so that the cycle of generations is interrupted but otherwise you wouldn't normally want to be pinching out the shoot tips (generating branching). Certain varieties show resistance: 'Ben Connan' and 'Ben Sarek' are two.

Birds

Not by any means top of the list of bird fodder but definitely there.

Big Bud Mite or Blackcurrant Gall Mite

This charmless little fellow multiplies in a bud to produce thousands of individuals, each only about 0.25mm long. These swarm in spring or early summer by leaping, crawling, being carried (by insects) or by being moved in rain or wind. They can carry with them Currant Reversion Disease, a virus (see below). Infested buds are fat and round in comparison to healthy elongated, pointed buds.

Healthy blackcurrant bushes are able to resist invasion by the mite quite well. However, when infected by reversion virus, that resistance is broken down and mites are able to infest more easily. A downward spiral.

Control: removal of the infested buds in the winter when they are more obvious. If this is done promptly spreading to neighbouring plants is reduced. Otherwise, in conjunction with the virus, remove the whole plant. There are some varieties that are resistant to the mite.

Currant Clearwing Moth

Affecting redcurrants and blackcurrants, this pest is so called because most of its wing area is transparent. Combined with a black and yellow body and flying during the day, it is a surprise we don't notice it (or maybe we do but just don't connect it with it being a mildly pesky nuisance). Easily spotted, however, is the damage: either stems break because there is a tunnel down the middle of it or we see the tunnel when we're pruning. The larva of the moth has eaten its way down the centre of a shoot, unnoticed until the nuisance part: the weakening (and breaking) and possible dying back of infested shoots.

This pest tends to be tolerated, though maybe a little cursed at, since control is limited. If a tunnel is uncovered, not totally dissimilar to a POW escape attempt, then action is required. Cut back the infected shoot to beyond the tunnelling – the grub may still be inside and so can be 'disposed of'. If, for some reason (perhaps there is a good strong lateral shoot) we don't want to cut all the way back, some gardeners have recommended pushing a piece of strong wire down the tunnel until no resistance is felt...

Currant and Gooseberry Leaf Spot

This seems so familiar: in May, dark spots develop on leaves, possibly enlarging and joining together. They start on the older leaves and work their way up the stem. The leaves gradually drop off and, in severe attacks, fruit can shrivel and next year's cropping can be affected. Yes, a fungus having fun just like rose blackspot, apple scab, and many others. Control is also familiar since re-infection is via the fallen leaves. Pick them off or collect them up.

Currant Reversion

This is a virus and is probably the reason for the premature end of cropping in most blackcurrants. When fully infected by the virus the bush continues to grow as before but cropping falls away. From an initial infection, it probably takes three years for a bush to become fully 'reverted'. The word 'reversion' refers to a subtle change in the appearance of the leaves: they become flatter (less corrugated), have fewer main veins, fewer serrations along the margins of the leaf and, at the point where the leaf stalk (petiole) meets the leaf blade / lamina there is less of an indentation (see picture). This all sounds very straightforward – well, maybe – but unless you have infected and uninfected leaves side by side for comparison, this is quite tricky.

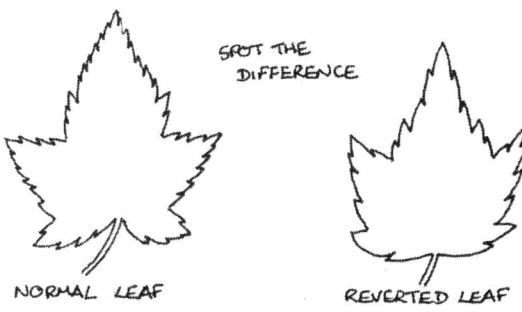

There are other symptoms that show when the first flower buds are about to open: they should be grey and downy but if they are infected they are hairless and brightly coloured. Unfortunately, this difference is more pronounced in some varieties then others.

It is usual for a grower to only notice that there is a problem when fruiting is seriously compromised. By then it will have been providing a constant supply of virus-laden mites to infest your neighbours' plants for some time. There are better ways to make yourself popular.
Control: dispatch the whole bush. Plant resistant variety 'Ben Gairn'.

American Gooseberry Mildew
This can be as big a nuisance on blackcurrants and redcurrants but, in honour of the name, most of the information is found under 'Gooseberries'. One difference with A.G.M. on blackcurrants, however, is that it is believed that re-infection in spring is from spores released from last year's fallen infected leaves. A little light clearing up in autumn might therefore be in order. The varieties listed at the beginning of the chapter are resistant to mildew.

Coral Spot
This is less a disease of blackcurrants and more a symptom of incompetence. It is a fungus that loves dead wood or wood that can't put up much resistance, such as stubs created by poor pruning. It shows up as lots of raised, salmon-pink spots scattered over the affected part. Like an uninvited guest taking over the conversation, coral spot moves on from its initial infection into live wood potentially leading to death of a branch. The currants seem very prone and it can be a particular problem if it gets into the dead stumps at the base of the plant.
Always prune to something – a bud or side branch – so as not to leave out the welcome mat. This is perhaps easier said than done especially when you're trying to squeeze the blades of some loppers in between the stems at the base of a blackcurrant. Cut out any infection that appears 15cm/6" below the visible symptoms and if the soil happens to be within that distance then have an overview of the plant (is the rest of it healthy? Has it been cropping well?) to decide whether it is worth continuing with it.

Hybrid Currants
A **Jostaberry** is cross between a gooseberry and a blackcurrant. It is more vigorous than either of its parents as well as being ungainly and the fruit not being an improvement (think large, dull blackcurrant). The best thing going for it is its disease resistance.

The **Chuckleberry** is a complicated cross of redcurrant, gooseberry and jostaberry meaning there is only a small amount of blackcurrant in there. Nevertheless, it is treated as a blackcurrant when it comes to cultivation and pruning, just as jostaberries are. Chuckleberries produce heavy yields of blackcurrant-like fruit in July, with a great flavour. It also gets extra marks for marketing.

Other interesting things concerning blackcurrants

The flowers (and therefore fruit) are produced on little branching stalks called a strig (try saying 'string' as though you have a cold). The first flowers to open, showing a tinge of red, are at the end of the strig nearest to the branch and when fully open are vulnerable to frost. The last flowers to open are at the end of the strig, hence the fruit developing there will be later to ripen than that from the first flowers.

Cold may cause issues in the spring but it is important to have low temperatures in the winter. Mild winters apparently cause poor and irregular flower bud development (so giving lower yields). 'Ben Lomond' and 'Ben Alder' are particularly badly affected.

The fruit is notoriously sharp-tasting yet the sweetness rating (in 'Brix') is commonly given as being higher (around Brix 13) than other fruit such as blackberries (Brix 7).

BLACKCURRANT TASTING

Vitamin C in blackcurrants is pretty spectacular – about 200mg/100g of fruit, which is not far off four times the amount in lemons. One dilemma we are faced with is how to eat the things.

Vitamin C is water soluble therefore a lot of it is lost when blackcurrants are processed – cooked in puddings or made into jam. The problem we have is how can we retain as much Vitamin C as possible yet still have fruit which is palatable? Some people love blackcurrants raw but for most of us they are so sharp / sour that, eating more than two or three, our faces try to fold inside out.

Cooking enables the easy incorporation of sugar so it would be splendid if a way of doing that was found without destroying vitamin C. The following suggestions carry no guarantee:

Make ice cream. Dairy or non-dairy blackcurrant ice cream requires some skill to avoid the production of purple-coloured bricks. Requirements – a freezer and some patience or an ice-cream machine.

Make a 'smoothie' perhaps with bananas added for the sweetness. Requirements: a fruit-squishing device (blender?).

Hide a few fresh berries in an existing dessert or muesli. Requirements: dessert, muesli, an ability to not overdo it.

Until you make up your mind what to do with them, preserve a good amount of vitamin C by freezing them, then using as required.

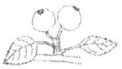

BLUEBERRIES *Vaccinium corymbosum*
(*Vaccinium*, L. for blueberry, *corymbosum*, flowers in a corymb
(flat-topped cluster))
Family: ERICACEAE

Why we should grow blueberries
Antioxidant-acting chemicals; anti-cancer; delayed memory loss, onset of arthritis and deteriorating eyesight (a.k.a. aging). Great autumn leaf colour.

Blueberry Essentials
Varieties
The following are all highbush varieties.
Bluecrop. Heavy crops, full flavour, vigorous, very widely grown, mid-late.
Chandler. Very large fruit with good flavour, heavy crops, mid-late, easy to control size.
Duke. Medium-large, early fruit, reliable with good yields.
Earliblue. Large sweet fruit but needing a sunny spot for the best flavour, vigorous and early.
Spartan. Large well-flavoured fruit produced mid-season, good yields.

SOME LIGHTLY-PECKED BLUEBERRIES

Size: Highbush varieties are 1.3-2m / 4.5-6' in height. The root systems can spread a long way, upto 2m / 6½' diameter spread with depth to over 60cm / 2' though most roots are in the top 30cm / 1'.

Spacing: The accepted spacing for blueberries is in the region of 1.5m / 5'.

Position: An acid soil pH 4.5 to 5.5, possibly 6. Full sun or partial shade. Tolerant of some exposure, but not sustained cold winds.

Feeding: Not that I was going to recommend them, but apparently blueberries don't like animal-based manures and fertilisers. So that leaves us with (obviously non-chemical) feeds which don't raise the pH. Home made compost should be fine as a mulch but not green waste / municipal compost which has a high pH of 7.5 to 8. There are dedicated organic feeds for ericaceous plants based on seaweed. Urine is slightly acidic.

Pruning: Mostly nothing, but if you insist see below.

Pollination: Only partly self fertile so better crops will produced with more than one variety.

Harvesting: As a nice comparison to blackcurrants, blueberries ripening is gradual, usually longer than four weeks. The berries should be completely blue and will indicate their ripeness by detaching easily with little force. Full ripeness means full sweetness. A wonderful plant for regular picking of a few berries for, say, every breakfast.

Propagation: Most successful is a greenwood cutting with a heel. Translation: a 10cm/4" piece of new growth pulled off the stem in June-early July and inserted in 'cuttings compost' in a propagator or polythene tent. Light shade is needed and the rooted cuttings are not re-potted until the following spring.

Weeding: The best control here is a mulch which not only suppresses the weeds but keeps the roots near the surface cooler.

Blueberry Origins

Garden blueberries are derived from the wild highbush blueberry found in the Eastern U.S.A., particularly New Jersey. They were introduced, grown and promoted in the UK, mid 20th century, particularly by the Trehane family of Dorset. There are many crosses between varieties and species including between the highbush and *Vaccinium asheii* otherwise known as the rabbiteye blueberry. The latter brings with it a tolerance of hotter conditions, perhaps of more value in certain areas of the States.

Blueberry Nutrition

As superfoods go, blueberries have to be one of the most disappointing fruits, certainly in terms of minerals and vitamins. On the positive side, there are the antioxidants, amongst the highest levels of any fruit with the remarkable level of 5562 TE (Tolex Equivalents). It would be even more remarkable if I had the remotest clue what a Tolex Equivalent was. Also, should you be trying to lose a pound or two, blueberries could take a more prominent role in your diet: just over 50 calories per 100g is not a lot. The vitamin content is best described as unexceptional: even rhubarb has double the level of Vitamin A. Vitamin C clocks in at about 10mg/100g which is slightly higher than the average apple and the only mineral which seems to be in reasonable quantity is manganese. Potassium is 77mg/100g, Calcium just 6mg/100g and Iron is not disastrous at 0.28mg/100g.

Discussion / rambling / elaboration
One of the first fruits to be outed as a 'super food', it leads by example: given the right conditions a blueberry bush can last a lifetime. Most of our more widely grown soft fruit species stagger on for about 15 years before needing replacing.

Growing conditions
Probably the biggest barrier to many of us growing blueberries is the need for an acid soil. So if you have a soil with a naturally low pH (pH 6.2 or below) you are in luck. Those of us on limey / alkaline soils can still join in by growing in containers, but thereby we enter another world of expense and maintenance (see below). It is even more expensive and arduous to try to convert a limey soil into an acidic one, though it can be done: replacing the soil itself is possible and will involve much barrowing away of limey soil and as much barrowing in of an acid loam. There are additives that will react with the moisture in a soil to lower the pH. For example, sulphur or sulphur compounds will react to produce sulphuric acid. Pine needles are acidic but not easy to come by. Moss peat will do the same but if you have any conscience at all you won't be using that.

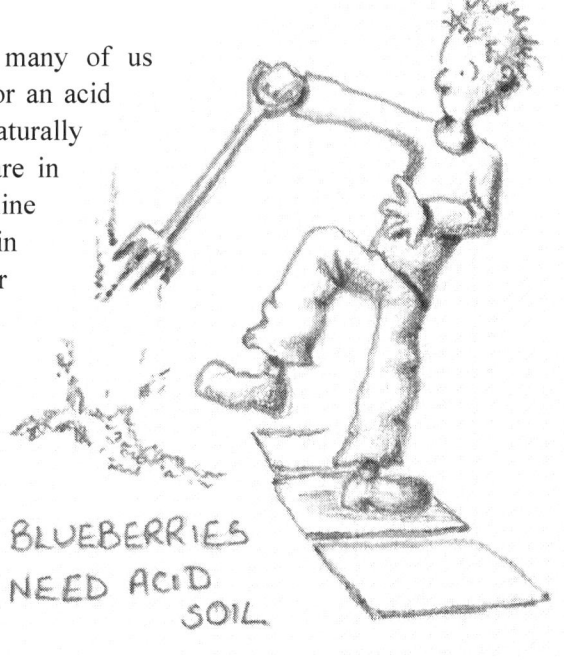

Also required by most blueberries is a period of winter cold (below 8°C) to set the flowers. The length of the period will vary depending on the variety but whatever it is, it's normally easily achieved in the UK. There is a chance that in a warm winter, in a warm part of the country, in a warm part of a garden, we could foul it up.

Growing in containers
Growing any fruit in containers is tricky with, perhaps, the exception of strawberries. Blueberries are generally quite amenable to the idea which is fortunate since, for many of us, it is the only way that we can have them at all.

Ericaceous compost is the growing medium to look for. Interestingly, but not reliably, the packaging of ericaceous compost seems to involve the colour pink.

Perhaps look for the words 'ericaceous' or 'acid-loving' to make sure. As ever, since you have bought, been given or shop-lifted this book because you are interested in organics and the environment, we should avoid using peat-based composts. This simple act is actually harder to do when sourcing acid / ericaceous compost since moss peat is acidic and therefore is the obvious and established choice from which to concoct a compost. But non-peat acid composts are out there. Good hunting.

When a plant has been newly purchased, its roots are likely to be fully occupying the pot. If they're not, they ought to be. This indicates that it can be potted on – in other words, put in a larger pot. The recommendation of when and how is little different to virtually all other container-grown plants, from houseplants to your collection of miniature standard roses: early spring, into pots that are one, no more than two, sizes larger. The idea is that the plant is not left in a sea of soggy compost surrounding the roots with too large a pot whereas the timing is to do with the fact that a blueberry will be about to come into active growth and there will be no check to that growth if it is potted up in February or March. The choice of container is up to you; whatever fits in with your surroundings is perhaps the main factor.

Formative Pruning
To produce stocky, strong frameworks, a young plant is best cut back. How much should be taken off depends on the plant but long shoots could be halved. No more than a couple of years of doing this should set up the plant for its future long life.

Regular Pruning
It is often said (by me) that blueberries are rare in that they need little attention, particularly pruning. And then someone will come along and spoil it by saying it is essential for rejuvenation and renewal of growth – if you don't prune them they will become woody. The idea is that by occasionally (every two or three years) cutting out the occasional piece of old wood that has previously fruited, new vigorous growth is stimulated. If you go to the trouble of this, then cut as low as possible.

This sound, non-interventionist approach is too often ignored by the enthusiastic gardener, wielding their secateurs, feeling that 'surely something has to be done'. Well, I like to feel that we can cater for all peculiarities here.

So, as ever, it helps to know whereabouts on a plant the fruit is produced. In the case of the blueberry it is all over the shop: large, good quality fruit is produced on the growth produced the previous year but slightly smaller berries will grow from older wood. It makes sense, therefore, that if you did nothing you would still have plants that crop well.

At the same time, however, a case could be made for a little shaping (removing congested shoots or those that bow down to the ground), pinching out the tops of long leggy shoots in summer to keep a plant compact and the occasional removal of the oldest, least productive growth down to ground level especially if it helps to open up a plant. Very old wood will have stopped fruiting – it has thickened, it is often in the centre of the plant or low down and it is shaded. But, as explained above, 'essential' it is not – 'desirable' might be a better word.

Blueberry Probems

Birds
The ripe fruit will simply disappear in a flurry of feathers and no matter which species is the perpetrator (usually pigeons, blackbirds and thrushes), netting is the main answer.

Mammals
Well, if we will breed plants that produce such attractive fruit. Mind you, deer, badgers, rabbits and small, uninvited children will go for any fruit within reach. Fencing may help, possibly plugged into a battery.

Vine Weevil
The adult vine weevil, a hard-shelled, brown-dark grey individual, is most likely to be female: hardly any males have been found. Although this may solve certain issues like the complications surrounding mating and whose turn it is to do the washing up, in the long term this is not a great policy. It is generally accepted that, in terms of evolution and coping with changing conditions, a bit of genetic variation is desirable.

Some people would be very happy to see vine weevils erased in one sweep. The adults themselves do little damage – a little light browsing around the leaf margins. It is the offspring that are the main problem and they revel in the roots of container-grown plants, being far less of a problem with plants grown in the open ground (though see 'Strawberries'). The larvae (grubs) are about 8mm long and a creamy white. They feed on blueberry roots in pots for most of the growing season; the plants don't show a lot apart from not growing. Any new growth that has started can wilt, just during the day to start with, then permanently before browning and dying. One of the first biological controls containing a parasitic nematode was developed for just this pest, marketed to us as 'Nemasys'. The product is added to water and the compost in pots is drenched. The nematode (or eelworm) swims to find the larvae and it, apparently, 'enters via any orifice'. Well, I'm not sure how many orifices a vine weevil grub has but I'm guessing at least a couple and that should be enough: the end is nigh. The biggest problem is applying the nematodes in time to save the plant – some growers will apply them prophylactically.

Chafer grubs can have exactly the same effect; they are a lot bigger with large swollen abdomens. There is a parasitic nematode especially for them, too.

Botrytis (Grey Mould)

This fungus is ubiquitous on fruit but blueberries have an extra problem in that flowers, leaves and stems can be affected, especially after some other damage such as frost. Stems with such a fluffy grey coating will continue to die back. Perhaps prompt pruning, plus protection, prevents premature partial plant passing-on.

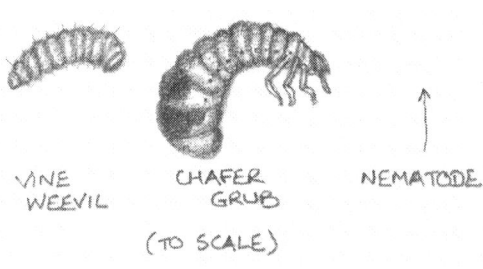

Rust

There is a rust for every occasion. Leeks, willows, runner beans, roses, hollyhocks and many others get rust (all different species) and the name describes the appearance: yellow-orange spots developing into patches are found on the leaves. Eventually the leaves drop off and are a source of infection for next year. Severe and / or repeated infections will weaken a plant and crops will be poor. Hygiene (removing infected leaves from the plant and collecting up those fallen) coupled with keeping the plants well-fed and watered should be enough. Some advocate spraying with potassium bicarbonate as a preventative.

CHERRIES *Prunus avium, P. cerasus, P. x gondouinii*

(*Prunus*, L. for plum, *avium*, L. a bird, *cerasus*, Gk. cherry)

Family: ROSACEAE

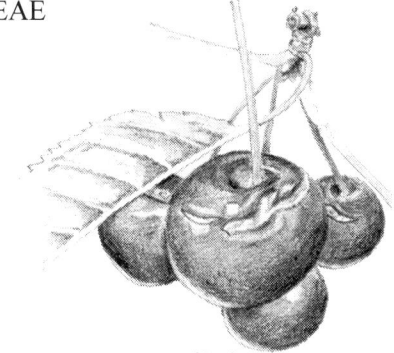

CHERRIES, SPLIT

Why we should grow cherries

The explosion of a ripe cherry in the mouth is hard to surpass – and they are hard to stop eating. There is superb blossom in spring and pretty good leaf colour in autumn.

Cherry Essentials

Varieties: *Prunus avium* is the sweet cherry (wild versions also called Gean or Mazzard). *P. cerasus* is the acid or sour cherry and *P. x gondouinii* is a cross between the two and is known as the Duke cherry.

There is a wide range of wonderful old varieties that are never grown nowadays for the simple reason that the most recent cherries are generally as excellent but without the pollination problems. For example, the sweet cherries are represented in our gardens by modern self fertile varieties, all reliable croppers – '**Celeste**' – early (early July), dark/black, sweet and mild, small stone meaning there is lots of flesh, '**Sunburst**' – mid-season, large, black fruit, picking lasting a week, '**Stella**' – mid-late, dark red, full flavoured. '**Sweetheart**' – late, red/dark red, full sweet flavour, cropping over a slightly longer period. These are all late 20th century varieties bred at Summerland Research Station, British Columbia, Canada.

The dark red acid cherry that most people are familiar with is '**Morello**' which produces fruit mainly used for cooking. If they are left long enough, however, they can become sweet enough (just) for eating fresh. They are produced later than a lot of sweet cherries and are slightly smaller. The name '**Morello**' is often used as an alternative to the common name of 'acid' cherry – it is actually a distinct variety. There used to be many more varieties available, not so nowadays; it is a struggle to find anything other than '**Morello**'. However, '**Nabella**' is another well-regarded acid cherry and might be in some catalogues.

Size: This is dictated by the (relatively small) range of rootstocks available. '**Gisela 5**' is the go-to rootstock for most of us: it reaches about 3m in five years and produces reliable crops. Unfortunately, it needs long term staking (or against a wall) and good feeding and watering. Sometimes offered but fairly uncommon are, in increasing size, '**Krymsk 6**', '**Gisela 6**' and '**Krymsk 5**' with the latter at about 4.5m. Far more available is '**Colt**', the next size up (3.5 - 5m) making it useful for large cherry fans or free-standing trees where you can't quite reach the fruit. '**F12.1**' gives a traditional orchard tree (over 6m) suitable for feeding birds. All rootstocks here are more tolerant of poor soils than '**Gisela 5**'.

Spacing: Rootstock dependent: 3m ('**Gisela 5**') to 5m ('**Colt**') is fine for both fans and half standards

Positioning: The soil requirements are the same for all types of cherry, notably lovely, deep, neutral, moisture-retentive, free-draining with good fertility. However, the aspect varies considerably. In fact, most of us should be able to squeeze in one of each of the cherry species listed above since most of our gardens are boxed in by fences or walls so providing a range of aspects. Sweet cherries prefer the warmth of a south-facing aspect, acid cherries cope with north-facing walls making them quite valuable and dukes should be fine with a west-facing aspect.

Feeding: As with most dwarf trees, cherries on the rootstock 'Gisela 5' need extra attention with an annual application of a compost mulch. Trees on the larger rootstocks are more tolerant of poorer soils but still wouldn't say no to the occasional feeding.

Pruning: Once a dwarf tree is into a routine of cropping, there is some new growth but not an excessive amount. As a result, pruning is at a minimum. There's a bit more on this later in the chapter.

Pollination: The excellent sweet cherries (that we don't grow anymore) are fine in an orchard setting where cross pollination is possible between different trees. For those of us with room for just one or two trees pollination is more of an issue: many cherries need cross pollination yet there are incompatibility groups where one variety may flower at the same time as a different variety yet not pollinate it. The answer therefore, to the detriment of those older varieties, is to choose a more recent selection which is self fertile and which also happens to have very tasty fruit. Acid and duke cherries are self fertile.

Harvesting: Pick when just ripe – keep testing until you get it right.

Propagation: Grafting or budding.

Weeding: Keep weed-free for the first three years, trees on 'Gisela 5' keep clean permanently.

Cherry Origins
The Romans, again. V*eni, Vidi, Et protulit cerasorum* – they came, they saw, they brought cherries (I studied German at school). This information presumably refers to cherries brought into cultivation about 2,500 years ago since wild versions of the species have apparently been in this country, way before our toga-clad friends turned up. The acid cherry *Prunus cerasus* may be a cross between *Prunus avium* and another species, *P. fruticosa*.

Cherry Nutrition
One of the highest levels of sugars of all fruits, on a par with some apple varieties and just behind grapes. Reasonable levels of most minerals and vitamins but nothing special. The juice of cherries is recommended for the relief of gout.

Cherry Botany
Like the other *Prunus*, a cherry is a 'drupe' which consists of several layers (skin, flesh and stone) which originate from the ovary wall (a structure in the flower) and, in the middle of the stone, a single seed. For those of us not familiar with flower and fruit structure, that last sentence was written in English. Suffice it to know that the cherry is a 'true' fruit.

Discussion / rambling / elaboration
Harvesting
Picking cherries is a delightful pastime in that it means you've actually got some cherries to pick and the birds haven't had the lot. You are also obliged to dispose of cherries that don't make the grade – known as eating them on the spot. Split or disfigured fruit tastes just as good as 'complete' fruit, so just ditch the rotten specimens.

Good news – unlike a lot of soft fruit, cherries are picked in the upright position, reaching and stretching – cherry-based yoga. Depending on the rootstock of the tree and the training system (if there is one) you may, however, have to take steps to get to the topmost fruit. This is fiddly. Climbing is, as always, immense fun but cherry fruit spurs are very easy to damage or knock off. Ladders have an element of risk about them and again, if the size of the tree allows, a stepladder with a large platform base is best.

We have the advantage over commercial set-ups in that we can easily return to a tree several times (perhaps every four or five days) to selectively harvest, each time picking just the fully ripe fruit. This spreads the load, so to speak, allowing you to deal with the yield gradually, as well as enjoying and / or processing ripe, best-flavoured cherries.

Orientate yourself as you work so that the fruit is not a silhouette (very easy to do when looking up). You need to be able to assess and compare colours, picking the darkest (ripest) fruits since sugar levels in the fruit rise dramatically as they become fully ripe. The aim is to remove cherries complete with the stalk – destalked fruits might just have to be eaten on the spot again since they don't keep as long. Sometimes, when pulling on a single fruit, another will come away with it – cherries are often borne in pairs or multiples. The twin or companions may not be as ripe. So be it. On the positive side picking is quicker when this happens. Worst of all is when the fruiting spur comes away with the fruit. Fortunately, if you are careful enough, this is a rare occurrence; if it worries you that much, separate from the shoot using scissors.

Still with their stalks attached, sound fruit can last for a week in a cool place. They can be frozen but it is often recommended that the stones are removed before freezing – this can be a little fiddly. Maybe, if you have a pie made from cherries complete with stones, you are constantly expecting them and therefore eat with care. This may take away some of the enjoyment but is perhaps better than chomping happily through a de-stoned-cherry dessert only to encounter 'the stone that got away', necessitating a lengthy wait reading old magazines at the dentist.

CHERRY-BASED YOGA

More on Pruning

Imagine a sweet cherry tree that is already in its productive phase. It is July and the fruit has just been picked. At this time, next year's flowers are initiated and where they are initiated can only be on older wood and a tiny bit of the new growth that has formed so far that year. As a result, the next year's flowers (and resulting fruit) will be produced on old branches and at the base of the new growth (most of that new growth has appeared after initiation). Actually, none of that is remotely helpful when it comes to pruning because any that is to be done is straight after fruiting. We are still within the recommended summer-pruning timeframe of May to July to avoid diseases and there is an in-depth investigation of this under 'Plums'.

It is different for acid cherries that can flower on new growth, in fact that is where most of the crop will be. If a tree is left it will produce small amounts of new growth (to flower and fruit) at the ends of all of the branches. But if it is regularly pruned, that pruning will stimulate more new growth to fruit and flower. It is referred to as a renewal system of pruning and is alongside all the other regulatory pruning that we might do. That makes it quite a different proposition to the sweet cherry which is more of a hands-off approach.

Cherry Problems
Blackfly
Lots of plants have attacks of aphids but for some reason cherry blackfly manages to stand out possibly even more than (a different) blackfly on beans. The young shoots are coated in black aphids, the leaves curl up and the shoots can actually die. They are at their worst in spring and into summer when either they migrate to their summer hosts (woodruff and assorted other wild plants) or they are wiped out by predators which could have done with turning up a few weeks earlier. They return to the cherries in the autumn to lay eggs ready for the next spring. Don't, as some books say, use a tar oil winter wash to try to kill off the eggs – it is horrible stuff, very messy to put on a tree and is self-defeating in that it kills predators also holed up on the tree such as acorid bugs. Also, it's not available any more, though other versions exist. Try instead to surround your tree(s) with a lovely mixture of predator-friendly plants or bug hotels: a good clump of nettles is always helpful, especially for ladybirds.

CHERRY BLACKFLIED CHERRY SHOOT

Birds
Blackbirds are the arch bandits when it comes to cherries but pigeons aren't far behind. Other birds will also have a peck. For some reason I begrudge pigeons a few cherries more than I do blackbirds: pure speciesism apart from the relative rewards for their busking, perhaps. It is easily possible to have absolutely no crop as a result of birds and for that reason the holy grail of cherry growing is a highly dwarfing rootstock so that the whole tree can be netted.

A tiny rootstock called 'Tabel' was tried but the tree was found to be unreliable so currently we get by with 'Gisela 5'. The alternative is to grow the trees as fans and hang down netting from the wall / top wire. It is best to net the trees soon after fruit set since some foul fowl even go for unripe fruit. Bird scarers work for a while (old CD's, ribbons, etc.) but then the scared birds get used to them: ring the changes regularly.

Bacterial canker

Bacterial canker affects a range of Prunus species but probably cherries are attacked most of all with plums coming in a close second. In the autumn and winter, bacteria can enter the stem through wounds or leaf scars. Spread of the infection is rapid in the spring. Strangely, the bacteria can then die out, leaving the damage achieved so far, such as dieback of shoots and sunken areas of bark lower down the branch. A common feature associated with these areas on cherries is oozing amber-coloured gum. One of my reference books describes a symptom of bacterial canker on the trunk or branches of plums as being a 'black depression'; this would be paralleled only by the black depression I develop on finding it.

Since infection in the summer is rare then is makes sense to do any pruning in the summer months. This coincides nicely with summer pruning recommended to avoid the disease silver leaf (see 'Plums' for an over-long discussion of this). If there is any dieback, including yellowing and stunting of leaves on just one branch, it should be pruned out, again in the summer. Leaves of cherries can be superficially affected in late spring when the same disease develops in round patches which then drop out leaving brown-edged holes. This goes by the name of 'shot-hole' to describe the similar effect one can achieve by firing one's shotgun through the foliage of one's cherry tree.

BACTERIAL CANKER CAN CAUSE A BLACK DEPRESSION

Splitting

Cherry fruits can split when there is uneven water supply: if there has been a dry spell followed by heavy rain, the fruit can expand rapidly and split. Picked promptly, these can be used but if left for a while before picking rots can set in. Perhaps a good mulch to buffer the effects of changing soil moisture may help.

Slugworm

A charming name for a poor little thing just trying to make its living destroying leaves. Actually, it sounds like something out of Lord of the Rings. Affected leaves have what is called 'window-paning' or 'skeletonising' where the upper layers have been eaten, leaving veins and lower epidermis to die in patches. The black, shiny, big-headed slug-like larva of a sawfly feeds for about a month in late spring, pupates in the soil and the adults emerge to lay eggs and do it all again in late summer. This second generation's pupae normally remain in the soil over winter. Let other creatures do the controlling since it is very unlikely to get out of hand.

Other Issues
- Short season and no fresh storage.
- Late frosts.
- Hail.

Random Nonsense
If music be the food of love, cherries aren't far behind. Luscious, succulent, red, suggestive – imagine dangling them into the mouth of your loved one. Strewth, I've come over all of a fluster.

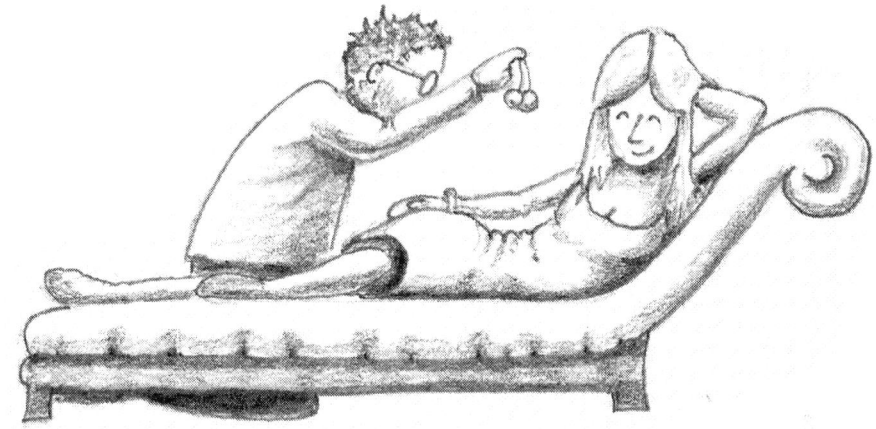

All parts of a cherry can be used, though most of us will just use the sensible bit – the flesh. The stones, sucked clean of all vestiges of edible cherry, can be collected and used as a kind of hot water bottle: in an appropriate bag, they can be heated up in the oven or a microwave, whichever you feel is safest, then popped between the sheets. Smaller versions can be used to ease aching parts especially if you've overdone the gardening that day (perhaps by picking cherries?). The stalks can apparently be used medicinally by soaking them in water. The resulting tonic seems to have quite wide–ranging properties, aiding with lung and blood issues as well as the ever popular steadying of the bowels.

Growing cherry trees as free-standing trees or as fans are the main options for most of us. There is some research to suggest that given the space we could get a reasonable yield by growing in a more informal way: a high hedge. The pruning technique has yet to be explained but it is an intriguing idea; closely planted trees giving blossom, fruit and autumn colour and a boundary marker.

There is reputed to be a custom in Yorkshire involving gathering around the cherry tree, singing to it, then taking it in turns to give it a shake. The number of fruits hitting the deck when you shake it will give you the number of years you have left to live. Probably as accurate as anything else, maybe even more so since the hale and hearty amongst us would be able to give it an extra vigorous shake, and the less able dislodging fewer fruit indicating a sooner demise. I'm slightly concerned, however, for those lower down the list who find all of the loosest cherries have already dropped. Maybe it is best not to look at this kind of thing too closely.

DAMSONS *Prunus damascena and other related fruit*
(*Prunus*, L. for plum, L. *damascena*, from Damascus)
Family: ROSACEAE

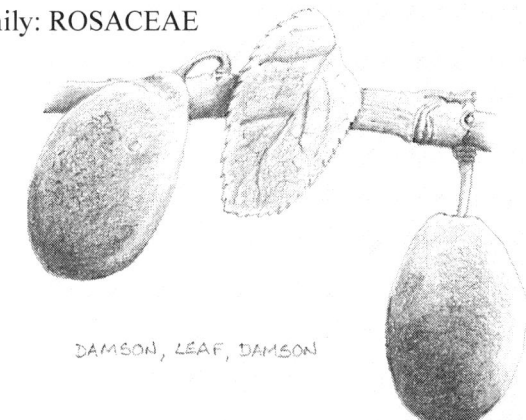

DAMSON, LEAF, DAMSON

Why we should grow damsons and friends
Wonderful blossom, terrific powerful flavour, less vigorous trees.

Damson etc. Essentials
Varieties
Damson Merryweather: Prolific and with a lovely rich flavour and though the fruit is smaller than a plum it is larger than other damsons; flowering group 3.

Damson Farleigh: A cooking damson, late season (mid September), the heaviest cropping damson with good disease resistance; flowering group 4. A third obtainable variety is **Shropshire Prune** which has an excellent flavour but is a lighter cropper; sometimes called **Westmoreland Prune** or **Cheshire Prune** – or just **Prune** to stop the bickering. There are no notable varieties of blackthorn or bullace and cherry plums are classed as red, yellow or black.

Size: In this chapter only the damsons are on rootstocks (the same as plums) and hence of variable size. Damsons are considered to be 'compact' anyway, so on, say, 'Pixy' rootstock they will make trees only about 2-2.5m/6-8'. The rest are limited only by their circumstances: blackthorn / sloe and bullace are in the range 1m-3m whilst the cherry plum or myrobalan was actually used as a rootstock for plums – pretty big ones: over 5m/16'.

Spacing: For damsons, spacing depends on the chosen rootstock, but for the aforementioned 'Pixy' it would be about 2.5m/8'. The others are nearly always planted closely, in hedges. Blackthorn, for example, would be planted as one-year-old whips in a zig-zag, 30cm/1' along the row.

Feeding: Unless the soil is very poor, there is little need for extra feeding. Perhaps a good mulch of rich organic matter for the first few years? Damson on 'Pixy' will need a little more input.

Pruning: Minimal. Three out of the four species here are, if not all naturalised, then at least used in hedges indicating that pruning is not such a fiddly affair as with other top fruit. Even damsons can be pretty much left alone with just occasional 'adjustments' once they have been set up with some simple formative pruning.

Pollination: Self fertile but, as usual, there will be heavier crops if there are more than one compatible variety in the proximity of each other.

Damson and Others Origins
Damson *Prunus damascena* or P. *insititia*: from the Middle East as the name suggests (Damascus = *damascena* and possibly 'damson'). The second possible name, *P. insititia*, doesn't contradict this but does offer the possibility that it is really a selection of the bullace.

Sloe / Blackthorn *Prunus spinosa*: a native tree with black bark, flowering before the leaves open. Lots of thorns. Fruit is small and black – large pea size.

Bullace *Prunus insititia*: a naturalised tree with brown bark, flowering after the leaves have unfurled. Not so many thorns. Fruit is twice the size of a sloe and black or green-yellow when ripe.

Cherry plum *Prunus cerasifera*: only known in cultivation, though supposed to have come from the same region as the common plum (Caucasus, Western Asia). Also known as myrobalan and used as a rootstock for plums and damsons. Purple versions are quite common as a street tree e.g. *P. cerasifera* 'Nigra'.

Damson Nutrition
Calcium levels are pretty good (damsons have twice that of plums at 24mg/100g).

Discussion / rambling / elaboration
Damson Problems
These species are smaller, tougher and less subject to the diseases hitting plums and gages.

Hedges
Some *Prunus* in this section can be used as hedges such as, not surprisingly, sloes and bullaces, which make an excellent barrier against whosoever you want to keep out. Just be aware of the suckering which again can be a feature of this genus: blackthorn stretches out, like the tentacles of octapi, and pops up quite a way away. The cherry plum *Prunus cerasifera* comes in different coloured forms and, if planted closely – about 1m / 3' – in a bush form, a fruiting hedge can be created. Stakes are knocked in between the plants and branches woven between them. Lumps

can be cut out if required to maintain the hedge since cherry plums are tough old things. The downside is that fruit may be produced only every other year. The wonderful flowering is regular, though.

Damson 'Farleigh', though basically a cooking damson, is very hardy and is used as a windbreak.

The downside to having a flowering, cropping hedge is when it comes to trimming it – it can't really be cut like other hedges which receive a short back and sides at regular intervals. If this was done, most of the cropping would be lost in the process. Still, a more selective, time-consuming pruning could be done to keep everything ticking over.

Character Assassination

What a bunch. This tough crew are the Peaky Blinders of the fruit world. Not only are they mostly pest and disease free but they can grow in the most hostile conditions. This is illustrated by the popularity of damsons in Cumbria. On top of that, if they don't actually have thorns, then they are very capable of presenting 'sharp bits'. Blackthorn is the worst of all in this respect: its thorns are reckoned to be amongst the most septic, being coated in algae and cleverly brittle. This ensures that, not only are you injected with bacteria and algae, but the 'needle' breaks off and makes itself hard to extract.

Effects of Damsons

Damsons and their relatives will activate the digestive system. I can testify to the effectiveness in this regard: as a teenager and therefore lacking a standard helping of common sense (whereas now I have no excuse) I came across a feral damson tree in a lane and helped myself to a considerable quantity of the terrific fruit. The after effects are too grisly to report in detail, just that I was grateful to have had a change of clothing.

What to do with Damsons and friends

Damson wine is particularly splendid. One of the most popular uses is the steeping of fruit in gin and the most popular of these is without doubt sloe gin. This may be because sloes are plentiful in the countryside coupled with the inability to find anything else to do with them. It is often recommended that they are picked after the first frosts so that they release their flavours most easily. Since frosts are unreliable in their timing and birds will also be interested in the ripe fruit before the frosts, this process can be mimicked by picking earlier and freezing. The manual version of this procedure to release the flavour of the flesh is to prick every fruit individually with a needle. This is quite time consuming

but, after getting punctured by evil thorns during the picking process, maybe this engenders a satisfying feeling of revenge. There are good reports of damson gin too, though when it comes to drinking fruit-flavoured alcohol, perhaps any skilled tasting goes out of the window after the second glass.
The process is as follows:

450g/1lb of Sloes (treated as above)
170g/6oz Sugar
1 litre/1.75pint Gin (since the subtleties of fine botanical gins can be lost behind the fruit flavour, it may be worth buying an economical brand)

Combine all of the ingredients in a screw top jar and store for three months, shaking every day for the first couple of weeks and then 'occasionally' thereafter (= when you remember). After the three months, strain off the fruit and bottle (keep the old gin bottles handy for this). Leave until the following winter before drinking: it should be sipped and relished, not knocked back in volume. Behave yourself.

While we are on the subject of concentrated alcohol… whereas buying cheap gin and converting it to something fruity in the home is perfectly legal, I'm pretty sure that any form of domestic distilling is strictly not allowed. Therefore I cannot condone Lawrence D. Hill's directions in 'Grow Your Own Fruit and Vegetables' where he suggests that a spirit of sorts, of unknown percentage proof, can be made by putting the aforementioned superb damson wine in a freezer and picking out the ice as it freezes. This is the water that has frozen first and the more that is removed before the whole thing goes solid will leave behind a concentrated fruity alcohol. Even if this practice was found to be highly enjoyable and a terrific damson brandy generated, it can't possibly be recommended. Most certainly not.

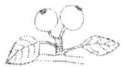

FIGS *Ficus carica*

(*Ficus*, L. for fig, *carica*, of Caria, a place in Asia Minor)

Family: MORACEAE

Why we should grow figs

It is very difficult to get hold of fresh figs without taking out an overdraft or growing your own. A fully-ripe fig fresh from the tree is swoonable overable. The tree, and particularly the leaves, give a terrific tropical / Mediterranean feel to a garden.

FIG, RIPE

Fig Essentials

Varieties: **Brown Turkey** is by far the most common variety offered for sale in this country, basically because it is the most reliable. **White Marseille** and **Brunswick** are also available.

Size: Up to 3.5m / 12 feet wide by 2.5m / 8 feet high (restricted size), up to 9m / 30 feet (unrestricted).

Spacing: 3m / 10 feet apart for restricted trees, 3.5m / 12 feet for restricted fan-trained trees.

Feeding: Unlimited feeding and watering is on a par with not keeping the roots restricted: lots of shoot and leaf growth, limited fruit growth. In practice, an established tree in a clay-dominated UK soil, will need little input. Perhaps a foliar spray of seaweed now and then.

Pruning: For a restricted free-standing tree, little pruning is required: the occasional removal of a branch to relieve congestion or to maintain a shape is fine in early-mid winter. For more challenging pruning, see later in this chapter.

Pollination: Self fertile, in fact, parthenocarpic (producing fruit with no pollination needed at all).

Harvesting: A fig is ready to eat when it has enlarged, changed colour from a bright green to a purple-brown ('Brown Turkey'), drooped to a more vertical position and has softened – give it a little squeeze to check. Another indication is that other creatures are exploring it too.

Propagation: Hardwood cuttings in November or layering in spring-summer.

Fig Origins
Middle East. One of the oldest of all cultivated fruits. Evidence of the consumption of figs (probably wild ones) is found in Neolithic sites of over 10,000 years ago. It is the sole representative of the *Ficus* genus outside in this country; indoors we have the Weeping Fig *Ficus benjamina* and the Rubber Plant *Ficus elastica* as well as one or two others.

Fig Nutrition
Low water content compared to other fruit (77.5%). Pretty good calcium levels (35mg/100g) and terrible vitamin C levels (2mg/100g). Relatively average levels of other minerals and vitamins.

Fig Botany
Concentrate, now; a fig is a flower which is turned inside out, called a syconium. Following pollination many tiny single-seeded fruits (achenes) are formed inside. We tend to think, incorrectly, of a fig as the fruit with little seeds inside, in the same way that a strawberry has the genuine fruits - achenes again - studded on the outside of the big, red, fleshy structure. But that's botany for you. More below.

Discussion / rambling / elaboration
Figs are surprisingly easy to grow provided that you don't expect too much, which is about as useful as saying Swahili is dead simple as long as you don't want to speak it. To clarify: they are undemanding to grow (in fact they normally need restraining) but in this country we expect the total annual yield to be considerably lower than in their native homeland, wherever that is. Actually it is probably the Middle East though figs are now very widely grown. We have too short a growing season combined with lower levels of sunshine and lower temperatures to get the best yields, but it feels that to get anything at all is a triumph.

Figs produce an early crop called the 'breba' crop which has formed from tiny figlets. These existed on the shoots from the previous autumn and had been waiting to burst into life ever since. In fact we are encouraged to remove anything larger than these pea-sized fruits in the autumn since it is only the tiny figs that will become usable fruit. So then the breba crop comes and goes and lots of figs of varying sizes develop, none of which will come to fruition apart from the next batch of tiddlers doing so next year. So spend a happy hour or two picking them off and ending up as sticky as a bucket of toffee on a hot day.
In warmer climes all of the figs we are removing would zoom away and become the main crop. In fact this fruit, developing on the new wood, is considered to be superior to the breba crop, and sometimes it is the breba crop which is removed when still young in favour of the maincrop. After our breba crop I have tried

leaving the very largest of these late figs, no more than one per shoot, plus of course the tiniest for next year. If there happens to be a warm, sunny autumn the idea was that some of these larger fruits may ripen, with the energy going only into these. It doesn't work. The most I've managed, after a hot summer, was a crop of small, almost-ripe maincrop figs with some flavour but little sweetness. In summary, to achieve two crops of figs in one year:
- Restrict the growth of the tree.
- Grow in a sheltered sunny place.
- Have a long hot summer.
- Or move to the Mediterranean.

Planting

Avoid rich, moisture-retentive soils. This doesn't mean figs don't like moisture and feeding – quite the opposite - just that if they get too much the plants will be huge and any crop will be out of reach. They produce good crops on quite small restricted plants so, to achieve this, take small plants and restrict them: planting can be in containers (45cm/18" minimum) or in lined holes in the ground. For the latter, the traditional way is to dig a hole 60cm by 60cm (2' x 2') and fit old paving slabs flat in the bottom and vertically around the sides. Wouldn't it be helpful to use 60 cm x 60cm slabs? (Five of them if you were wondering). Fill the pit with good topsoil including some organic matter such as compost, all on top of some drainage material.

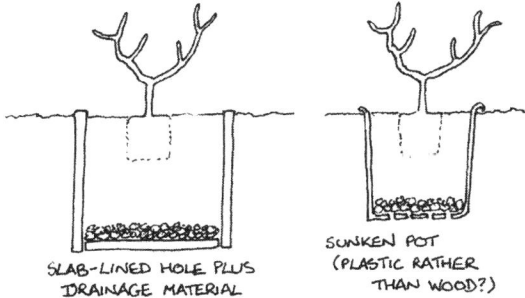

SLAB-LINED HOLE PLUS DRAINAGE MATERIAL

SUNKEN POT (PLASTIC RATHER THAN WOOD?)

The idea is that the fig starts off enjoying growing in the lined pit to produce a small plant and then slows down when the roots encounter the sides. It is expected that roots will find their way through gaps in the slabs but will still be restricted enough to control the size. The same effect can be achieved by plunging a container in the ground. Make sure that, if planting is on heavy clay, the hole you have dug doesn't act as a sump, that is, collect water.

Pruning

Pruning is best done early in the winter. This is unusual for the majority of our fruit which, given the choice, would be done later, perhaps February. Figs, like vines – perhaps it is a feature of hot climate plants – will bleed if cut late in the dormant period: the sap rises early.

For a free-standing tree / bush little pruning is required apart from the occasional removal of pieces to shape it. This is particularly the case if you have remembered to restrict the tree (see planting, above). It is important to understand that the fruit is produced in this country on the growth produced the previous year. So if it was decided to give a plant a haircut in the winter by cutting back all of the ends of the shoots then the fruiting growth will have been removed. Result: no figs. Therefore if you need to reduce a plant, do so by taking out only a few selected branches and then repeat the operation the following year, maybe getting into a regular cycle. Hopefully the plant will be positioned and restricted enough in its growth to mean pruning is not required.

This is where you say 'What happens if you have a friend who might not have planted their fig in a way to restrict its growth?'. All is not lost though you do need to pay attention – and put in some work every year. Firstly, you (or your friend) will need a framework at a manageable height. What is meant by this is a permanent structure, a thick stem or stems, should rise from the ground to a height of about 1.5m (5'), give or take a bit. Ideally you would have created a framework gradually from when the plant was quite small in the same way you would formatively prune an apple tree.

Since you might have realised quite late on that this tree hasn't been restricted in any way, then you really need to start the process by pollarding the plant; that is, cutting through thick stems, ideally at junctions, at about the desired height. The response of the tree will be to send up a cluster of young shoots. This is the growth that will fruit next year (the breba crop) and is called one-year old wood. When you come to do the pruning in, say, December, strictly speaking this growth will be less than a year old. All you will remove of these one year old shoots is weak and congested growth plus a small proportion of the strong, vigorous shoots. "You fool," you cry, "they were going to fruit." And this is true, but you need to get into a routine of some shoot removal each year in order to promote new fruiting growth for the following year.

An illustration: a particular branch ends in just ten new shoots. For the reasons given above you might remove five of them in the winter. The following summer two

FIG TRUNK POLLARDED   REACTION - ONE YEAR LATER   THINNING TO LEAVE WELL-PLACED SHOOTS TO FRUIT things happen. Fruit is produced on the five remaining shoots and new growth is produced at the base of the shoots which were removed and this new growth will fruit the following year. So, let us say that at the end of that year there are the old five shoots that fruited (now termed two year old wood) plus eight brand new shoots: we will now remove the two year old shoots (principally to keep the whole tree under control) so, again, stimulating new growth for the next year. Plus, of the eight new shoots, we might remove a couple of weak or badly placed ones. From now onwards, our annual pruning will consist of the removal of two year old wood and a few feeble one year olds. It is usual at this point for someone to ask about the fact that there is new, one year old, soon-to-fruit wood at the end of the two year old branches. Well, so what? It is now over 3m (10') up in the air and you are losing control over the growth. So do as you're told and stick to that annual removal.

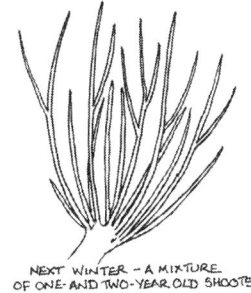
NEXT WINTER – A MIXTURE OF ONE- AND TWO-YEAR OLD SHOOTS

TWO-YEAR OLDS REMOVED PLUS 2 OR 3 WEAK SHOOTS

Pruning is required if a trained tree has been created: to maintain a fan with its evenly spaced branches, new growth is cut back to 5 leaves in the summer. Outward-growing branches are either tied into a space or removed and it might occasionally be prudent to prune out an old branch and replace it with a new one.

Dried Figs

Figs can be dried, at a domestic level, by using a small dehydrator. However, lovers of fresh figs will find this heresy. It almost goes without saying that figs produced in this country will be eaten fresh, unless there has been a remarkable crop on a particular tree and the digestive systems of consumers will be seriously compromised if they ate any more fresh fruit. It has often been pointed out that figs grow with little in the way of inputs (a.k.a. chemicals) in their native habitat (Turkey, for example) and therefore it is not worth paying extra for organic figs. However, it is the post-harvest treatment that is worth considering.

Non-organic figs are treated with particularly toxic chemicals such as methyl bromide to deal with the fig moth, a pest that would love to hitch a ride to countries which are fig moth-less. Incidentally, organic figs are also treated but in more complicated and expensive ways such as freezing or exposing to high levels of carbon dioxide. Some people find fresh figs not that easy to eat, especially when a helpful friend has pointed out the similarity between the red, moist flesh and unnamed body parts.

Pollination

A fig fruit is a strange structure in comparison to more conventional fruits. The skin develops from a part of the flower called the receptacle, which is unusual to start with, but the rest of the flower is hidden inside the receptacle. This inverted flower is called a syconium and the inside is composed of male parts bearing pollen and two types of female parts (called carpels): short and long. Most figs grown are self fertile: they will produce fruit without the need for an insect to exchange pollen between flowers. In fact, pollination is not required, full stop – the fruit is formed parthenocarpically. This is just as well since the insect that would normally do the pollinating is not found in the UK. It is required for the older 'Smyrna' varieties which aren't grown here. As a result, we don't need to know about this complicated and fascinating procedure. So here it is (you do need a degree in botany or to have read the bit in the Introduction on flower and fruit structure).

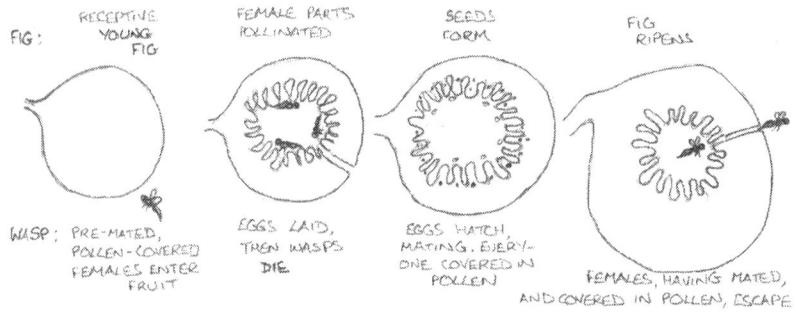

A tiny wasp (1 mm long) squeezes through a hole in the base of the syconium (flower-enclosed-by-a-receptacle if you weren't paying attention earlier). This hole is so small that the wasp, a female, loses her wings in the process of entering, meaning she can never fly away; a captive carrying pollen from outside. She will pass the pollen to the stigmas of the long carpels (collective female parts of the flower, remember) – cross fertilisation for the figs. The seeds will develop in the ovaries of the long carpels.

Having already mated, the wasp lays eggs in the ovaries of shortened carpels and these eggs, on hatching, release a brood of wingless males and winged females. As long as other female wasps have entered the syconium, too, and laid eggs, there will be lots of males and females hatching that can eventually mate without the worry of incest – cross fertilisation for the wasps. The other function of the males is to make a tunnel to the outside through which the females can escape. The females (having mated) will now go off to another fig tree carrying pollen and start the whole process over again. The males die after reaching the outside.

Now, you might feel a little uncomfortable about all of this going on inside something you want to eat. But most of the occupants will have vacated by the time the fruit is ripe. The only wasps that are left behind are the original females who died after laying their eggs. Incidentally, even they aren't really there since the fruit releases an enzyme called ficain which dissolves the dead wasps and utilises the nutrients in the developing fruit and seeds. Remember, none of it is happening in home-grown crops anyway. So relax.

Random Nonsense

I have occasionally wondered if the phrase 'I don't give a fig' refers less to the limited value of said fruit and more to the fact that there has been a poor yield ('I don't give a fig because I haven't got any'). Or maybe more accurately it is that the word 'fig' is a simple short word beginning with 'f' that makes a snappy substitute for less acceptable F words.

Figs are in the MORACEAE family which is only a surprise if you know that mulberries are also in it. Mulberries related to figs? That is like saying a recent American president is related to the rest of us (he is, but not obviously).

The leaf of the fig has long been used as a modest covering for the nether regions, certainly in classical and religious art. I've found it hard to see how the leaves are attached (barely visible vine tendrils? Velcro?) and to understand what happens on a hot day. When it is old and shrivelled, for example, is a leaf necessary at all? Who said innuendo was dead?

Ever been short of paper glue? Need to seal up that envelope? Just pop out to your fig and sacrifice a small shoot. The white sap that emerges from the cut surface (beware – it can be an irritant) is latex and apparently is as good as paper glue. I have tried this and can confidently say, what a load of horse excrement. The Inland Revenue was not convinced when I explained that the cheque for monies owed must have fallen out of the envelope because my fig-sap glue hadn't held. No imagination these people.

GOOSEBERRIES *Ribes grossularia* or *R. uva-crispa*

(*Ribes*, from Arabic, acidic, *grossularia*, L. for gooseberry, *uva-crispa*, curly grape)
Family: GROSSULARIACEAE

THE LITTLE DANCING LEGS OF A GOOSEBERRY FLOWER

Why we should grow gooseberries
Masochism, reliable, long-lived, versatile.

Gooseberry Essentials
Varieties
The Leveller: my granddad's favourite, a heavy cropper with excellent yellow-green fruits. **Careless**: with a good-sized green fruit this is one of the most popular gooseberries but is susceptible to mildew. **Hinnonmaki Red**: medium sized ruby red fruits ready mid July with good disease resistance, also **Hinnonmaki Yellow. Whinhams Industry**: a good-flavoured red gooseberry from 1850 which crops well in shade and poorer soils in late July though not great resistance. **Rockula**: red, early fruit with some mildew resistance and slightly drooping habit. **Pax**: large red fruit on upright almost-spineless plants with good mildew resistance and 'moderate' dessert flavour. **Invicta**: large green fruits (if they are yellow they are over-ripe) and mildew resistant; late July.

Size: 1.2-1.5m / 4-5'.

Spacing: 1.2m apart, depending on variety.

Position: The plants will tolerate light shade and still crop well so are suited to planting underneath top fruit, for example.

Feeding: Regular top dressings of a rich organic matter such as compost or manure in spring preceded by a couple of handfuls of wood ash. During the early part of the growing season, dilute urine and / or comfrey liquid can be watered on. All of these have reasonable levels of potassium, a deficiency of which is the most common.

Pruning: Initial formative pruning is desirable to create a framework and give early cropping. Pruning also involves removal of the 3 Ds and maintaining an open shape for good light distribution and ease of picking.

Pollination: Self fertile.

Harvesting; Carefully, making sure small children are not within hearing distance. Pick early for cooking, always leaving some to ripen fully and eat fresh. Start in early June, usually.

Propagation: Hardwood cuttings in October-November.

Weeding: Avoid weeds, especially perennial ones, from establishing initially because the roots of gooseberries are near the surface and will be damaged by excavations. Every year spread a mulch underneath possibly combined with a good square of well-anchored cardboard.

Gooseberry Origins
A European native, though mainly North Europe where it prefers the cooler conditions. Apparently first noted in this country in the thirteenth century, though it might be that the first importers and growers of gooseberries weren't terribly good at writing earlier than that.

Gooseberry Nutrition
Middling levels of minerals and vitamins e.g. Vitamin C is 14mg/100g compared to the average apple at 6mg/100g and blackcurrants at 200mg/100g. Lowest sugar levels of all temperate fruit, though that must be variety and ripeness-dependent.

Discussion / rambling / elaboration
Propagation
Hardwood cuttings should succeed but they are not as bomb-proof as blackcurrant cuttings. With their tendency to produce low branches, gooseberries also layer well (the branches naturally root into the ground, usually where you don't want them). Cuttings should be removed from, preferably, young vigorous plants, taking growth produced that same year: it is quite pale grey in colour.

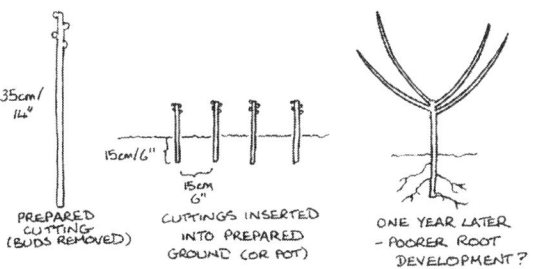

The prepared cuttings should end up being about 35cm / 14" long so pieces are removed from the parent plant longer than this: the soft tip is removed to just above a bud and the bottom of the cutting is removed to just below a bud.

Now we have a discrepancy: usually gooseberries are grown on a bare stem or, technically, a leg. The resulting plant should look a little like our open centre bush apple tree – a wine glass shape. To achieve this we don't want any shoots below the crown which itself will form at the top of the cutting. The problem we have is that if we remove all of the buds (and thorns) apart from the top four or five as we would normally do to grow a plant in this way, then root formation is not as good as when all of the buds are left. But if all of the buds are left, then shoots will appear below the crown.

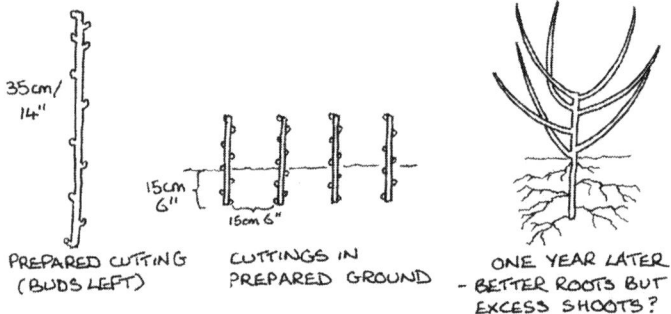

Well, if you were concerning yourself with trivia like the existence of a deity or extraterrestrial life or What It Is All About, then pull yourself together and consider the serious matter of your gooseberry cuttings having suckers. The answer might be to leave the buds on and any shoots that arise below the top 4/5, remove them a year later when you come to move the new plant. It is a compromise because it is not ideal to waste the plant's energy and resources producing unwanted shoots. Still, if it means you get a rooted cutting rather than a de-budded rootless stick, I'd go for the former. Alternatively, stop worrying and grow your plant as a multi-stemmed thicket (a.k.a. a stool) which is probably better for poorer soils anyway.

Whatever you do, the prepared cutting should be inserted in a deep pot of gritty compost – deep enough to cover the bottom 15cm / 6" of the shoot. This will leave 15cm / 6" of bare stem before those top four or five buds (perhaps try removing the buds and thorns from this middle section if you still want that leg). It could also be positioned in a trench of well-prepared soil outside: a slit is made in the soil and sharp sand or grit is trickled into the bottom. Cuttings are lined out in this slit 15cm / 6" apart before it is firmed back together.

It is normal to plant two-year old plants (that's what you'll probably get if you buy one): in a year's time the successful cuttings can be spaced out to 30cm / 12" apart and grown on for another year or left in their original spot for a further year before transplanting to their final position.

Pruning

Formative pruning is extremely similar to setting up an open centre bush apple tree. The new shoots on a bought plant or one raised from a cutting are halved to an outward-facing bud. 12 months later, the new growth which has resulted is treated in the same way. In fact, in pruning system number one, below, the halving of the new growth at the end of a shoot continues for the rest of the shrub's life. Cordons are dead easy. Treat them as a single vertical branch as in pruning system 1, spur pruning (below).

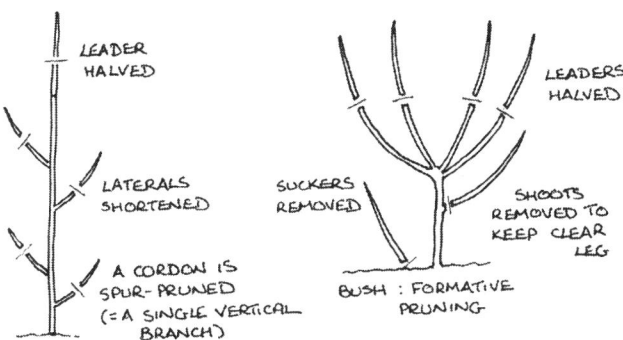

It would be wonderful to have a fruit for which the maintenance pruning is simple and straightforward. Unfortunately the gooseberry isn't it. Well, it might be if you ignore most of the following and go directly to number two, below. The first point of interest is that gooseberries flower and fruit on the old wood and at the very base of the new growth. It makes sense, therefore, to suggest that the majority of new wood is disposable. Pruning regime one follows exactly this, with the removal of much of the new shoots, not only in winter but partially in summer, too. The idea is that it clears out congestion leaving a very open plant with good air movement and high quality, large fruit great for dessert use. There is also the appearance; as George Glenny said in 1878 in 'The Culture of Fruits and Vegetables': 'Gooseberries may be… grown to miniature trees, they are very ornamental, and therefore pleasing…'

Some jolly good reasons not to go anywhere near this approach include:
1) The amount of time and effort to carry it out, especially any summer pruning when there is, of course, hardly anything else to do.
2) The pain involved. Also, exactly how much blood do you want to keep in your veins?
3) It is not necessary: a government leaflet on gooseberries states that this kind of pruning stimulates excessive shoot growth. This is a waste and is using resources of the plant that could be going in to fruit production.

So let's have a look at it.

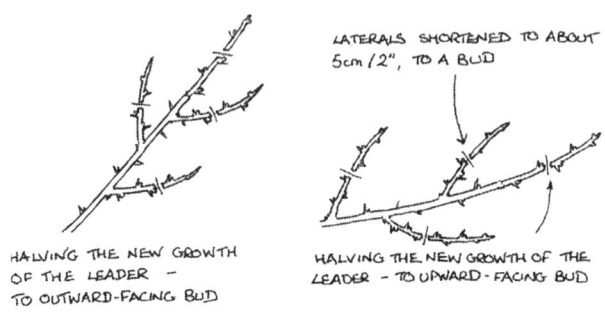

Pruning regime #1 Also known as spur pruning.
In the winter, halve the new growth at the end of each branch. This young piece is called the leader. As ever, cut to a bud, often an outward facing bud, unless the branch is quite low in which case choose an upward facing bud. Next, shorten all of the new growth which is sticking out from the side of each branch. These are the laterals. Don't remove them completely however, because, as indicated above, fruit can appear at the bottom of the laterals. Prune away the laterals leaving about 5cm / 2". Try to find a bud to prune to. Summer pruning can be missed out but it is recommended by some to, again, keep the plant open as possible for picking, plus dispatch some encroaching P & D. The new laterals arising from each branch are shortened to 10cm / 4" in July. If summer pruning is carried out, then the winter pruning will consist of reducing further those laterals. This system of pruning is used for a cordon gooseberry where there is a single vertical stem – effectively a branch with a leader.

Pruning Regime #2 Also known as regulatory pruning.
Leaders are left untipped. Laterals are left untouched. Whole, undesirable shoots / branches can be removed entirely but we need to establish what is meant by 'undesirable'. In a couple of words, the answer is 'apple tree' – it is again the same as for an open centre bush apple tree: removal of the 3 D's, removal of low branches including those below an established canopy (if there is one), removal of crowded or crossing branches to achieve an open centre with lots of air and light and evenly spaced branches. There should be a larger crop using this method but the individual fruits could be smaller. In answer to that, if you are desperate for

large gooseberries and don't want to follow the spur pruning approach, thin out the fruit as it forms or make an early picking of fruit for cooking leaving the remainder to ripen and grow for dessert use.

Gooseberry Problems
Birds
If you think that our feathered friends aren't interested, just wait until the fruit starts to ripen and get a little sweeter. The bush itself is not terribly hospitable but that doesn't matter too much when the branches are low and getting lower under the weight: a pigeon will happily reach from ground level. Those plants hidden in amongst other trees and shrubs à la forest garden seem to suffer least. Are fruits harder to spot with a mixed foliage background or do the birds feel more uncomfortable foraging in that situation as opposed to a stark, bare-soil gooseberry bed? Control? Prompt picking and tolerance of loss seems a very popular approach, about as popular in fact as netting a spikey bush is unpopular: it is more likely to get you to fork out for a fruit cage than any other reason.

Gooseberry Sawfly
Not one but three: the common, lesser and pale gooseberry sawflies. The common is……the most common, about 15mm/1/2" in length and a pale green with black dots along its length and a black head. Eggs are laid in spring on the underneath of the leaves and larvae emerge in a week, meaning that their presence is detected usually when damage (leaf-eating) starts. After feeding for a month, they move to the soil to pupate. There can be three generations, the third one's pupae staying in the soil over winter.

This pest possibly shows up the principle of natural balance as well as any other. The worst damage is often found in the third year after planting when the whole plant can be defoliated, and a sensible question would be 'why?'. Well, I'm making this bit up now but it makes sense that it takes that long for the little blighters to find the plants and build up in sufficient numbers to cause the defoliation. It also makes sense that, thereafter, the predators of the sawfly will have discovered them and so will begin the to-ing and fro-ing between the dominance of one or the other. For that reason, once year three is out of the way, in some years there will be little or no damage whilst in others there will be a noticeable but tolerable level of damage.

Disturbing the soil underneath for birds to investigate the possibility of a pupal snack is one possible control measure, as is hand-picking, even worse in terms of puncture wounds than picking the fruit.

George Glenny, 1858, comes up with three suggestions: 'Set children to pick them or brush them off' (presumably when they have time off from cleaning chimneys), 'Smoke them by burning rubbish on the windward side of the plantation' (a good one, particularly if you enjoy kippered gooseberries) and 'Wash them off with the garden-engine' (don't ask).

My favourite method of control is described in Beeton's Shilling Gardening Book. 'If the caterpillar has begun its ravages, the ground beneath the bush should be sprinkled with new lime, and a double-barrelled gun fired two or three times under it to shake  the caterpillars down into it.' I have often imagined trying to explain to the local constabulary that the demise of several neighbouring allotment plot holders due to shotgun pellets was entirely acceptable collateral damage resulting from caterpillar control. I also wonder if it occurred to Mr. Beeton (I somehow think it wasn't Mrs. Beeton) that he might have achieved a similar success by using a big stick to shake the bush. We will never know.

American Gooseberry Mildew
This goes by the snappier name of *Sphaerotheca mors-uvae*. Like most mildews the symptoms involve a white coating on plant parts, especially the young stems and leaves and even the fruit. Leaves can become distorted and shoot tips die. The coating on the fruit turns brown and, curiously, the berries are still edible underneath – all you need to do is remove the mildew coating (I remember Bob Flowerdew suggesting the use of a stone polishing machine), though they are less appetising being a muddy colour. It is encouraged by high humidity around the plant (solution: good spacing and pruning). And by excess Nitrogen (rarely a problem in an organic system). Remedies (not corroborated) include spraying prophylactically with a bicarbonate solution (sodium or potassium) or compost tea. Perhaps the sensible approach is to plant resistant varieties in the first place: from the list above we have 'Pax', 'Rokula', the 'Hinnonmaki' varieties and, especially, 'Invicta'.

Aphids and Leaf spot can be problems. Have a look at 'Blackcurrants' for more information on these.

More Fascinating Information
There are few fruits which we in the UK have taken to heart quite so comprehensively over the years as gooseberries. The excitement and tension

as the annual gooseberry show approaches, allowing the esteemed members of the 18th and 19th century gooseberry clubs to present their new varieties or biggest specimens, is hard to imagine. The weight of a wild gooseberry fruit is about 7g yet the winning weight in 1786 was 14.2g. The following century, the variety 'London' clocked in at 57g (2oz). Until perhaps more recent decades, gooseberries were a feature of most gardens, reflecting their ease of culture and the need to deter small children from playing in the fruit cage.

The names of some varieties of gooseberry dating from the 19th century perhaps reflect more on the plant breeders themselves rather than the qualities of their fruits: Conquering Hero, Bang Europe, Slaughterman, Broom Girl, Hit or Miss, Climax, Thumper. A fine selection, there, not out of place in yet another sequel of 'Fifty Shades of Grey'.

The name 'gooseberry' is shrouded in mystery. In other words, nobody seems to be able to make up their minds. Here are the options:
- A corruption of the word 'gorseberry' because it is so spiky.
- The thorns, when they are removed, have an uncanny resemblance to a goose's foot.
- The fruit was quite often cooked to make a sauce that goes with roast goose.

The two pruning systems described earlier, spur pruning and regulatory pruning, produce smaller crops of large fruit and larger crops of small fruit respectively. The reason given for spur pruning, which is a lot more work, is that the resulting large fruit are more suitable 'for dessert'. But what does that mean? Eating fresh? Maybe, but not many people do that (some fully ripe varieties are actually lovely). So does it mean 'making a dessert' i.e. cooking? If so that's exactly what you're doing with the far more plentiful but smaller fruit from a regulatory-pruned bush.

The esteemed food writer, Nigel Slater, recommends freezing ready-stewed gooseberries and then, when the time arises, defrosting and stirring in lightly-whipped cream of some sort (oat cream works well) plus a dash of elderflower cordial and you have an instant fruit fool. Incidentally, he also reckons that gooseberries make the best crumble of all. To be discussed. Or disgust (particularly if you are a big fan of rhubarb).

GRAPES *Vitis vinifera*
(*Vitis*, L. for vine, *vinifera*, wine-producing)
Family: VITACEAE

Why we should grow grapes
Wine and juice, autumn leaf colour, fresh unsprayed grapes, long-lived.

Grape Essentials
Varieties: **Triomphe**: good yields of black fruit suitable for wine or eating fresh. **Regent**: a vigorous cross between a *Vitis vinifera* variety and an American species which produces blue-black seeded grapes of a sweet flavour; generally resistant but there can be problems with Botrytis apparently.
Interlaken Seedless: green medium-sized seedless berries ready mid to late August; 'refreshing tangy flavour' suggests not very sweet but it has good disease resistance and good for raisins (if you live in California). According to Bob Flowerdew's 'Complete Fruit Book', the best dessert grapevines for outside in the UK are **Boskoop Glory** – large, dark, sweet berries, very reliable and disease resistant, and **Siegerrebe** – sweet, pink grapes, not the highest yields though.

Size and Spacing: This depends on the growing system and pruning chosen.

Position: Sunny. Warmth between flowering in June-July and harvest is crucial for ripening the crop. Avoid frost pockets to spare the young growth in spring. Ideally, use a south-facing wall: plant about 30cm / 1' away from the wall and angle it on to that. On an allotment, try a backing of other fruits such as a row of raspberries about 1.8m / 6' away. They can be grown through trees, though the positioning and vigour of both vine and tree are important, and pruning can be an issue, there.

Feeding: Decent compost as a mulch in spring, otherwise seaweed meal and something with a good helping of potassium (potash) wouldn't go amiss.

Pruning: Once the framework has been established, pruning is twice a year. Summer pruning is to remove the ends of new branches two leaves beyond developing bunches of grapes and the winter pruning is to remove virtually all of the season's growth back to one bud.

Pollination: Self-fertile.

Harvesting: Cut the whole bunch using a pair of secateurs, taking a section of stem if for dessert.

Propagation: Grafting or hardwood cuttings.

Weeding: Ideally keep weed-free for a good 1m / 3'+ diameter. 'There must not be a crop, or plants of any sort, on any part of the border, larger than a radish or seedling vegetables for planting out, for the vine is selfish.' George Glenny in 'The Culture of Fruits and Vegetables'. Thank you, George.

Grape Origins
Europe. Grapes have been used for making wine in the UK for getting on 2,000 years.

Grape Nutrition
The highest levels of sugar of any fruit: good news for winemaking, bad news for wasps or rather it's good news for wasps but bad news for us because of the wasps. Moderate levels of minerals, poor levels of vitamins. Presumably red and black grapes would have decent amounts of antioxidants.

Grape Botany
The plant itself is a woody, scrambling perennial. An individual grape is a true fruit called a 'berry' – a thin skin enclosing fleshy tissue and usually multiple seeds. Other famous berries include tomatoes and currants but, confusingly, not blackberries.

Discussion / rambling / elaboration
Pruning
At the beginning of virtually all pruning and training of grapevines, the first years are spent building up a framework of mature wood. From this framework, every year, new shoots will arise. The fruit is produced towards the bottom of this new growth. At the end of the season it will be removed, back to the framework and the following year it starts again.

The complications occur when you look at the range of frameworks that are used and the approximate positions of the annual new growth. Lets get the pruning out of the way first. Pruning is the big feature of growing grapevines, perhaps more so than any other fruit – there are whole books on the subject yet the information under 'Grape essentials' at the beginning of this chapter, plus a little extra detail, is really all that is required.

Do we need to prune at all? There are reports of a chap in the 19th century (a Richard Webb from Calcot near Reading) who grew a 'Black Hamburgh' grapevine and never pruned it. The interesting thing about that is not just the size of it (over 500m total length of shoots) but that it still produced lots of fruit, reputedly a ton of fruit per year. Conclusion? Vines are vigorous and, like many of the fruits in this book, produce good crops without being pruned. So let's see how to prune them.

Routine pruning

Whatever the framework, the following approach of summer and winter pruning can be followed. There is some slight variation with the more complicated frameworks but for most of us this should suffice:

Summer Pruning

When fruit starts to form on the new shoots, it is time to carry out summer pruning: cut off the end of the shoot two leaves beyond the bunch. If a shoot hasn't produced any fruit, cut it back anyway to a total of five or six leaves. Summer pruning contains the plant and makes it more manageable; it is the reason you may decide not to tie in the shoots. Any new growth that emerges after the summer pruning can be pinched out to one leaf.

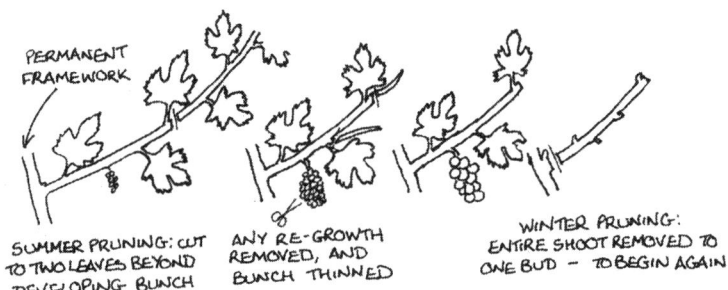

As well as pruning the shoots in summer if might be wise to thin out the grapes too, even on an established plant. For our climate (variously described as 'relaxed' or 'changeable' or 'bl**dy awful') we might be asking a bit much of our vines to produce many full bunches of grapes. So one recommendation is to remove half of all bunches that have started forming (i.e. take away every other bunch) and, of the remaining ones, when you can get a pair of scissors in there, remove part of the bunches. The remaining grapes, now possibly only 1/3 to 1/4 of the grapes that the plant was originally intending, should be larger and sweeter so this is particularly worth doing if they are dessert grapes; the size is less important if they are for wine.

If you haven't got anything better to do, there is more. Leaves that are next to bunches can be removed to allow more light on to the fruit and speed up ripening as well as increase its sweetness, though, of course, removing too many leaves will reduce the amount of sugars produced by the plant. It is all a balance.

So far in summer pruning, there is the possibility that you have removed the ends of shoots, pinched out re-growth, cut off bunches or parts of bunches of the fruit and even taken off a few leaves. You may be forgiven for thinking that there is nothing left to prune, though you are destined to be disappointed: some books recommend removing any tendrils that appear. The reasoning is that you are doing the supporting (if any) with bits of string and wires, and tendrils are just another drain on resources.

Winter Pruning

Winter pruning is traditionally done between Christmas and New Year, possibly as way to remember to do it. Personally, during that time I'll be immobile in an armchair having sampled plenty of the previous year's processed produce; smugly, the pruning will have been done a month before. In practice, you have a lot of time to do it. The main thing is not to leave it too late: whilst most of the other fruits that need pruning can be left until February or even March, grapevines will bleed. The sap is 'rising' and will drip from a wound if made this late, weakening the plant. The technique is very simple: remove all of the new growth produced that year, fruited or not, back to a single bud. The idea is that, presuming you had enough shoots that year, you'll want the same the following year: they will arise from the single bud to which you have pruned. There are many advocates of pruning back to leave two, maybe even three buds, to ensure that there will always be enough shoots. If that approach is taken it means there will be extra work later on to remove the weaker shoots of those that form if there are more than required.

Forming a Framework

There is scope for a little improvisation here. As we have seen, we need a plant structure to hold up the branches that are going to be produced each year.

The Standard. The shape of that structure depends on the space and location but a simple (and rarely-used framework) is a single, free-standing yet supported stem. New shoots will burst from the top of that stem like a firework or the hair of someone with their finger in an electrical socket. It is a kind of 'pollarding' system and isn't the best in

terms of shoot spacing, but it is certainly one of the easiest. The issue is, and this is one reason why there are so many different pruning and training systems, what happens to all of those new shoots? Are they left to float around mid-air or do you provide, say, a post and wire arrangement to hold them still and space them apart so that each shoot gets an even amount of air and light? If there is plenty of room around them, you can perhaps afford to be laissez faire about it, otherwise construct a support to hold them in place.

The shape itself is very straightforward. Start with a single-stemmed vine and plant it next to a post. It might be worthwhile using a metal pole as the initial support since it is going to be needed for many years – a vine can last well over 40 years, in fact remember to put it in your will. If the stem is already long enough, remove the top to a good bud. The point at which you make the cut will be where all the new growth is intended to come from, from now onwards. If side shoots (laterals) arise lower down, pinch them out to a single leaf as soon as you notice them – the longer they are left, the bigger the waste of resources when they are removed. If your new plant isn't long enough wait a year for the single stem to extend then, again in the winter, cut the top off to the desired height (somewhere between 90 and 120cm / 3-4').

The new shoots produced at the top of your stem will radiate outwards and, once you've decided how many of these shoots to keep, you might want to think about supporting them. The first time it fruits allow a maximum of only three or four bunches in total to develop, so that the plant is able to continue to develop and establish strongly.

The more uniform, productive and better-looking arrangement is the cordon.

The Cordon. The idea here is to have the same single stem as above but this time shoots are allowed to, seasonally, develop at intervals up that stem, running out horizontally. Clearly, there is the advantage that the shoots aren't all congested together at the apex and they get better light distribution as a result. On the

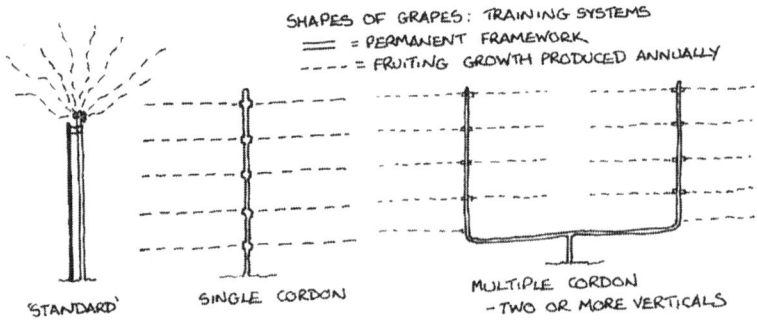

other hand, the action is spread from ground level upwards as opposed to the eminently sensible all-at-the-top less-bending approach.

The Double Guyot System. This sounds very grand and it is the system of choice for many commercial vineyards. It encompasses many of the features discussed already along with a big helping of 'renewal', a.k.a. butchery. Each year, new shoots (three) are left to grow in the middle: the two lower ones will, at the end of the season, be lowered to replace the horizontal framework arms which are removed completely. The remaining shoot is cut back to stimulate three new shoots for next year.

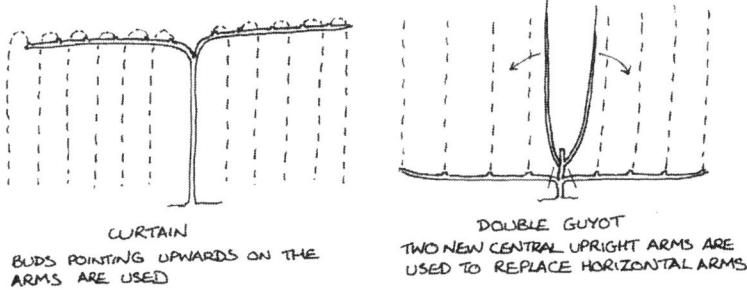

CURTAIN
BUDS POINTING UPWARDS ON THE ARMS ARE USED

DOUBLE GUYOT
TWO NEW CENTRAL UPRIGHT ARMS ARE USED TO REPLACE HORIZONTAL ARMS

Grapes and Weather

Protection of vines may be required. Back in the mists of time (2017) there was a late frost – in some areas it reached -6°C, which is very low for that late in the spring – and the newspapers were full of reports of the UK's grape crops being devastated. The parts of the plants being affected weren't the flowers, as can often be the case with many fruits, but the young shoots which withered. The end result was effectively a delay (up to a month) in producing replacement shoots which could then flower and fruit. As it 'appens, it was warm and sunny right through to July so some almost caught up. Unfortunately, August and September were cooler and wetter… The end result was that there was an overall reduction in the UK's production but some vineyards had exceptional years. Such is the nature of growing and the location of plants.

Propagation

Most vines bought from a nursery will have been grafted. This is because the rootstocks provide protection from diseases. However, these are less prevalent in the UK so it is perfectly acceptable to propagate by cuttings, and they are some of the most straightforward. They can be propagated as per hardwood cuttings or a special technique which enables lots of plants to be produced from small amounts of material. The technique is called 'leaf bud cuttings' or 'vine eyes' and is successful when done in the late autumn, making it a hardwood leaf bud cutting – without any leaves. Here is the detail:

In November, take a section of stem (this year's growth, removed when pruning) of your chosen variety and make a cut about 5-7.5cm / 2-3" below a node (the bit where a bud is). Make the next cut immediately above the bud at that node. This cut will be slightly angled. A sliver of bark can be removed from the side away from the bud near the bottom to encourage roots to form – called quite rightly 'wounding'. The cutting is then inserted in gritty compost in a suitably deep pot and topped with more grit.

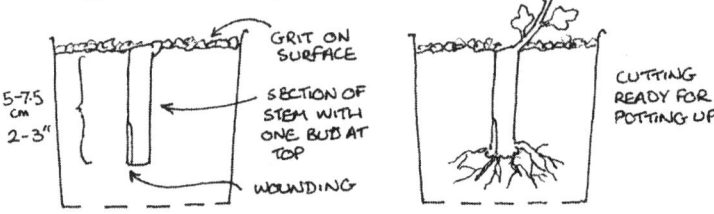

The section of stem you have is partly to anchor the cutting and a new shoot will come from the bud which should be level with the surface of the compost. Place the pot in a greenhouse or cold frame. The more warmth there is the sooner it will root; check for the very occasional need for watering.

Storage

Sounds strange, but grapes can be stored fresh for weeks. All you need is a cool, dark and dry location – a lean-to shed on a north-facing wall perhaps, though a cellar would be rather handy... The lightly handled bunch has its stalk attached to a piece of stem which is inserted into a bottle of water and that's it. There are a number of complicated devices to hold the bunch in position and the bottles are usually laid horizontally – scope for improvisation.

Grape Problems

Wasps

The bunches are attacked particularly as they ripen and the fruit sweetens. Grapes are a favourite perhaps because the skin is thinner than, say, an apple's. In many books, control seems to focus on destroying the wasps' nest, a process of such joy it is presumably on most people's bucket list. There are effective modern traps now available if they become an extreme nuisance, as opposed to the jar-of-jam-solution solution in which they come to drown in immense jammy happiness. A few bunches can be protected individually with fine mesh bags – fiddly, mind.

Grey mould / Botrytis

The fruit rots and the there is a growth of cuddly grey fur. Problematic because the berries in a bunch are so close that it moves from one to another easily. Botrytis is actually used to deliberately shrivel grapes and make them more concentrated (= sweeter) for winemaking, so according it the name The Noble Rot. I originally thought that was a comment on the upper classes. Another thing to do with naming is the scientific name for grey mould – *Botrytis cinerea*. The cinerea bit means 'grey', so far so good. But the genus, *Botrytis*, comes from the ancient Greek (*Botrys*) for 'grape' referring to the fact that this fungus was noted in its incidence and importance on grapes and was named in honour of them. Of even greater interest, cauliflowers are named *Brassica oleracea* 'Botrytis Group' not because they get the fungus too but because the curd looks a bit like a bunch of grapes.

NOBLE ROT

Any control involves a combination of hygiene (remove any damaged or affected fruit) and prevention (try to avoid damage in the first place – see 'Wasps' – and keep good air movement by following the pruning and thinning procedures).

Frost
This can damage flowers but more problematic is the effect on young growth before flowers have formed. Some of the best vineyards in the UK are on the slopes around a lake or river, benefiting from the warming effect of the water (a kind of storage heater). Plant your vines in a frost-free position or grow them so that you can protect them in some way.

Powdery mildew
A familiar disease on fruit. The leaves and shoots develop a powdery white coating particularly when conditions are hot, dry and humid. Maybe these are more likely to be achieved in the great wine-growing regions of the world which have higher temperatures and more sun than in the UK. Still, it is worth keeping your vines well watered and mulched.

Commercially, prevention and control has often centred on fungicides. Copper-based chemicals (Bordeaux mixture) were used so frequently that vine leaves had a blue coating and eventually there were reports of copper poisoning of the plants. Copper as an organic control was pleasingly withdrawn several years ago. Viticulturists have to be careful using chemicals, especially if the natural yeast on the fruit is used as the agent of fermentation and it isn't added separately (yeast is a fungus just as powdery mildew is). Growers producing grapes for fresh consumption are not similarly inhibited and vines can be among some of the most heavily sprayed fruits. A great reason to grow your own.

Shanking

Worth mentioning for the name alone. Shanking of grapes is where individual berries in a bunch fail to develop their full colour and then shrivel and taste sharp: black grapes stay red and white grapes remain transparent. It is presumed to be due to unfavourable growing conditions: low nutrition, impeded drainage or inadequate watering. So, a seaweed foliar feed, improved drainage or watering. Sorted, as they say.

Woolly scale

Flattened, shield-shaped insects surrounded by white waxy fibres – the eggs – stick to the branches. They suck the sap and, like aphids, can deposit the excess on leaves which are sticky as a result, possibly combined with sooty mould. Use a small brush to remove them, especially if localised, and sprays of soap / fatty acids and rapeseed oil are possible.

HYBRID BERRIES *Rubus sp.*

(*Rubus*, L. red)

Family: ROSACEAE

Why we should grow hybrid berries
They're different. Hardly ever seen for sale. Some great flavours.

Hybrid Berry Essentials
Varieties: *Rubus* **Tayberry Group**: Spiny, moderate yields, crop for over a month (mid July to August), excellent flavour, Brix 9-11. Assorted other raspberry-blackberry crosses described below.

Size: Variable, and can be manipulated to fit in particular gaps.

Spacing: 3m / 10 ft between plants grown on wires should be enough for most hybrid berries. The wires should start at about 60cm/2ft above ground, be spaced 30cm/1ft apart and end around 1.8m/6ft.

Position: Generally, the sunnier the position the better the cropping. However, perhaps to make the most of difficult locations, it may be worth trying some of these on a north-facing wall and accepting a lower yield. They need a moisture-retentive, free-draining soil just like most fruits, but the 'moisture' bit is especially important. Maybe forgo the south-facing wall because of that and aim for a good half-day's sun.

Feeding: An annual helping of compost, preferably, or a general fertiliser.

Pruning: Dead easy – every late autumn remove the canes that fruited and leave the canes that grew that year to fruit next year.

Pollination: Self fertile.

Harvesting: Just like many soft fruits, the advantage we have over supermarkets with the hybrid berries is being able to harvest and eat them fully ripe. The tricky bit is knowing when they are fully ripe – see 'Tayberries' below.

Propagation: In late summer, bury the tip of a young shoot in a pot of compost or in the ground. It can be severed and transplanted a year later when new growth will have emerged from that tip.

Weeding: Keep mulched and weed-free: the roots are quite shallow so it is hard to remove perennial weeds once they have insinuated themselves amongst them.

Hybrid Berry Origins
Hybrid berries – crosses backwards and forwards between blackberries and raspberries and others – have been produced in many nurseries and research stations around the world, particularly over the last couple of centuries.

Hybrid Berry Nutrition
Generalising because of the variability between different hybrids, these fruits are above average in terms of minerals and vitamins, especially potassium, calcium and magnesium. Vitamin C is in the region of 35mg/100g – not bad.

Discussion / rambling / elaboration
Types of Hybrid Berry and Others
These are not to be confused with hybrid currants which, annoyingly, have the word 'berry' in their name e.g. Jostaberry. Most hybrid berries are crosses between blackberries and raspberries and back with themselves again, which sounds a bit worrying but that's ok.

For example, the very wonderful Tayberry originated from a cross made at the Scottish Crop Research Institute in the 1970s between blackberry 'Aurora' and a tetraploid raspberry. The canes are bristly rather than prickly, but can still be less than pleasant to get in an intimate embrace. The fruits themselves are like a raspberry in front of a fairground mirror, stretching it to twice its length. It is also a lot darker. And tastier. But that's personal.

Loganberry has a longer history being introduced into the UK in 1897 sixteen years after the Californian judge, James Logan, found a chance cross between a blackberry or dewberry and a raspberry. It is sometimes listed as the species *Rubus x loganobaccus*, the little 'x' indicating it is a hybrid – a cross between two other species. There are thornless clones available which perform well.

Different varieties of blackberry and raspberry were used to produce the obscure / hardly-ever-seen Veitchberry, whereas Boysenberry, sounding alarmingly close to 'poisonberry', is a cross between raspberry, blackberry and Loganberry. The equally popular Tummelberry (remember to read this stuff with a hint of irony) is a 1985 cross of Tayberry and... Tayberry. The ambitiously named Phenomenal Berry is an 'improved' Loganberry but doesn't crop as heavily.

The exception to these hybrids is the Japanese Wineberry which is a

species in its own right, *Rubus phoeniculatus* (a mouthful without even growing the thing). It looks terrific – beautiful red bristles on the canes which glow with sun behind them. Some consider the fruit to be a little bland.

With any of these plants, the good news is that you grow them exactly as you would blackberries. Another good reason for growing hybrid berries is that they're not blackberries. Variety is the spice of life. Bad news: along with Japanese Wineberry, most aren't an improvement. In fact, once you've tried a fully ripe Tayberry, the rest are considered by some gardeners to be insipid, repulsive, loathsome, flavourless or, for the younger growers, gross. But don't be swayed – grow them and judge for yourselves and then come to the same conclusion.

Incidentally, Tayberries (sublime, rich-flavoured, glorious or, for the younger growers, wicked) are dark purple not red and should come away easily from the 'plug' when they are fully ripe.

Pruning and Training

To accompany the ease of pruning (removing the oldest canes – those that have fruited – leaving the youngest canes – those that will fruit next summer) are some interesting training techniques. Often the canes of hybrid berries (and blackberries) are trained to keep the two ages separate, not just for ease of pruning but to reduce the transfer of diseases from old to new growth. The

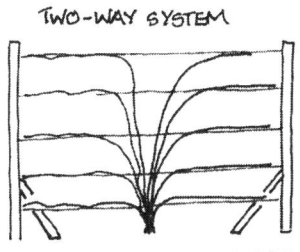

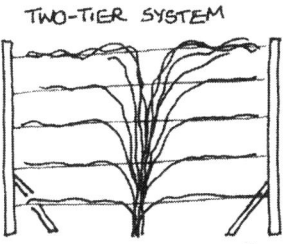

simplest training is to have the new canes tied in one direction on the wires as they grow, and the fruiting canes tied in the opposite direction. When the fruiting canes are pruned out, there is a big gap on that side ready for training-in the next lot of new canes.

Another option is to fill all of the wires except the top one, in both directions, with the canes about to fruit. As the new canes grow they are tied in loosely all together, vertically and then onto the top wire. When the older canes have been pruned out, the loosely-bunched new canes are released and tied into their place.

Harvesting

In order to have one of the best flavoured fruits on offer such as Tayberries, you have to undergo a certain amount of angst when picking. You must wait until the fruit is dark purple, not just purple. To remove a berry, bend it sideways and don't pull it. If it comes away cleanly, it's ripe, if it separates complete with the calyx (the little green star at the top of the fruit) then it isn't. The colour should have told you that but, well, everyone can make a mistake.

Pests and Diseases

There is a fine selection of pests and diseases that affect raspberries, which will also affect the hybrids with varying degrees of success. For example, Loganberry and Phenomenal berry are susceptible to Raspberry Yellow Dwarf Virus, but not others. Raspberry beetle will have a go at any of them.

Raspberry Cane Spot is a fungus which produces purple spots on canes early in the summer and then possibly on the leaves. Loganberries can even have the fruit affected. The bark of canes may split, leading to dieback. Prune out any infected canes as soon as they are seen.

KIWI FRUIT *Actinidia deliciosa* and other species

(*Actinidia*, Gk. a ray (referring to flower parts like spokes of a wheel),
deliciosa, delicious)
Family: ACTINIDIACEAE

Why we should grow kiwis
Vitamin C content, sense of achievement when you produce a home-grown kiwi (or abject failure when nothing materialises), a lush, leafy climber.

Kiwi Fruit Essentials
Varieties: '**Hayward**': a female variety producing typical kiwi fruit. '**Tomuri**': a male variety producing nothing (except pollen for the female). '**Jenny**': a self-fertile variety producing kiwis the size of a large plum. *Actinidia arguta* '**Issai**': as for 'Jenny' but the fruit is hairless. There are several more varieties of *A. arguta* most of which are more vigorous and are not self fertile. Fruiting versions with the same issues can be found of *A. purpurea* and *A. kolomikta*.

Site: Sheltered (i.e. not windy), sunny – south or south-west facing, no frost pocket, ideally against a wall for additional warmth especially if grown in the midlands. Not suitable for the north of England and Wales or Scotland unless in a protective structure. But then, with global warming…

Soil: pH 6.5, fertile to produce new growth and crop well. Avoid excessive nitrogen to reduce the chance of shoot and leaf dominating at the expense of fruit.

Size: Considerable. But can be contained.

Spacing: 5.5-7m (18-23 feet) depending on the vigour of the variety.

Feeding: A balanced feed with good helpings of potassium should do it. How about a spring mulch of compost?

Pruning: Shorten all new shoots in summer, and again in winter.

Pollination: Male and female plants are required for (insect) pollination. Provided there is an abundance of pollinating insects (see the chapter 'Pollination') there is no need for the pollinating by hand advocated in some books. There are a handful of self-fertile varieties.

Harvesting: The fruit is ready when, if you give them a little squeeze, there is some give. They are often ripe really quite late in the year, even in the middle of winter when there are no leaves on the plant.

Propagation: A semi-ripe cutting taken in August-September or a hardwood cutting taken in November are the main methods, though both types will be more successful with 'bottom heat'.

Weeding: Keep weed-free especially when the plant is establishing. Later on it is less critical though still desirable.

Kiwi Origins

The somewhat mis-named kiwi (it is from China / East Asia) achieved fame by being grown in vast quantities for our delectation in New Zealand. Chinese gooseberry is perhaps more accurate except for the gooseberry bit, the only real similarity being the fruit shape. The less common common name of Monkey Peach is simply unhelpful.

Kiwi Nutrition

Over 100 mg of vitamin C is possible per 100g of fresh fruit, which is close to half the best blackcurrants but grapefruit is 40 mg/100g and oranges are 50 mg/100g. You may say 'Well, an orange is twice the size of a kiwi' to which I'd say 'Eat two kiwis – besides, you can't grow oranges outside in this country'. Reasonable levels of potassium, calcium and iron.

Kiwi Botany

The kiwi fruit is technically a 'berry' which takes some getting used to, mainly because we are accustomed to thinking of berries as small red or black things. Can contain over a thousand small black seeds per fruit.

Discussion / rambling / elaboration
Kiwi Gender
A couple of important points to do with the kiwi are:
1)   It has particular sexual preferences.
2)   It is a sun-lover.

Well, that doesn't narrow things down hugely – I even know a few humans who fit those criteria. Much of the fruit we grow here has male and female parts within every flower and can still manage to be exceptionally tiresome when it comes to pollination. The kiwi plant, on the other hand, will be either male or female. This arrangement is called 'dioecious'.

Should we care about this? If we want fruit rather than just an overenthusiastic leafy climbing plant, the answer is 'yes'. Just having a female plant means no fruit because a male's pollen is required for fertilisation and fruit production. Only having a male plant is simply asking for trouble – male plants don't produce fruit. The solution, of course, is the same as for apples, but for a different reason: two plants are required for fruit. If you had the room, one male kiwi would pollinate at least four female plants and an oft quoted optimum is one male to eight females – a veritable harem. The drawback here is, as mentioned, space. One kiwi alone can cover a huge area of wall, fence etc. Nine would clothe Clifton suspension bridge.

If you only have room for one plant, don't be downhearted. There are a number of varieties that have been developed that will produce fruit all by themselves and are relatively restrained. For example, 'Jenny' and the different species but still recognisably a kiwi, *Actinidia arguta* 'Issai', will crop alone. The minor downside is that the fruit tends to be small to middling in size. 'Issai' fruit also happens to be bald.

Pruning and Training

The aim of growing any chosen fruit plant is usually to maximise the yield. It makes sense that if you've given space to a particular plant, you want it to produce as much fruit as possible: a low-yielding apple, chosen for its flavour will still be grown to give of its best. In the case of the kiwi, almost as important is restriction. Because the plants are so strong-growing and can be huge, we rarely have the space required to let them reach their full size. Plus, like tomatoes, if side branches aren't contained, there is a great tangle with fruit hidden and the whole plant becoming unmanageable and even unhealthy.

For that reason, the kiwi is often trained as an espalier: a central vertical stem with permanent horizontal branches spaced about 30cm (12") apart. Growing from this permanent framework will be a mixture of (temporary) new growth on longer term fruiting spurs.

The growth of kiwi plants is a little strange – it is often far from steady. The young plant, a teenager perhaps, is surly and reluctant to get a move on. A little older and the thing won't stop.

Formative Pruning of an Espalier

The framework is formed gradually as with an apple or pear espalier. Usually a single-stemmed young kiwi is planted and the top removed to a bud, typically about 30cm (12") above the ground. This stimulates the stem to produce shoots which are reduced to just three by removing all others. The lower two are now tied in horizontally in opposite directions and the third (top) shoot is tied in vertically and again its top is cut off, leaving about 30cm (12"). This cut results in more shoots which are trained as before to create the second tier, and so on. The horizontals should be 'stopped' at about 1m (3'ish), to stimulate side shoots, the end one of which will then continue the horizontal growth.

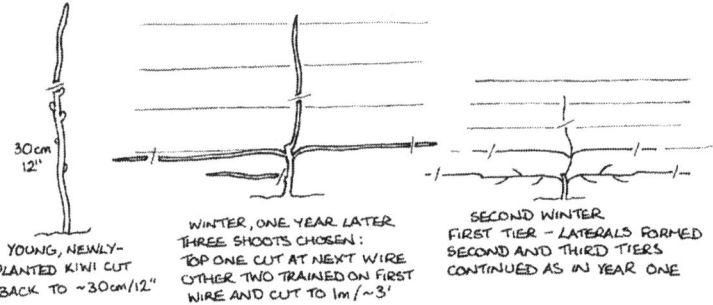

Spur Pruning an Espalier

As part of our formative pruning above, we have stimulated side shoots to form along the horizontal branches. These are dealt with by pruning twice a year and it helps to know the reasoning behind it: fruit develops in clusters at the leaf joints of shoots produced the previous year and at the base of brand-new shoots. This is already sounding complicated but by following the summer and winter pruning below the locations where fruit is formed is maximised.

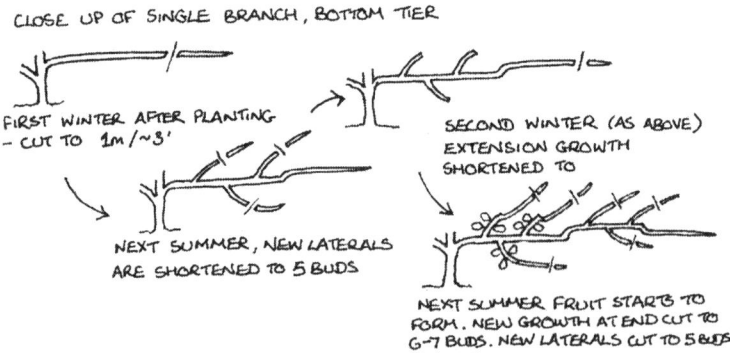

Summer pruning: This involves removing the tips of new shoots to five buds / leaves, called 'pinching out'. The tips of new growth from fruiting shoots are similarly removed, though to six or seven buds / leaves. Any new growth that develops subsequently is removed completely. This is called summer pruning though it starts when the shoots are long enough to have the appropriate number of buds / leaves to cut back to: May onwards.

Winter pruning: Those shoots which haven't fruited and were cut back to five buds in the summer are left. So winter pruning involves further shortening of the young shoots at the base of which there was hopefully some fruit, to two buds outside the last fruit (this develops into a 'spur' system).

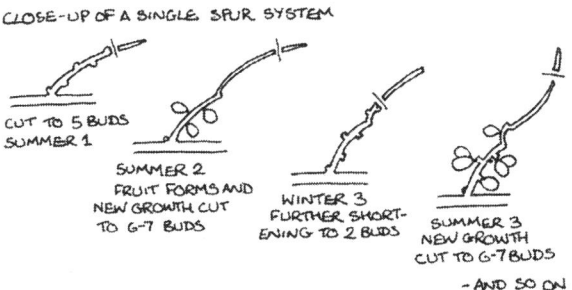

There are alternatives to the spur system, notably the New Zealand renewal system which requires a free-standing framework – but since most kiwis in the UK will be at their best with a backing of a wall or fence, the spur system is probably the most useful. Strong emphasis is placed on tying in shoots to the surface of a framework rather than feeding them around the structure and allowing them to twine. If they do, they will apparently constrict growth and development.

Kiwi problems

Kiwis are refreshingly pest and disease–free, though there will always be something looking to have a go. Slugs and snails are interested in the leaves but are not normally considered a nuisance because of the vigour of the plant. However, that sluggish young plant, taking its time to get on with it, can be defoliated by our mollusc mates. There is also the possibility of a general, non-host-specific pest like capsid bugs, red spider mites and the ever-popular aphids. Even these are less of an issue, perhaps because of the unshaven nature of stems and leaves: lots of bristles slow the restless ramblings of little creatures.

Cold weather in the winter isn't the main problem – it's cold weather in the spring, specifically when new growth has commenced. Young shoots can be frosted, making protection and / or a sheltered site desirable. The flowers appear later so tend not to be affected. In Yunnan Province, a Chinese hot-spot for kiwis, there are considerably fewer frosts yet enough cold for flowers to be promoted: over 400 hours below 7°C are required.

Kiwi Consumption

Slightly surprisingly, kiwis can be stored for several months if wrapped and given low temperatures. They can be left on the plant for ages provided that birds don't start to have a go at them, which is more likely when the fruit is fully ripe and the winter makes other foods more scarce.

The biggest question with kiwis is, of course, not how to grow them but how to eat them. Do we go for the 'whole in one' approach? – small kiwis can be popped straight into the mouth like sweets. Or do we go for the way of the apple? – simply eat everything bit by bit. The issue for many, here, is the texture of the skin. Variously described as being somewhere between a piece of suede and a badger's rear end, the skin is both rough and manure-coloured. So, if this presents itself as a problem, does one peel 'n' slice, which provides for versatile use such as in fruit salads or drinks, or eat 'out of the skin', perhaps a little like a boiled egg: cut off the top and spoon out the insides (recommended)?

MEDLARS *Mespilus germanica*

(*Mespilus*, Gk. half a ball, *germanica*, of Germany)

Family: ROSACEAE

Why we should grow medlars
Tree shape, white flowers in spring, autumn leaf colour, even the fruit.

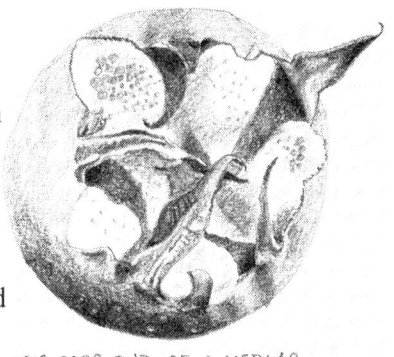

THE REAR END OF A MEDLAR

Medlar Essentials
Varieties: '**Dutch**' and '**Monstrous**' – the largest fruit 9cm / 3.5 inches, '**Royal**' and '**Nottingham**' – smaller but reputedly tastier.

Size: On rootstocks Quince A or BA29 – 3-4m / 10-14', on Quince C – 2.5-3m / 8-10'.

Spacin: You'd really like more than one? If so, try 5m / 16 feet for Quince A trees and 4m / 13 feet for Quince C trees.

Position: Most soil types, sun or partial shade.

Feeding: Initially, to help establish the tree and get good strong growth, it is worth mulching for a few years with compost or manure, particularly on a poor soil. Thereafter, some general and high potash feeds can be given but it is not the most demanding tree.

Pruning: Don't bother trying, certainly not to shape it. Size can be restricted a certain amount by pruning but choose the appropriate rootstock first.

Pollination: Self-fertile.

Harvesting: Pick in October when some of the fruits start softening, with patches of brown.

Propagation: Most often propagated by grafting the chosen variety on to a rootstock. Can be grown from the large seeds but it takes longer to get a fruiting tree.

Weeding: Keep weed-free when young. Later on they tolerate under-planting.

Medlar Origins
Eastern Mediterranean, Turkey – cultivation has been for thousands of years. In Britain, medlars were very popular in the Middle Ages, which doesn't tell us much especially when the main vegetable was a leek and entertainment was a bladder on a stick.

Medlar Nutrition
Probably the lowest water content of all the UK fruits – perhaps they'd be marginally more palatable for some people if there was more. Good levels of Potassium and Calcium, nothing much else exceptional to report

Medlar Botany
The medlar fruit is a 'pome' (like apples and pears) meaning that most of the structure has developed from parts of the flower other than the reproductive parts. So a pome is a false or accessory fruit. The very central part housing the seeds has developed from the female parts of the flower as a true fruit would do.

Discussion / rambling / elaboration
Harvesting and Storing
The fruit should be picked before it starts to fall, usually around October. When one or two have dropped maybe that is a good indicator to pick the lot. The next stage is relatively unusual in that the fruits are 'stored' by setting down on their flat bottoms, made just for that purpose. By keeping frost-free but still cool, they will gradually soften and turn brown, taking about three weeks. Despite having the appearance of a decaying apple, this is not, as is commonly suggested, 'going rotten' but is a special procedure called 'bletting' – it just seems as though it has gone rotten. It is at this stage that the fruit can be eaten fresh. They last a while in the bletted state but eventually do go mouldy, an attractive blue growth being the most common fungus.

The Medlar Tree
The tree is, regardless of the fruit, a lovely plant; the framework is anarchic with branches in all directions, a wonderful characteristic shape, the tree looking quite old even when just a few years of age. It is relatively short in stature, rootstock dependent, but well-spreading. Large, clear, simple, five-petalled flowers are produced in late spring, May-ish, after the apples – white, sometimes tinged pink. The leaves give good autumn colours, particularly yellows. The fruit is a great talking point if nothing else. It refuses to grow in the intended direction despite careful pruning. This makes it a straight forward proposition: don't bother pruning, at least not to influence the direction of branches.

Flavour

This seems to be a 'love it or hate it' fruit. On one side of the fence, lounging in a hammock, surrounded by the wreckage of umpteen medlar skins and pips, sucked clean of the pulp, like Alien feasting on a good helping of brains, is me. On the other side are... quite a few people. Edward Bunyard, in his

'Handbook of Fruits' 1925, doesn't distinguish between medlar varieties, saying '... as I cannot appreciate this fruit I should personally consider them equal in unpleasantness'. Well, that showed me.

The flavour, again divided into the two camps, has been described as 'apple puree', 'fruit cake' 'rich dates' and 'toffee apple' on the one hand and 'sewage' on the other. For some, it is the texture that defeats them, it being a thick, slightly cloying, brown mush embedded with large pips – as the modern phrase goes 'what's not to like?'

Medlar Jelly

Medlars are perhaps at their most acceptable when they have been processed in some way. One of the most popular is medlar jelly, whereby this maligned magnificence is simmered and strained and prepared as with many sugar-based preserves (see recipe below). The result is a lovely clear, glowing, deep pink jelly though, to achieve the best colour and flavour, apparently a few unbletted fruit should be added to the preparation.

Because it is quite a dry fruit, the downside is the relatively low return on the amount of jelly produced to the number of fruit required. Some might say that that is positive. Also, with the processing of lots of different soft fruits such as blackcurrants being likely, the question has to be asked 'How many jars of this kind of thing do we actually need?' There is perhaps a limit to the number of times that you can tie ribbons round your jars and liberate them as festive gifts. Medlar jelly is lovely simply spread on toast though some use as it an accompaniment to various dead animals that have been liberally peppered with lead shot.

Briefly boiling bletted medlars in plenty of water, passing through a colander to remove the pips (and some skin) and consuming with a generous helping of cream-like substance is a surprisingly acceptable dessert, in terms of flavour if not appearance (sort of cow pat). Medicinal properties: reputed to be a cure for an upset stomach.

Medlar Jelly recipe
2kg / 4.5lbs of bletted medlars plus two or three unbletted fruits
2.5 litres / 4 pints water
Sugar and lemon juice
Wash the fruit and simmer slowly in the water until it has broken down. Pour the pulp into a jelly bag and allow it to drip through overnight. No squeezing allowed otherwise you end up with cloudy juice. The collected liquid should be measured and put in a big pan adding a tablespoon of lemon juice for every 600ml / 1 pint. Bring it to the boil before stirring in sugar at 350g / 12 oz per 600ml / 1 pint of liquid. Bring back to the boil and leave it there until it reaches setting point. Put in heated, clean jars and affix lids. Attach a handsome label.

Medlar Problems
Hardly anything. Birds? Squirrels?

Random Nonsense
The name 'medlar' doesn't describe the fruit for us particularly well, whereas the French who apparently provided us with that name, with no holds barred themselves go for *Cul de Chien*. It receives this name because of the appearance of the underneath of the fruit, which is sunken and puckered. A few centimetres make all the difference: a fruit can go from being the Dog's Wotsits to a Dog's Wotsit in no distance at all: I'm not feeling like more of a translation than that, sorry.

The botanical name is a lot friendlier, with the Greeks coming up with *mesos* and *pilos* (*Mespilus*) meaning half and ball respectively, the fruit looking as though it is a round russet apple that has been cut in half. If we wanted to be pedantic it could be said that the Greeks were being a trifle pessimistic in that it is more like three quarters of a ball. The species name, *germanica*, means 'from Germany' not surprisingly, which is a shame since they're from Persia. Maybe they arrived via a tour of northern Europe.

MULBERRIES *Morus nigra*
(*Morus*, L. for mulberry, *nigra*, black)
Family: MORACEAE

Why we should grow mulberries
A wonderful, long-lived, trouble-free, messy old tree, full of character.

Mulberry Essentials

Varieties: There are few selections of *Morus nigra* such as '**Chelsea**' – found at the Chelsea physic garden – which has large fruit of an intense, rich flavour. '**Wellington**' is a heavy yielding variety, with fruit medium-sized at 3cm and also a good flavour. '**Charlotte Russe**' is a brand new dwarf mulberry getting to 1.5-1.8m / 5-6' which crops (apparently) all summer. Most of the time you'll just be offered 'Black Mulberry'.

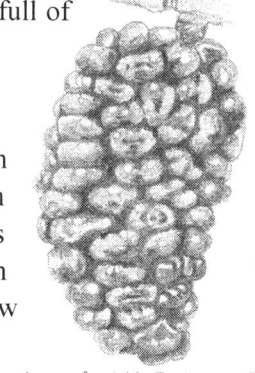

A SLIGHTLY DEFORMED MULBERRY

Size: One of the few top fruits not to be grafted. As a result, there isn't a range of sizes possible for the 'normal' mulberry. The full size of this is 9m / 30' high by 6m / 20' wide but it is quite amenable to being restricted by pruning. As far as fruit trees go, this is quite a substantial size but, compared to trees in general, 10m and less is considered small. Then we have the diminutive 'Charlotte Russe', above.

Spacing: If you are going for more than one, which is a unlikely, or you have such a large garden that perhaps one of the under gardeners should be reading this, then go for 5-6m / 16-20'. Try 'Charlotte Russe' at 2m / 6' spacings.

Position: Sunny site. Free-draining soil. They can actually grow in the north of Scotland with a wall backing.

Feeding: Unless the soil is particularly poor and a young tree needs some help (in which case a mulch of compost is fine) then let it be. Would you feed an oak tree that you have planted?

Pruning: None unless you're really desperate: weak shoots, misplaced branches, weak forks. Actually, just leave it alone.

Pollination: Self fertile.

Harvesting: Gently, when fully ripe, wearing old clothes.
Propagation: Cuttings, of various sizes – see below. Can be from seed but it is a lot slower to get a fruiting tree.

Weeding: Keep clear until the tree gets going and probably permanently clear around the dwarf variety.

Mulberry Origins
China, arriving here in the 16th or 17th century via France. Apparently there are forests of mulberry along the south coast of the Caspian Sea and on the Iranian steppes.

Mulberry Nutrition
Most minerals and vitamins are nothing special except, for some reason, iron in which it excels beyond any other temperate fruit at 1.6mg/100g.

Mulberry Botany
Mulberries: like raspberries, but on a tree, except they're darker. And being more succulent (meaning they are hard to transport anywhere without them going to mush). And being less trouble to grow. Though they are more troublesome to pick, being up a tree.

Ok, so they're nothing like raspberries, though both have what are called 'compound fruit'. A compound fruit is one which is composed of lots of small individual fruitlets. In the case of raspberries these fruitlets are called drupelets whereas mulberry fruits are made up of lots of individual fleshy flower parts, giving the superficial appearance of a raspberry.

The botanical names of mulberries unfortunately don't always reflect the colour of the fruit, particularly *M. alba* with berries of a pink-red ('*alba*' means white). The fruit of M. *nigra* (= black) is purple.

Discussion / rambling / elaboration
Propagation
Propagation is relatively straightforward: normal hardwood cuttings are used when the leaves have dropped off (November), though they are often taken with a heel – see the 'Propagation' chapter. They are perhaps slightly longer than normal cuttings at 30-60cm / 1-2', being inserted to about half their length. Abnormal hardwood cuttings can also be used - at the same time of year - consisting of a thick section of older wood called a 'truncheon': a branch with sideshoots shortened to a few buds: up to 10cm 4" wide, length negotiable but aged 2 to

4 years. One reference book suggests a piece of 1.8m / 6' in length and 15cm / 6" thick, which is not so much a truncheon as a roof truss. Whatever size of truncheon you choose, it is inserted directly in its permanent position. When you step back and think about this as a method of propagation, it is pretty unusual: firstly, sticking a cutting in the ground where you want a tree. Normally it is done elsewhere and then transplanted when the success – or otherwise – of it rooting has been determined.

Secondly, it is no ordinary cutting but potentially a whole branch. Very strange.

Pruning

This is a splendid fruit tree to plant and forget about, providing you have the room. Pruning and training can be done if you are desperate for the activity. You might snip back branches initially – formative pruning – to encourage the head to form in a particular way, or you can train it as an espalier. However, it might be an opportunity to grow a fruit that needs no input whatsoever.

Harvest

Mulberries are slow to come into fruit especially seed-raised plants. Other options are to choose a more mature specimen (3-4 years old) or get hold of a quick-fruiting variety. The picking season is over about four weeks in August and September though if given a favourable position (say, with a backing of a south-facing wall) mulberries can start cropping as early as July. If the normal, large tree is planted in a lawn, conveniently the dropped fruit can be collected off the grass or off sheets laid down for the purpose. It is probably best to use old sheets unless you want to snuggle between bed covers bearing a mulberry-juice tie-dye effect.

A Bit of History

The usual species to grow is *M. nigra*. The story goes that thousands of trees were imported into this country in the reign of James I, James II or Henry VIII (take your historical pick) to beat the Chinese monopoly of silk production: silk worms feed on mulberry leaves. Unfortunately, their main food plant is *M. alba* not *M. nigra,* so the disappointment of not having home-grown silk underwear was offset by having lots of tasty fruits falling on the bed sheets. James I seems to get most references having decreed that 'every county town should make mulberry available' - 1610.

More recent history is the selection of a different species of mulberry, *Morus rotundiloba* 'Charlotte Russe' which was voted plant of the year at the Chelsea Flower Show. The only similarity between this tiny tree and *Morus nigra* is the messiness of the fruit. It fruits for ages (May to September) and starts at a very young age. Unfortunately, though it is still early days, there have been a number of reports suggesting that the flavour doesn't match up: the small fruit are sweet and juicy, but bland. To be confirmed.

Mulberry Problems

None, apart from the need to develop a charitable disposition towards feathered thieves which will go for the highest fruit first, the ones you couldn't reach anyway. Plus the fruit often hangs inside the foliage protecting some of it. The new dwarf mulberry can be netted. There is the possible issue of slugs and snails on young trees – they are very attracted to the leaves.

Random Nonsense

Just in case you weren't already aware of it, the nursery rhyme 'Here we go round the mulberry bush' has been attributed to a mulberry planted in the grounds of a female prison, HMP Wakefield. Prisoners apparently circulated around the tree / bush for exercise, though some commentators suggest that the circumnavigation was prior to execution, others saying that the whole thing is a load of tosh and that it was really a blackberry bush. If it is true then it may at least illustrate two useful horticultural features: a mulberry growing in Wakefield which, whilst not located in the permafrost of the Arctic Circle, still illustrates a certain degree of hardiness. Also, unless there was another tree planted elsewhere in the establishment they're not telling us about, (and presuming it fruited) then it demonstrates the mulberry's self-fertility.

Another useful piece of information is that, because mulberry fruits tend to squish easily it is very likely that you will be covered in juice. If they weren't your mulberries to pick in the first place and the owner would have preferred them not to be scrumped, then there is a possibility you will be identified as the culprit – you will be caught 'red-handed'. True.

PEACHES *Prunus persica* and **NECTARINES**
Prunus persica var. nectarina
(*Prunus*, L. for plum, *persica*, Persia)
Family: ROSACEAE

Why we should grow peaches
Home-grown peaches can contain as much pesticide as you want them to (hopefully none), whereas non-organic shop-bought are near the top of the list for contaminated fruit. Terrific blossom. Peaches: a taste of summer.

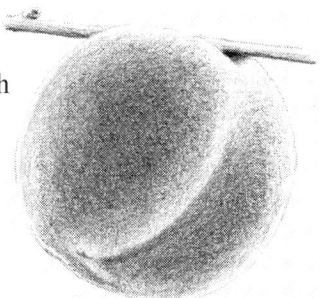

A FUZZY, 'CHEEKY' PEACH

Peach Essentials
Varieties: Nectarines are bald peaches or, the other way around, peaches are nectarines in need of a shave. Established varieties are, for peaches, '**Rochester**' (yellow flesh, adapted to the UK climate), '**Peregrine**' (best flavoured white flesh for UK), '**Red Haven**' (yellow flesh, some resistance to peach leaf curl), '**Saturn**' ('donut' peach, reputedly the sweetest but needing good conditions; regarding its flat shape it is sometimes amusingly called 'Sat-on'), '**Amsden June**' (white flesh, freestone type, ripe in June / July) and for nectarines, '**Lord Napier**' (white-fleshed, good for UK conditions), '**Humboldt**' (orange-fleshed, ripe mid to late August), '**Fantasia**' (yellow flesh, mid season).

The more recent introductions include the resistant Peach '**Avalon Pride**' and the genetic-dwarves Peach '**Garden Lady**' and Nectarines '**Nectarella**' and '**Snow Baby**' – for more of these, see the end of the chapter.

Size: Established rootstocks for peaches and nectarines include 'St. Julien A' which gives a tree of height and spread 5m / 16'. More recent introductions include 'Torinel' (better disease resistance and tolerance of wet soils, also slightly smaller) and with a more dwarfing nature, 'Montclare', and the plum rootstock also suitable for peaches, 'Wavit', both about 3m / 10'. The Russian rootstock 'VVA-1' (a.k.a. 'Krymsk 1') is perhaps the smallest at 2.5m. See also the very small genetic dwarves at the end.

Spacing: Dependent on the rootstock – the spacing is (approximately) a bit less than the spread.

Position: Sunny, ideally a south facing wall. Peaches typify the universal request for 'a moisture-retentive, free-draining soil', but more so: they like lots of water in the growing season yet hate it hanging around for any length of time. Witness the rumblings about California's desert of (the closely related) almond trees, taking up vast quantities of the state's water resources with irrigation.

Feeding: As with the water, so with the feeding. A good, annual mulch with compost is extremely helpful in retaining water as well as feeding.

Pruning: As for apples but more so. We have the additional reason for pruning: stimulating the tree to produce more new wood on a regular basis. All maintenance pruning should be done, as with any stone fruit, between mid May and mid July – remember, prune a prune in June.

Pollination: Self fertile, but running around with a little paintbrush, dabbing it into as many flowers as possible, is recommended particularly if the tree is being protected. Even if it isn't, there is a chance it will be too cool for many pollinating insects: at this time of year we are reliant almost exclusively on a healthy population of bumble and solitary bees…

Harvesting: Like apricots, one of the joys of growing peaches is plucking a fully ripe, sun-warmed specimen and eating it on the spot. Probably best not to wear your evening dress when doing so – it could get messy. It is tricky checking an individual fruit for ripeness without bruising it, which, if it isn't ripe, means it will deteriorate. Commercial peaches are picked under-ripe for transport and rarely achieve that sublime tree-ripened flavour.

Propagation: Grafting (in late winter) or budding (in summer) of material from your chosen variety onto one of the rootstocks listed above.

Weeding: Keep weed-free for at least the first three years and continue to do so with dwarf trees.

Peach Origins
Probably a native of China and arrived via Persia (hence the name) to the UK in the 16th century.

Peach Nutrition
Average in all departments, disappointingly. if you look at figures from the 1990s quoted in The New Oxford Book of Food Plants. Go back another 30 years and Temperate-Zone Pomology gives excellent figures for Carotene and Potassium, equivalent to those of apricots.

Peach Botany
A true fruit. Often referred to as stone fruit, it is technically a 'drupe' – the skin, flesh and the stone itself have all developed from the ovary wall. The single seed has developed from one ovum in the ovary.

Discussion / rambling / elaboration
Pruning
The most useful piece of information regarding pruning is the fact that the best quality and largest fruits are produced on one-year-old wood. It will be produced on older wood too but it makes sense to generate a regular turnover of new shoots which are used to replace older shoots. For more on this including fans, see the chapter on 'Pruning and Training'.

Thinning
It is strongly recommended in the literature that peaches are thinned, once to reduce fruit numbers to two per cluster, and again at walnut size. It is quite easy to remove the whole cluster or damage the young shoot by accident when tugging on the thinnee so it is quite interesting to hear of a technique used in France. The fruit to be removed is simply cut in half across-ways, through the soft stone. The piece remaining, still attached to the stalk, will shrivel and drop off in its own time. Neat, eh?

Too much fruit on a tree not only reduces the quality but reduces the vigour of the tree itself and how well it will crop the following year. It is better to even out the cropping over the years rather than the feast and famine approach. The resultant final spacing to aim for after thinning is one fruit every 15cm / 6" (nectarines, and for peaches in very favourable situations such as a south-facing wall) or 22cm / 9" (for peaches).

Peach problems
Peach Leaf Curl
This alone is probably responsible for relatively few peaches and nectarines being grown in the UK. There are ways to deal with it, however. Firstly, the symptoms: in spring, leaves are puckered and shrivelled and in a rather fetching range of colours including reds and pinks. They become marginally less attractive as a white coating develops followed by the leaf going brown and dropping off. It is a fairly sad sight, a partially defoliated tree with little in the way of usable fruit.

The fungus overwinters in the buds and bark of branches, and spores from this infection spread to the leaves in spring, aided by rain splash. It doesn't take a huge amount of imagination to realise that this disease will be worse in a wet spring. Some solutions:

- Remove affected leaves before they produce the white bloom that will release spores to infect the shoots, and so complete the life cycle. This might not be so straightforward with a large specimen.
- Keep rain off the plant between January and March. Dead easy…… When peaches were grown for the 'big house', they were often trained against the south-facing walls of the walled garden. This, being a very warm aspect, was perfect for the ripening of peaches and it also gave the opportunity to construct an angled roof: a glazed metal frame stuck out from near the top of the wall. To protect the blossom on cold nights, hessian could also be hung from the lower edge of this frame. It is unlikely most of us will be in the position to do anything similar, but it was fun mentioning it anyway. Instead, by growing small specimens, they can either be covered individually or, if in a pot, they can be moved inside for January to April.

WALL FRAMES CAN PROVIDE PROTECTION

- Use a resistant variety (see 'Avalon Pride' below) or grow an apricot instead.

Brown rot

This is a fungus which develops mainly as a dark brown blotch on the fruit, spreading rapidly to produce concentric rings of dirty white pustules. It can also affect young shoots and flowers (given the name 'blossom rot'). Most infection is from infected mummified fruits on the tree (occasionally on the ground) and, with the fruit, entry is via a wound. The simplest remedy is a couple of strong doses of hygiene: firstly, promptly remove rotting fruits as you see them, not only to reduce the re-infection but to stop it spreading to neighbouring fruits (see 'thinning', too) and, secondly, remove any mummified fruits in the winter, which are, let's face it, rotting fruit which you have missed in the first round of hygienic activities. And, of course, try not to damage the fruit in the first place – inform any naughty insects and birds likewise.

There is a lovely selection of other diseases which affect Prunus but peaches seem to get away with fewer incidents: silver leaf (worse on plums) and bacterial canker (worse on cherries).

Aphids

There are very few plants immune to an aphid attack and Prunus species are particularly susceptible. Witness the leaf curling and general ugliness of a cherry branch infested by black aphid. Peaches even have an aphid named after them indicating the two main hosts of the pest: the Peach-Potato Aphid. As it turns out, this aphid has seriously diversified and attacks a huge range of plants, not just the peach and the potato. Leaf curling seems to be a fairly popular activity amongst these little suckers (it affords a bit of protection) but they rarely affect the tree badly especially if the surroundings are quite diverse as they should be in an organic system – there is a strong argument to be made against allowing large monocultures of any crops to be called 'organic'.

You'll have guessed that one control measure for aphids, a favourite of mine, is 'do nothing': the beautiful, uplifting mixture of plants in a true organic system will provide the support system for control. On small trees, a little light brushing is possible. Spraying with soft soap, rapeseed oil, pyrethrum or even home-made rhubarb spray is, yes, organic but is also counterproductive and messy with a tree: any predators such as hoverflies and ladybirds will be eliminated in the process (they won't be affected by rapeseed oil) so giving the pest the upper hand in re-establishing. If there aren't any predators, the question must be asked 'Why not?'.

Wasps

There is no doubt that wasps can be nuisance. I once had a crop of Apple 'Discovery' that, when I went to pick them, my discovery was that they were lanterns, the skins hanging there with the flesh completely wasp-hollowed. They are even more of problem with sweeter fruits like peaches. Still, I'd find it difficult to try eradicating them – they are slightly schizophrenic since, apart from being a pest, they can be beneficial by eating caterpillars and pollinating fruit plants. Lawrence D. Hills in 'Grow Your Own Fruit and Vegetables' had a novel method of attack. Following a wasp back to its nest, he suggested waiting until they were all putting their feet up at home in the evening before inviting us to insert into their hole an equal mixture of flowers of sulphur and saltpetre. This 'weak gunpowder' was detonated using an inserted fuse, not to blow the nest to bits, but kill them with a fumigation of sulphur.

Weather, the effect of

Peaches need a cold period, commonly referred to as 'winter', to stimulate flowering. They also like a hot summer to produce fruit. Then we have the spring to contend with: with early flowering (March-April) there is the strong likelihood of frosts that can kill the blossom. This is a bit of a design fault you might think but on the continent where peaches fruit their socks off, spring lasts about a week: winter frequently switches to summer over a very short period and this means there is a much reduced chance of a late frost.

The other thing we, or rather the peaches, have to contend with is peach leaf curl and the conditions that encourage it are found in a wet early spring as described above. If you add all of that up, you'll see it is quite hard to win: springs are a mixture of wet and mild (PLC) and clear and frosty (damaged blossom).

Peaches in the U.S of A.

Other countries with endless days of heat and beating sunshine find it a bit easier to grow peaches and nectarines, and as a result can get carried away studying peaches, perhaps in the same way we might with apples: you can probably get a BSc in Advanced Peach Fluff at the University of Incontinent Rock, Calif. The west coast of the USA is indeed a major player and has categorised fruit as follows:

Flesh: Yellow – more tart, earlier ripening.
White – sweeter, later ripening.
Melting – soft texture, mainly for fresh eating.
Non-melting – best for processing.

Stones: Clingstone – the flesh sticks to the stone.
Freestone – flesh and stone are separate; nectarines and some peaches.

Who would have thought stone fruit could be this fascinating?

Some Recent Introductions of Special Note
Peach 'Avalon Pride'
An interesting development in that this is the first peach that is claimed to be truly resistant to peach leaf curl. It can be made dwarf, too, by growing it on a

small(ish) rootstock and restricting in a container – nurseries cleverly describe these as 'patio trees'. In a way, it doesn't need to be dwarf because the resistance should be enough to protect it when grown outdoors. The cropping abilities of 'Avalon Pride' may be overstated by some nurseries, with reports from growers of fewer numbers of fruits than those claimed and of weak branches allowing breaking. The recommendation therefore has been to ensure, with formative and renewal pruning, that there is a strong framework there constantly. The fruit itself is highly flavoured and is yellow-fleshed.

Peach 'Garden Lady'

SOME PEACH TREES CAN BE TINY

Very dwarf peaches, such as the genetic dwarf 'Garden Lady' at less than 2m, are naturally tiny without being on a special rootstock. This makes them desirable simply because, grown in containers, they can be moved in and out of a sheltered area: dry stems (and later leaves) in January to March mean peach leaf curl is less likely to be a problem. This tree is early (early August) producing a clingstone fruit with yellow flesh. It is precocious, starting fruiting really quite soon. It has attractive pale pink blossom and politely requests full sun. It's from New Zealand but seems to cope with being planted the right way up for here.

Nectarine 'Snow Baby'

Another genetic dwarf, this time only 1.2m / 4' high after ten years making it very easy to move around to protect. The name, incidentally, refers to the white flesh of the fruit.

Nectarine 'Nectarella'

This genetic dwarf (less than 2m) is late (mid to late August), with a good sweet flavour. It is a freestone nectarine and is quick to start producing, becoming a regular cropper.

PEARS *Pyrus communis*
(*Pyrus*, L. for pear, *communis*, common, in groups)
Family: ROSACEAE

Why we should grow pears
Often long-lived, pear trees are very attractive in themselves with craggy bark and increasing gnarliness. The blossom is lovely and some varieties have excellent autumn colour. Oh, and the fruit's not bad either.

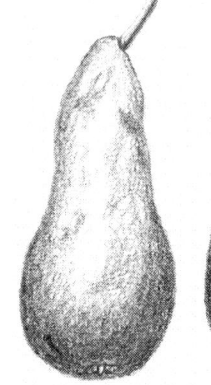

CONFERENCE AND COMICE – THE LAUREL AND HARDY OF THE PEAR WORLD

Pear Essentials
Varieties
'Onward': one of the more recent varieties, it is a reliable cropper and produces pale yellow fruit with a suntan of red / brown on one side. A useful variety for cooler areas because it flowers later and so can avoid frosts.

'Doyenné du Comice': the 'Cox's Orange Pippin' of the pear world, this can be a strong-growing tree unless restricted by the rootstock. It needs good conditions so no sticking it in some shady, out-of-the-way place – in the north, perhaps try it against a south-facing wall. The fruit is picked when ready, mid October onwards, and can be stored until the end of the year; it can be quite large and has a reddish patch on the sunny side of an otherwise yellow-green skin. Some russetting is likely. The flesh is white and the texture is smooth. It is also juicy and sweet.

'Beurré Hardy': as the name suggests, this is suitable for growing in most parts of the country not just Dorset (a minor literary joke, there): it is hardy and reliable. It has a russetty skin, sweet, smooth, juicy flesh and it ripens in October. Good autumn colour.

'Williams Bon Chrétien': an 18th century selection ready in late September. The fruit has been described as 'dumpy-looking' and changes from green to yellow as it ripens – harvesting should be when it is slightly under-ripe. It is sweet and juicy with a noticeable amount of acidity making it a very suitable cooking pear, too.

'Concorde': a pleasing selection of the cross between 'Conference' and 'D. du Comice', released in the 1980s. Those splendid folk at East Malling Research Station managed to capture the best bits of both: reliable, high yields and quality of the former and, despite looking superficially like 'Conference', the fruit has properties of the latter. Pick unripe in late September.

'Conference': an old favourite in the UK with narrow fruit and a dark skin turning paler and a bit russetted as it ripens. It is ready from mid September onwards and is at its best when picked just under-ripe to be ripened naturally indoors. It is considered to be self fertile (it will produce fruit all by itself) but will perform far better if there is a suitable pollinator nearby.

'Beth': a cross between 'Beurré Superfin' and 'Williams Bon Chrétien', this is an early season pear to pick in late August / early September and use as soon as possible. It produces chubby little pears with thick necks, like a prop forward just slightly smaller. The skin is smooth, thin and a typical pear green/ yellow. The flesh is sweet and has the characteristic 'melting' texture. It appears to be fairly recent in that it was released for sale in 1974 but was actually bred much earlier than that.

Size / Rootstocks: Quince A (3-4m / 10-14'), Quince C (2.5-3m / 8-10'), BA29 – another quince but bigger than Quince A, Pyrodwarf (4-4.5m / 13-15'), Hawthorn. More on these later in the chapter.

Spacing: Trees on Quince A are spaced about 4.5m / 15' about, on Quince C about 3.5m / 12' and the others about 5m / 18'. This is for most tree forms but the distance will be less for cordons (75cm / 30") and dwarf pyramids (1.2-1.5m / 4-5').

Position: Pears need more sun and less winter chilling to make good blossom than apples meaning sunnier aspects are preferable: a west-facing wall is ideal for an espalier. Save the south-facing wall for even fussier trees.

Feeding: A full range of essential nutrients is required as a starting point, as with any fruit plants, but a little extra nitrogen in spring along with the obligatory potassium is ideal. Dilute urine combined with a good compost mulch should do the trick

Pruning: The same pruning requirements, opportunities and hassles as apples. Pears tend to have a more upright growth making it trickier to form an open centre bush. It may be worthwhile using festooning in the formative stage to ensure that the new branches fix in a wide-branching position. However, they readily form fruiting spurs making them superb fruit for growing as espaliers.

Pollination: Despite the availability of one or two self fertile pears (e.g. 'Conference') the best yields are found when there are two different compatible varieties in reasonable proximity. For more fascinating information, see later in the chapter.

Harvesting: Earlier pears are picked ripe, later pears are picked slightly under-ripe and stored to continue ripening.

Propagation: Grafting in spring or budding in summer.

Weeding: Small and trained trees need keeping clean of the most pernicious weeds permanently and all pears kept weed-free when establishing.

Pear Origins
Brought to the UK by the Romans or the Normans (take your pick), the sweet dessert pear came originally from eastern Europe / western Asia. It is thought to have crossed with the native or wild pear (*Pyrus pyraster*) in this country to produce trees with inedible raw fruit that happen to have high levels of tannin and acidity – the perry pear. Dessert pears have been bred for centuries and the French seem to have got the knack quite well: many varieties have their origin over the Channel.

Pear Nutrition
Some reasonable levels of potassium, calcium and iron (slightly above apple levels, but not exciting) and about the same as apples for vitamins.

Pear Botany
A pear is a pome as per apples.

Discussion / rambling / elaboration
Pollination
Pear pollination starts off very similar to apples; usually you need two different varieties that flower at the same time or close to it. So there is the first hurdle – understanding the groups that are arranged according to flowering time. All of the varieties given at the beginning are in pollination groups 3 or 4, meaning that they flower at the same time or the flowering overlaps to a sufficient degree. Overall, pears flower earlier than apples so are more subject to late frosts, possibly giving rise to the claim that pears are 'fussier'. Those of a group 4 flowering may be marginally less susceptible, e.g. 'Onward'. Next we have varieties that are termed incompatible: under 'Pollination' in the Essentials bit at the beginning of this chapter I sneaked in the word 'compatible' while nobody was looking. It is not surprising that cross breeding with a close relation is not advisable (just look at the royal family in the 19th century) and plants try to avoid this. As a result, you can choose two pears that flower at the same time but, because they are closely related – maybe one has been bred from the other in the first place – they won't successfully cross pollinate and are therefore 'incompatible'. Consequently, the second hurdle is to find your tree(s)

from different incompatibility groups. The only two varieties of those listed above in an incompatibility group are 'Onward' and 'Doyenné du Comice' (the latter is a parent of the former), so those two won't pollinate each other. As usual, in city gardens, it is quite possible to plant a single tree and have it pollinated by one of your neighbours' trees, quite often without you even knowing they have them.

Incidental fact: if the blossom of your pear tree is pink, it's an apple. Pears only have white blossom (though some apples can have white blossom too).

Pear Ripening

The ripening of pears is a mystery to most of us, alongside what men are thinking about or what women do in the bathroom. The problem seems to be one of speed – not the narcotic but the seemingly very short time between a rock-hard, tooth-challenging specimen and a fluffy, cotton wool disappointment or prematurely-composting catastrophe. The technique espoused by some is to pick the lot when they are still hard at around the time

THE UNRIPE   THE SLIGHTLY OVERRIPE

when they are supposed to ripen. Then you can keep an eye on them and check them every few minutes at your leisure. The main problem with that is, in any particular year, when actually is the time that they should ripen?: variation can be up to four weeks.

Some prefer the more natural but somewhat haphazard method which is to check the fruit regularly while it is still on the tree. For example, with the excellent variety 'Onward', look for a change in colour from greenish to yellowish, gently press near the neck of the fruit and if there is any 'give', 'tis time. Or, finally, cup the fruit in one hand and gently lift, perhaps include a slight twist if you feel up to it – if it parts from the branch, well, you've just picked it and it's ready to eat. The last technique is probably the better of the three since it seems to catch the fruit a tiny bit earlier than the colour or softness. Some say that smelling the fruit is not to be sniffed at, but normally a strong 'ripe' smell means the pear is overripe.

The downside of the ripening-on-the-tree technique is that all of the fruit has to be checked on a regular, almost daily, basis – not a problem with a small back garden tree or an espalier, but not so convenient with a large specimen. The tree-clearance method is a lot simpler in that case.

There are stories of gardeners saying they have to stay up all night with their 'Conference' pears to catch the change from rock hard to fully ripe: that's a great indicator how alert you have to be. Maybe employ the compromise technique – when the first few pears are tested as ripe, then pick the lot: you know they won't be far behind.

Storage

This is not as easy as with apples and they rarely keep well into the New Year. For the best chance, however, choose the right varieties: 'Conference', for instance, can keep until March given the best conditions. For most of us, without the advantage of special storage rooms, the 'best conditions' means getting the temperature frost-free and low for as long as possible, ideally 1 or 2°C. That isn't very likely unless you have a specially set fridge so the next best is a shady outbuilding / shed where cool air can be trapped during autumn nights and shut in for the days. This is not looking good: you haven't got a dedicated pear fridge, your shed isn't in the shade of a structure (a north-facing wall) or evergreen tree, it's not very insulated anyway since the felt blew off in recent gales, and you'd never remember to get down to the allotment to shut the shed door first thing in the morning anyway.

Bit of History

'Williams Bon Chrétien' has a vaguely interesting past. It was obviously very popular in a number of countries, hence the tendency to try to appropriate it. It was raised as 'Williams' in Berkshire in the late 18th century. In Europe they apparently had a bash at attaching a legend to the variety, resulting in the addition of the 'Bon Chrétien' bit. In the states, it was Mr. Enoch Bartlett of Massachusetts who bought an orchard in 1817 and instead of identifying the pears as 'Williams' he simply gave his own name to the variety. A little bit of a nerve, you might say, especially since, over the pond, that name has stuck: 'Bartlett' pears are identical to 'Williams'. This variety is also famous for being the one most used in the canning industry; maybe we have the right, if we were so inclined, to be slightly miffed when we read the ingredients on a tin of pears and it says 'Bartlett pears and syrup'.

MR. BARTLETT, THIS IS MR. WILLIAMS

Perry Pears

Pears, particularly perry pears, can live to a ripe (thank you) old age – up to 300 years which is going some for a fruit tree. This is significant because it gives plenty of time for an amazing range of wildlife to develop in pear orchards: in the same way that the numbers of insects in, on or around an oak tree increases with its age, good long-lived fruit trees can build up the range too. Perry orchards in Gloucestershire have recorded over 1,800 species of plants, animals and fungi.

Rootstocks

There's apples sitting there saying 'If you want to grow me, then graft me on to another apple. As far as rootstocks go, nothing else will do'. Pears come along and the next thing you know they're stuck on all manner of things. Related things. In fact the rootstocks are in the same family but then apples are in the same family. Strangely, the one plant which isn't that much use when it comes to grafting pears is pears – see below. So the species that has taken up the slack is the quince: selections of quince are responsible for the majority of rootstocks for pears grown in the UK. Even then, some varieties are a bit grumpy and don't fuse well such as 'Williams Bon Chrétien'.

So how does one grow a 'Williams'? Basically, stick a more amenable variety in between it and the rootstock. This is called double working in that a friendlier variety such as 'Beurré Hardy' or 'Fertility' is grafted onto the quince rootstock and the 'Williams' is grafted or budded on to that – double the amount of work. This variation in the grafting compatibility is found throughout top fruits. 'Fertility' is so accepting that it will fuse to a range of plants that other pear varieties wouldn't even look at, including apples: yes, it is possible to have a pear and an apple on the same tree, but in a fairly limited way.

Probably of more interest is the ability of a wide range of varieties to be grafted to hawthorn. This isn't terribly helpful if you want a free-standing tree and certainly not if you want to train it (a hawthorn rootstock gives an uncontrolled pear tree). What is more intriguing is being able to convert part of a hawthorn hedge into a row of pear trees. Also, of course, it is easier for the majority of us to get our hands on a hawthorn seedling than any of the other rootstocks.

Pyrodwarf is a rootstock of German origin and is bred from two varieties of pear. This makes it very compatible to graft on to. Unfortunately it is too vigorous for a lot of gardens and it also suckers freely.

In order to grow an espalier, which pears lend themselves to admirably, see 'Pruning and Training'. Choose a weaker rootstock like 'Quince C' if there are to be just two or three tiers and 'Quince A' for four or five tiers. It could be 'Quince C' for four tiers if the arms of each tier are quite short, say, 1.5-1.8m / 5-6'.

Pear Problems

Pear midge
Female midges emerge from hibernation in spring, mate and lay eggs in blossom. The eggs hatch in a week and the larvae feed for a month on the developing fruit. The young fruits can distort then blacken and drop off. They will be full of tiny (2-4mm) grubs which will pupate in the soil and stay there until the following spring. Pick off as soon as odd fruitlets are noticed and collect up any that have fallen so interrupting the midge lifecycle: if you're feeling up to it, crush them or put them in the council collection, but don't compost them in the normal cold heap.

Pear leaf blister mite
Too good to miss: this one is mitey small – it is microscopic, and inhabits the leaves instead of the fruit which is a nice change. Raised, pale blisters, only about 2mm wide, are found either side of the midrib and they turn black with age. Leaves can be removed when the damage is noticed but it's not considered to affect the tree or its cropping – my kind of pest, one where you don't have to do anything.

Pear and cherry slugworm
See under 'slugworm' in cherries.

Scab
Fruit can be made inedible and if there is a lot of leaf fall too, future cropping can be affected. Unlike apples, pear scab affects the fruit of pears first. This fungus is closely related to the apple version and is equally disappointing. The dark patches can be barely worth bothering with or it can cover the entire fruit accompanied by cracking and other fungi wanting to join in with the party. The leaves differ from scabby apple leaves in that they can end up looking as though they have been dipped in brown paint. Pruning and thinning helps prevent it establishing since it is encouraged by wet conditions: good air circulation will help leaves to dry out more rapidly and slow down infection.

ANOTHER SCABBY LEAF

Pear rust
Other rusts consist of a scattering of small yellow or orange dots on the leaves. Not so pear rust. Comparatively huge, bright orange spots appear on the leaves – bit of a show-off, really. Being so obvious helps in its control – we can pick off the leaves whenever they are encountered and send them to the council's hot composting facility. Because pear rust is rarely a major problem this should be all that is required. This level of leaf-removal is fine. For other diseases such as

scab, if this approach was used then we'd just end up helping the fungus in its mission to defoliate (and weaken) the tree.

Stony pit virus
The dreaded word 'virus', feared because once in a plant there is rarely a cure apart from removal (though I'm not sure killing a tree by removing it really counts as a cure). Stony pit is apparently only transferred by grafting so at least you won't have yourself to blame for this one. The fruit is knobbly and the flesh is extra gritty with many 'stone cells' throughout. Stone cells are, as the name suggests, the same tissue (sclerenchyma) of which the stone / pit of plums is made. Buy certified trees.

Canker
This is identical to apple canker (it is the same species) though pears don't seem to suffer quite so much. When spores get into a branch via a natural opening or a wound, the fungus develops to create a dead, sunken patch of bark. It can girdle the branch so killing all of the growth above the canker. Early on after infection, the tree often reacts and tries to grow over the dead area, resulting in lumps which can actually be the first thing to draw attention to the problem. Mild attacks are best dealt with by pruning to the next available junction below the canker, at the same time being aware that pruning cuts can be a site for infection. For that reason, a tree with lots of canker is probably not worth continuing with, especially since cropping is likely to be quite poor. Any cankers on the main stem can be cut out with a knife, back to a ring of live tissue.

More Nonsense
Before the advent of decent rootstocks, pears were grafted on to random pear rootstocks which resulted in the huge trees of old orchards. These are rather wonderful but unfortunately don't come into fruit for upwards of 20 years, giving rise to the saying, 'plant pears for your heirs'. I note that pears contain some folic acid (not much but more than Apple 'Golden Delicious') in which case you could say 'plant pears for your hairs'. Rabbits etc. can nibble low branches and young stems: 'plant pears for your hares'? It is probably time to move on to Plums.

PLUMS *Prunus domestica* and other related fruit (including Greengages)
(*Prunus*, L. for plum, *domestica*, domesticated)
Family: ROSACEAE

Why we should grow plums
Wonderful blossom; rich, juicy flesh; high levels of antioxidants; good fun with stone-spitting competitions.

Plum Essentials
Varieties:

A PLUM WISHING THAT, WHEN IT COMES TO BROWN ROT, IT HAD CHOSEN ITS NEIGHBOURS BETTER

Plum 'Victoria': late season (late August-early September), heavy cropping, superior flavour, mid season, disease prone, fruit skin is yellow with a pink blush; the most famous and widely grown plum; flowering group 3.

Plum 'Opal': early season (mid July) with good pest and disease resistance but needs a favourable position to develop its excellent flavour (i.e. lots of sun); flowering group 3.

Plum 'Kirke's Blue': late season (early September) with a dark purple skin and yellow juicy flesh, reckoned by Lawrence Hills as being the 'Cox's of plums'; flowering group 4.

Plum 'Blue Tit': mid season (mid August) and reliable with regular good crops; the RHS describe it as having a 'pleasant' flavour which is not an over-the-top enthusiastic description; flowering group 5.

Plum 'Marjorie's Seedling': dual purpose, late season (mid September) making it valuable for plums-in-succession should you have room for a number of trees; dual purpose though used as dessert only when left to fully ripen on the tree; good disease resistance; purple to blue/black skin and a good strong flavour; flowering group 5.

Plum 'Jubilee': mid season (mid August), a more recent introduction, larger and darker than 'Victoria' with which it is favourably compared; flowering group 3.

Plum 'Czar': mid season (early August), principally a cooking plum, but valuable on two counts: it has frost-resistant flowers and it crops well in shady positions. Heavy cropping. Flowering group 3. An indication of when it was developed: the Czar of Russia was visiting the UK at the time. Unfortunately, I don't know which Czar.

Greengages
'Cambridge Gage': mid-late season (late August) typical round-and-yellow gage easy to grow; flowering group 4.

'**Early Transparent**': mid season (mid August) rich and sweet with a pink blush on the shoulders (flowering group 2) and 'Golden Transparent'(flowering group 3) – all wonderful flavour. 'Transparent', incidentally, refers to the translucent nature of the skin and flesh meaning you can see the stone if a fruit is held up to the light.

Size: Rootstocks include 'Pixy' – 2.5-3m/8-10', 'Plumina' – as 'Pixy' but with larger fruit, 'Wavit' – 3-3.5m/10-12' and 'St. Julien A' – 4-5m/14-17'. 'VVA-1' is newly arrived (so not so established / tested) but gives the smallest trees at up to 2.5m.

Spacing: Plant trees apart the same distance as their height (the lower figure if a range is given).

Positioning: Most plums prefer a good half day's sun (so east or west facing walls are fine to train against). One or two varieties will crop adequately on a north-facing wall such as 'Czar'. Greengages need better conditions – more sun and drier conditions.

Feeding: As for all other fruits but with a little more emphasis on nitrogen (but not at the expense of the other nutrients). As always, good compost as a mulch would be fine.

Pruning: The more you prune plums the more you're asking for trouble – if possible just leave them alone. For trained trees such as fans it is a different matter. Formative pruning is done in the early spring whilst any regulatory / maintenance pruning should be done around midsummer.

Pollination: Cross pollination is required so two different varieties that flower simultaneously need to be planted relatively close to each other. The varieties listed above are mid season flowerers (groups 2, 3 or 4) so will mostly cross pollinate (not 2 with 4); exceptions are Plums 'Blue Tit' and 'Marjorie's Seedling' (both late flowerers at 5 meaning they can pollinate each other and 4s). See 'Pollination' to understand what these wretched numbers mean.

Quite a few varieties will produce fruit all by themselves, notably 'Victoria' and 'Czar', but will yield better if there is another variety nearby. It i s unlikely to crop up (ha!) but there is a handful of varieties that won't cross pollinate each other ('incompatible'), 'Early Rivers', 'Old Greengage' and 'Jefferson', for example.

Harvesting: Pick when the fruit starts to soften and has coloured well – this indicates full flavour as well as ripeness.

Propagation: Budding in summer, grafting in late winter.

Weeding: Keep weed-free when establishing (three years) and permanently for the smallest trees.

Plum Origins

Common plum *Prunus domestica* – from the Caucasus, probably a cross between the sloe and the cherry plum. Originally thought to have been brought to the UK by the Romans (who had them via Greece), they have been re-introduced at various times since. When that last bit is read, it sounds as though we have been a little absent-minded and have somehow mislaid the original specimens ("Please, Sir, can I have some more?"). It actually means that over the years, new versions, 'varieties', have been found, selected and / or bred and have then been brought here. And that is the case with a lot of fruit, including in the reverse direction. There are 320 varieties in the National Collection at Brogdale, Kent. Greengage *Prunus domestica* or *P. italica*. Native to Western Asia though the second possibility of a name indicates how greengages made it to the UK and other parts of Europe. Once again it appears we were a trifle negligent, needing later re-introductions (particularly the 18th century) to get a range of varieties. The name 'greengage' comes from the inability of this fruit to hang on to a common name: when it arrived here in the 18th century, label-less, it was called the green Gage's plum after the recipient, Sir Thomas Gage.

Plum Nutrition

This lot have good levels of Potassium, in the range 240-300mg/100g, and Calcium is not bad but variable. They have middling levels of vitamins with the exception of Carotene (precursor of A) at 300μg/100g (greengages have one third of that). Vitamin C is pitiful – about the same as Apple 'Golden Delicious' which is not a particularly desirable comparison. Good news: lots of antioxidants / anti-inflammatory compounds (procyanin, neochlorogenic acid and quercetin): one plum (red or blue, not yellow) equals a handful of blueberries.

Plum Botany

This bit is fascinating: the plum fruit is, botanically, known as a 'drupe' – a single-seeded structure with three outer layers: the skin, flesh and stone. Maybe that wasn't so exciting as it first seemed. But at least it is a true fruit with no complications. As a result of the botany, plums and friends are grouped in the Prunus

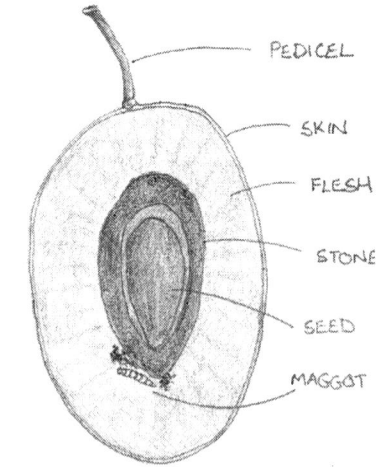

genus (which also includes apricots, peaches and cherries) collectively known as stone fruit. Incidentally, the same drupe structure is seen in blackberries and associates where mini drupes (correctly 'drupelets') are joined together to make a 'compound fruit'.

Discussion / rambling / elaboration
Pruning
Formative pruning is pretty much the same as for apples: halving of new growth each year for the first few years to an outward-facing bud to create an open centre. Other shapes are available. This builds up a strong framework which is even more important for plums which seem to suffer from a self-destructive trait. Even with a strong structure, branches are prone to breaking under the weight of fruit, wind and rain so the more effort we put in during the early years the better.

It is probably fine to do this formative pruning in the winter because the plant is young and vigorous plus the cuts that are made are generally quite small. When we move from formative pruning to the regular, maintenance pruning things change. The cuts can end up being quite large, particularly with older trees requiring renovation. Anyway, the main change is that maintenance pruning should take place around midsummer. Remember the phrase 'prune a prune in June', which only works if you know that a prune is a dried plum. This may appear like madness but it hasn't stopped us so far. It is hard to see what you're doing in the summer because of all of the leaves and, harder still, there are lots of fruit forming that will be knocked off in the process. If this is too irritating to contemplate, you have the option of looking at the tree in winter and selecting branches for the chop; mark them in some way, perhaps with string or ribbon, and then cut those out in June. If you know what branches are to be removed you could even pick off the flowers or little fruitlets from those branches to reduce the energy that the tree will put into them.

You may be curious to know why you're having to go to all of this trouble (if you're not, move on to something else). In a word, it is diseases. More on this can be found under 'Plum Problems' and the rambling bit at the end. In practice, we don't actually need to do much pruning of plums and damsons. Flowers (and hence fruit) are initiated on old branches in the stumpy little spurs and on the growth produced that same year – usually late in the summer. In other words, the following spring, blossom could appear anywhere on the tree (except for the oldest wood / trunk etc.) so it makes sense not to remove much at all. Occasionally, as a branch gets too old it might be worth pruning out and replacing with a young shoot, especially with fan-trained trees. And of course, the usual dead, diseased and damaged and any congested branches.

Thinning
This book is an attempt to help you grow fruit and, what do you know, we're pulling them off. Thinning apples is a pastime that is achieved when then there's nothing else to do. Plum thinning is essential. It is not so much to give them space and get bigger fruit as to stop the tree falling to bits. Plum 'Victoria', for example, will overload so much the branches can rip off. So do as you're told. Leave one fruit every 8-10cm / 3-4" (or for smaller fruits 5-8cm / 2-3") and do this after the tree has naturally shed fruitlets in June.

Storage
Plums etcetera tend to ripen over a relatively short time and there is a limit to how much crumble can be made and consumed before they all go off. In short: freezing, bottling or wine. In long: freezing works well but we are left, on defrosting, with fruit suitable only for more crumbles. Maybe to eat fresh plums is a seasonal delight and will only remain so if we can't access them the rest of the year – remember, don't confuse those out-of-season imported abominations with home-grown fruit. To extend the fresh fruit season for as long as possible, plant a mixture of varieties, potentially providing plums etc. from July to September. Bottling is a more traditional storage technique and, because they are processed (heated and combined with sugar syrup), the fruit no longer has the fresh appeal. Still, you will retain an essence of plum joy for a considerable time.

Plum Problems
It appears that Plum 'Victoria' is everyone's favourite, including most of the pests and diseases that follow.

Brown rot and Blossom wilt
These are caused by the same organism, a fungus. The symptoms are the same as those described in 'Apples' (though with apples, they are caused by two different fungi).

Plum rust
There is a rust for every occasion. The one that goes for plums also, bizarrely, affects anemones – normally it is one species of rust to one genus of plants. Anyway, the symptoms are the same as usual with orange spots on the upper

surface of a leaf and spore-releasing pustules corresponding underneath. Affected leaves fall prematurely and if the tree is attacked several years on the trot it can be weakened the first result of which would be a yield reduction. Either do nothing (a minor showing) or pick off infected leaves or rake up fallen leaves and dispose of.

Pocket plum

The fruit develops in an odd shape, like a little fat banana but without any other useful banana properties. They are hollow and stone-less. Take it off before it develops a white coating of spores. Rarely affects more than a proportion of the fruit and will quite often not appear in successive years.

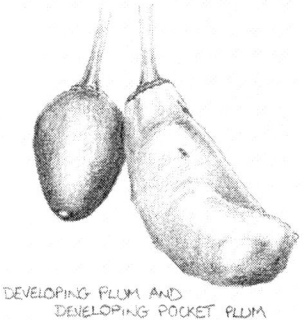

DEVELOPING PLUM AND DEVELOPING POCKET PLUM

Silver leaf

This is a fungus that can get into the system of the tree and eventually kill it. Leaves on a particular branch can have a silvery sheen to them often followed by that branch dying back. Spores of the disease get into the tree in the first place via cuts, wounds or natural openings. Dead wood can produce fruiting bodies, semicircles of bracket fungi that are brown and hairy. The recommendations against silver leaf are, one, preventative – only prune between mid May and mid July ('Prune a prune in June') or, two, remedial – cut out affected branches. If the resulting cut surface has a dark stain in it, cut back further until you are at least 15cm beyond the last bit of staining. A whole tree affected should be removed completely since the fruiting bodies will grow and spore on stumps: it's hygiene, you know.

Plums are most affected, Plum 'Victoria' being particularly susceptible, whereas Plum 'Marjorie's Seedling' is resistant to both silver leaf and bacterial canker. Damsons are less affected.

Slightly annoyingly there is a condition where the leaves turn silvery, called false silver leaf. It is temporary (being caused by malnutrition or soil conditions) and the tree is unaffected unless, that is, you've just lopped a branch off thinking it is real silver leaf. Coupled with the fact that some trees can get silver leaf and recover from it, makes the whole business quite tricky. Perhaps the best advice is, if leaves are silvering, to leave it until there are 'further developments' – any dying back – and then act quickly. Incidentally, the silver appearance is due to a separation of the layers within a leaf; with air inside, the leaf looks silvery.

Bacterial canker

Another nasty one affecting *Prunus* but more of a problem on cherries than plums.

Aphids

Specifically, it is the leaf-curling plum aphid which overwinters as eggs on plums and lives up to its name by curling the leaves. It actually hatches before the leaves open in January so the poor, shivering little things start by feeding on the dormant buds. It is a small, yellow-green aphid that, when it has (literally) got fed up with the declining nutrition in plum sap, develops winged forms which migrate to summer herbaceous hosts that are too numerous to contemplate getting rid of. They include *Chrysanthemum*, *Aster* and *Myosotis* (forget-me-not).

Most of the time, provided you have a mixed planting around your trees including nettles and a range of open flowers, predators will sort them out. The positive aspect of that is you don't have to do anything (plus you are sustaining a vital food web). The negative is, for whatever reason, the predator might not turn up to the party: they never will if the trees are sprayed – a messy process at the best of times. Even so-called organic winter washes (made from plant oils, no longer tar oil), applied to kill the aphid eggs, will also kill predator eggs and hibernating adults (such as acorid bugs).

WINTER WASH

Plum moth

What a delightful little fellow. If you have ever eaten a plum which looks good, is ripe yet has a slight graininess in the flesh then you have encountered plum moth or at least its toiletry habits. The grainy bit is frass, also known as caterpillar poop. The female moth lays eggs in June on the young fruit, one per plum. The eggs hatch in a week or two and the little larva or grub enters the flesh. It feeds near the stone for about a month before emerging, pupating in the soil to emerge as an adult the following year and start it all over again.

First of all, beware of prematurely ripe fruit – it is distinctly early – remove it and eat what parts you can cope with. Pheromone moth traps will catch a good number of males and prevent any of that procreation nonsense – but not all. Birds will be very interested in the pupae in the soil, such as robins, but to ensure more effective control, rent a chicken.

Plum sawfly

Corresponding to apple sawfly, this likewise attacks young fruitlets as opposed to the slightly more mature fruit attacked by plum moth and codling moth. Damaged fruitlets have a hole bored in them out of which extrudes black, sticky frass. One grub can attack four fruitlets before dropping to the ground, the little stinker, where it will pupate and remain until next year. Check fruitlets in late spring and remove (possibly as part of a thinning programme) in the hope of removing the larvae in them at the same time. Birds, as with the moth.

Random Nonsense

The 'Orange Pippin' website is quite rightly fond of plums and a description is as follows '… the flavour of ripe home-grown plums is vastly superior to shop bought fruit. Indeed, in our opinion, freshly picked dessert plums can offer the most exquisite sweet flavours of any fruit available from the temperate garden'. Another take on that, via 'The Guardian', was commentary calling shop-bought specimens as hard, squeaky-skinned, flavourless fruit. So, the same story as with apples: commercial varieties of plums are there for yield (= profit) and transportability; in other words, flavour comes way down the list if you can't get them to the consumer in one, intact piece. Answer? Grow your own.

The reason we are doing most of our pruning in summer as opposed to winter is in relation to a couple of diseases, specifically, a fungus called Silver Leaf and a bacterium called Bacterial Canker. For more details of these charmers, see under pests and diseases above. Actually why we prune like this is a trifle murky – there are differing opinions:

Apparently plant tissues are more resistant in July and August to Bacterial Canker. It is also possible that the wounds dry and are harder to infect at this time… though August is actually one of the wetter months of the year – maybe they are able to dry out quickly between wettings. The wounds will actually heal more rapidly at this time of year too (yes, but only small wounds will have completely healed in that time). It could be that it is the live tissue that is important (the bit around the edge of a cut) and it may be 'more resistant' or, more likely, heal up quickly even if the central, woody, dead part of the stem isn't covered. H.G. Witham-Fogg ('Fruit Growing' 1963) goes for this one: in the summer, trees resist attack by forming a gum barrier that seals off the wound and stops the infection getting a hold.

Spores of both diseases are less prevalent at this time of year. This is the most convincing reason. Silverleaf, for example, will infect wounds via spores between September and May. Pruning at the end of the disease's hunting season (June) will mean the cut is spore-free for the longest period and has a chance to heal, dry or whatever else needs to happen.

The stones of plums and related species can be used to identify specific varieties, just like fingerprints though less messy. The patterns on the surface of the stones, coupled with their size and shape, are completely individual. Because the stones are tough and a bit wooden (they are composed of a plant tissue called *sclerenchyma*, botany fans) it means they can be used to identify what was around centuries ago, as on Henry VIII's flagship, 'The Mary Rose'. It must have been very reassuring to His Royal Decapitator to know that despite his number one boat hitting rock bottom, we'd find out at a later date what kind of *Prunus* they were consuming on board.

QUINCE *Cydonia oblonga*
(*Cydonia*, L. for quince, *oblonga*, oblong)
Family: ROSACEAE

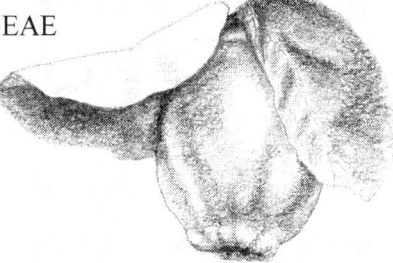

A SHY QUINCE

Why we should grow quince
No apple pie is complete unless a few slices of quince have been included. A lovely, ornamental tree.

Quince Essentials
Varieties:
'Vranja': perhaps the best known, with large fruit on an upright-growing tree.
'Meech's Prolific': quick to produce and keep well.
'Portuguese': a vigorous tree which is slow to crop. All of these are pear-shaped.
'Champion': rounded fruit with a more subtle flavour.

Size: This is dictated by, effectively, the choice of one of two rootstocks, Quince A (3-4m / 10-14'), Quince C (2.5-3m / 8-10').

Position: Moist, free-draining soil, preferably in a sunny spot.

Feeding: A seaweed spray occasionally during the growing season will keep the tree in good shape.

Pruning: Formative pruning is to generate an open centre bush or half standard just as with apples. Thereafter, maintenance pruning is removal of dead or crowding branches. In other words, the absolute minimum.

Pollination: Self fertile, but the best crops are found when there is cross pollination (more than one variety).

Harvesting: Picking is in October before frosts really get going and they have to be stored until they change colour: green to yellow. Then they are ready to use: the ripening process takes up to a couple of months. Store them in a cool frost-free place as you would apples and pears but in separate boxes or rooms – they can be tainted.

Propagation: Grafting. Since the rootstocks that are used are also quinces, some folk think that taking some suckers from an appropriate rootstock will give them a quince tree, and that is true except it is a quince selected for its rootstock properties rather than its fruiting abilities. Choose a specific variety.

Weeding: Definitely for the first three years, thereafter, it depends on the situation. In a garden, it could easily hold its own as a specimen lawn tree or in a mixed border, in both cases with other plants in close proximity. Lawrence Hills in 'Grow Your Own Fruit and Vegetables' reckons that quinces prefer to be 'grassed down' underneath; it certainly enables a control method of quince leaf blight (see below). In a modern orchard, there might not be a weed in sight.

Quince Origins
From the Middle East, Persia, that kind of area and arrived here in the 13th century. At least, that is when they were first recorded – 'Edward I planted four at the Tower of London in 1275'. The chances are that plenty were planted before he got around to it. Also, when I say 'Edward I planted....', it is unlikely said monarch pulled on his wellies and got down to a bit of hard graft: the place would have been teeming with peasants.

Quince Nutrition
Minerals and vitamins are seriously unimpressive apart perhaps from Vitamin C at 15mg/100g which is over twice that of the average apple.

Quince Botany
The fruit of quince, like its relatives pears and apples, is a false fruit – the majority has been formed from a part of the flower other than the ovary. The seeds are also poisonous like apple pips, containing 'nitriles' which are converted to hydrogen cyanide in the body. Oops. Like a lot of temperate fruit, quinces need a number of 'cold hours' for them to flower well. In other words, it has to know it has been through a winter. With our warming winters (?) this may become a problem, though with quinces the requirement is only between 100 and 400 hours below 7°C per winter.

Discussion / rambling / elaboration
Quince Problems
Quince Leaf Blight
This is a fungus that manifests as red and yellow then dark spots on the leaves and fruit. The leaves curl, shrivel and fall prematurely and occasionally the young shoots can be distorted before dying back. It over-winters on fallen leaves so, like apple scab, mowing the grass underneath chops up the leaves enabling rapid decomposition whether they are collected or not. Otherwise, rake them up and dispose of. Quinces prefer a moist soil which helpfully reduces stress-induced mildew (below) but can mean that if the site isn't also open then we have the

conditions that encourage blight: damp, stagnant air and cold. So choosing a good location is important, as is pruning if branches become congested. All of the varieties mentioned above, with the exception of 'Portuguese' have certain levels of resistance.

Quince Powdery Mildew
Possibly the biggest problem for quinces, especially in dry conditions and / or in a free-draining soil. There is a powdery mildew specially adapted for most plants and they're all different species. Well, usually. Interestingly, quince powdery mildew is actually the same species as the one that affects apples. The conditions that allow the fungus to develop are the same no matter what the species or the plant: there is dryness at the root, the plant is stressed and there is enough damp on the leaves to allow spores to germinate. These conditions are surprisingly easy to achieve. Simply, the answer is to obey the requirement of quinces for a moist soil by watering and mulching in prolonged dry spells. Prune the tree also as directed, to allow good air circulation. Collect up leaves as with leaf blight.

Fireblight
Many fruit plants are in the rose family, ROSACEAE. Of these, the 'pome-fruits' (ones which have the same sort of structure as apples) are susceptible to the bacterium fireblight, *Erwinia amylovora*. This manifests itself as wilting, then browning leaves and stem dieback. It is called fireblight because the affected stems and leaves look as though they have been a bit too close to a bonfire. Quinces are no more susceptible than the others but it needed to get a mention at some point. Fireblight spores usually enter via the open blossom eventually spreading into the shoot which becomes a reddish colour in the centre. Prompt pruning out is the answer, 60cm/2' into healthy wood. And clean your tools.

Brown rot (as on apples and pears) can occur occasionally and is best left at 'remove affected fruit when seen'.

Depending on the rootstock used, suckers may be a nuisance.

Uses of Quinces
The start of this chapter, 'Why we should grow quinces' could be countered by the question 'What the blue blazes are we doing growing quinces?'. They are rock hard, gritty, tart and, basically, inedible when raw. It seems that there are plenty of alternative uses to make up for their recalcitrance: quince jelly, quince cheese, room-fragrancer, talking point, addition to other cooked fruit especially apples (in an apple pie the recommended ratio is 20% quince to 80% apple), and that is without even looking at the tree itself. It is characterful, a lovely scented

flower that appears after apples and is not affected by frosts, the leaves turn a great autumn colour and they are traditional. Tradition is a mixed blessing – there are plenty of traditions that it is an immense relief not to have to encounter any more, such as using small boys to clean chimneys and charging across the countryside in fancy dress to rip foxes apart. But there are a few worth hanging on to like morris dancing and growing quinces.

Quince Names
The names of the varieties available to us reflect how widely quinces are grown ('Portuguese' – from no-points-for-guessing, 'Vranja' – from Serbia, 'Meech's Prolific' – UK, and from USA we have the slightly disappointingly-named 'Orange' and 'Pineapple'). There are over 20 varieties in the national collection based at Norton Priory, near Runcorn in Cheshire, whilst the National Fruit Collection at Brogdale has a mere 19.

The Spanish enjoy 'quince cheese' or 'quince paste', though they call it *membrillo*. It involves lots of cooking (three hours) to reduce the fruit combined with sugar to a sweet rubbery blob (a membrillo pad?).

The Portuguese, presumably using the variety 'Portuguese', make quince preserves from the pulp, called *Marmelo*. This, of course, gives us the name for the Seville orange-based preserves in this country – chutney. Seriously, marmalade is a major tradition in the UK but the name nowadays seems to be for oranges only. The original quince marmalade was said to have aphrodisiac properties and in the 17th century the prostitutes of London were called 'marmalade madams' as a result.

Fruits-other-than-oranges boiled with sugar now tend to be called jam or jelly. The Portuguese branch out by using vegetables, including the ever-popular carrot jam.

Quince Alternative
There is an ornamental shrub called *Chaenomeles* or, alternatively, Japanese quince. It has very attractive early spring blossom, red, pink, white, that sort

of thing. It also produces rock hard fruit very like a smaller version of the *Cydonia* fruit to which it is closely related. The Japanese quince is edible in much the same way that the one we're interested in here isn't, but is simply inferior.

History etc.
The quince has quite a classical mythology, right from Adam and Eve where the tree of knowledge bore, in some interpretations, a quince not an apple. Maybe the first piece of knowledge imparted was don't try eating this fruit raw again. The golden apple of love given to Aphrodite by Paris was a quince. Apparently.

Pete Brown in his book 'The Apple Orchard' went to considerable pains to suggest that 'apple' actually means 'fruit' and that early references to apple simply meant any old fruit. Why they should be quinces is equally interesting. And then, of course, in 'A Midsummer Night's Dream', there is the character Peter Quince, which really bares no relevance to this chapter at all since his name relates to woodwork not fruit.

As an indicator of how popular the quince was from the Middle Ages onwards, by the 17th century it was mentioned in more recipes than any other tree fruit. It might be, of course, that the choice of fruit was considerably more reduced than nowadays. Also if you have had several centuries of planting quince orchards there might be more of an incentive to find things to do with them. Perhaps the summers were hotter and more Mediterranean back then, because in good years the fruit can ripen and soften on the tree, so that it can be eaten fresh.

Other Useless Information
In his book 'The Culture of Fruits and Vegetables', George Glenny presents us with an interesting final sentence in the Quince chapter. 'If, as is sometimes the case with the quince, the bark turns rough and becomes tight, or what is familiarly known by the term "bark-bound", you must remove these evils by having recourse to the scraper, or use the draw-knife.'

There is so much in that, it is hard to know where to begin. Perhaps it is worth trying to decide what these evils really are: 'bark-bound' and 'tight' suggest that quince has an issue with its bark. Is it restricting the growth of the tree or

will it split unless drastic measures are taken? If so, it is a bit of a design fault and it is a wonder that the quince has managed to survive so many millennia in this perpetual state of malevolence. And what does 'The Scraper' actually do? Sounding like some medieval instrument of torture, it suggests a reduction or removal of bark. Certainly the draw-knife, a two-handed tool, is nowadays used to de-bark poles, posts etc. It makes one wonder what the effect on a 'bark-bound' quince is if strips of its bark are removed. Maybe some experimentation is in order. Just not on my trees.

The shapes of quince fruits seem to be a major identifying feature: principally round or pear-shaped. If you grew a quince expecting it to be the former and then discovering it is the latter, you might find yourself tempted to say 'My quince has gone pear-shaped'.
Or you might not.

RASPBERRIES *Rubus idaeus*
(*Rubus*, L. red, *idaeus*, from Mount Ida)
Family: ROSACEAE

Why we should grow raspberries
Consistently voted as the favourite soft fruit; reliable; off the ground; versatile in how they can be used; easy to prune.

Raspberry Essentials

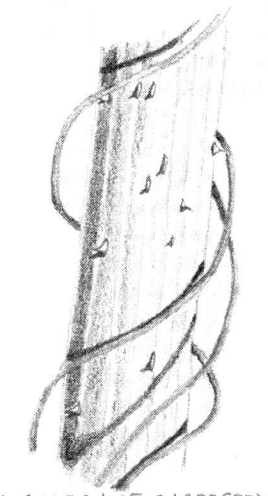

A SECTION OF RASPBERRY CANE COMPLETE WITH BINDWEED

Varieties: The majority of varieties are 'summer fruiting' which produce greater yields than the more recent 'autumn fruiting' varieties.

Summer: many including the splendid '**Malling Jewel**' – slightly more compact, reasonable resistance, good flavour. '**Glen Moy**' is relatively early, producing heavy crops of good flavour. The canes are shorter like 'Malling Jewel' and free of spines. '**Glen Ample**' is a lot more vigorous, producing heavy crops of large, tasty fruits on tall spine-free canes. All of these have the RHS's Award of Garden Merit.

Autumn: '**Autumn Bliss**' – still probably the best in terms of yield and flavour, but '**Polka**' gives a heavy yield, '**Joan J.**' has large fruit and '**Allgold**' is yellow.

Size: 1.2-2.1m / 4-7' high.

Position: At least a good half day's sun is best to give sweet fruit. Moisture-retentive, well-drained soil with a pH on the slightly acidic side.

Spacing: Planting spacing is 30-40cm / 12-16" and row spacing is 1.5-1.8m / 5-6'. Eventual spacing of canes is 7-10cm / 3-4".

Feeding: High potash (potassium) feeds such as comfrey liquid. Avoid wood ash which will raise the pH too high (unless you are on a reasonably acidic soil to start with). A mulch of compost or manure would be splendid just before growth starts in spring.

Pruning: Dead easy. In the winter, remove the old canes of summer varieties and all of the canes of autumn varieties.

Pollination: Self fertile, worry not.

Harvesting: When the berry easily detaches from the plug.

Propagation: Raspberries sucker, meaning that new shoots can pop up from below ground from the spreading root system. If these are carefully detached in the dormant season, the new shoot complete with roots can be moved to a new site or to the end of the row to extend it. Use only suckers from a recently planted row to avoid the transfer of diseases which will have built up in an old row.

Weeding: By using a clear bed just prior to planting and being very strict thereafter, perennial weeds should be permanently kept out of the canes.

Raspberry Origins
Well, the botanical name suggests one of two places, both a Mount Ida, found in Greece and Turkey, which is interesting because apparently raspberries are one of the few plants in this country to have been through the ice age.

Raspberry Nutrition
Whilst not spectacular, it is interesting to discover that raspberries have one of the highest protein contents of any home-grown fruit at 1.4g/100g and is one of the best fruits for fibre. Which is just as well since the figures for everything else are seriously underwhelming with the possible exception of Vitamin C at around 32mg/100g (the same as the best apple).

Raspberry Botany
A raspberry is a compound fruit consisting of several individual 'fruits' called 'drupelets', each with a single seed inside: each one is like a mini-plum.

Discussion / rambling / elaboration
Planting
When buying raspberries the cheapest option is to get a wrapped bundle of five or ten bare-root plants. The expensive option is to get individual plants in pots. The purchased plant in a bundle is effectively a root system. There is a stump attached, a leafless cane of about 30cm / 12", to make us feel better about what we've just bought as well as help us remember where we've planted it. Such bare root plants are best planted in the winter, as ever the preference being November / December.

When it comes to moisture, raspberries are surprisingly fussy. They definitely don't like being in very wet soil (the roots rot) to the point that some growers will plant them on a ridge or in a raised bed. On the other hand, if they don't get enough moisture during the cropping season, fruit size and yield can be considerably affected.

In the same way that cordon apple trees or espaliers can be used across a plot as a divider, so can raspberries. The effect is marginally less impressive, particularly after pruning, but it is a useful feature nevertheless. Apart from that, a row of raspberries is usually confined to the perimeter of the fruit and vegetable area, not surprising considering the height of them – over 2m / 6ft 6" in some cases. The aim of planting in rows is to make access as easy as possible. We have the 'proper' way and the lazy way; I couldn't possibly comment on which of these I have chosen. The proper way is to have a well-secured post at either end of the row and at least two wires, preferably three, strained between them. Note the word 'strained': this is where you find out how secure those end posts are.

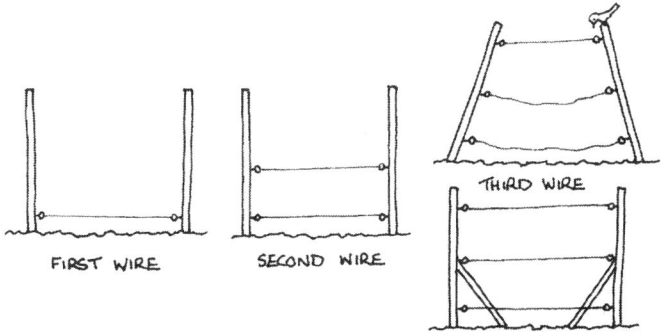

The lazy way is to plant in the same way (in a line, 30-40cm / 12-16" apart between plants) and avoid not only the post and wire system but any inclination to confine them to that single line. This is also known as the thicket approach and is used for varieties which are shorter growing. They can be grown in clumps supported by a central stake but the same problem will affect this, only more so, as with our rows: the desire of the raspberry plant to wander around.

Training

Yes, they have a suckering root system meaning that wherever the roots spread new canes can theoretically appear. Sometimes they appear to have a perverse desire to produce a new cane in any position other than the one you want them to. Particularly with a newly planted row of canes there is plenty of scope for the suckers to fill in the gaps within that row, but wouldn't you know it if they emerge several feet away to the side, thumbing their noses at your careful training system. There is a small question therefore about what to do with them. If they are relatively close and there is a gap, they can be bent in and tied to the wires. The spacing between canes along wires is 7-10cm / 3-4".

If they are too far away (more than 30cm / 1' either side), the simplest technique is to pull it off; this doesn't affect the roots in any way. It may be a more pleasant experience to do this by wearing gloves or to have planted a spineless variety. Some will hoe them off using a very sharp hoe. Since most of our hoes are  about as sharp as a house brick, perhaps stick to the glove method.

They can be dug out and re-used elsewhere, either to fill in gaps, to extend the row or to make a neighbour happy. In this case some roots must be taken with the cane and it's best done in the dormant season as soon as the leaves are off – just as we'd do when planting in the first place.

This propensity to stroll all over the shop is the reason many growers end up, not with a neatly tied-in 2-D line of canes, but the broad thicket. If this is the case then it is good to remember that the canes still need thinning within that thicket, a little wider than between the canes in a line.

Picking

Tying to wires can be done with lots of individual bits of string which might be better than plastic-coated twist ties in terms of cost and no-plastic-ness. I have tried using a single long piece of string looped around each cane and the wire, in the hope that I can re-use it each time – it usually breaks or ends up needing cutting.

I am often asked (actually, I've probably been asked twice, but that's at least one more time than I'd expect) when is the best time to pick raspberries. The simplest answer is 'in a relaxed, calm frame of mind'. Picking fruit shouldn't be a last minute thing, when it can get a little frenetic. More practical, some might say sensible, answers include when they are dry and ripe. Out of these two, the former is the easiest. However, if it is a choice between picking wet, ripe fruit or leaving it until it dries (whenever that is) go for the soggy alternative. The raspberries can still be processed (jam, puddings, etc.) or eaten fresh straight away: they won't keep but at least you were able to use them.

Deciding when a fruit is ripe is one of the trickier aspects of gardening and the best advice is to eat it. You'll quickly learn that the flavour will tell you and then you can relate that to the appearance. Certain varieties of raspberry are quite pale when they are fully ripe whereas others need to be more the colour of my nose after a hot spring day, not to be confused with a 'strawberry nose' which doesn't have a lot to do with fruit apart from perhaps grapes. A reasonable measure of ripeness, coinciding well with the colour change, is the ease with which the raspberry detaches from the little white cone, called a plug or core: if you have to tug on it, it's unlikely to be ripe. If a fruit comes away complete with core, calyx and stalk then it certainly wasn't ripe. Plus you will have risked breaking the whole fruit stalk which carries a cluster of unripe fruits.

We are encouraged by some books to discard damaged fruit and this is sound advice – you don't want your day ruined by a rogue raspberry. However, a little damage shouldn't stop you scoffing it at the time of picking. For example, one or more of the drupelets in a fruit (the round, bobbly bits that go to make up a raspberry) may have been deflated by a puncturing pest like the shield bug. As long as the offending creature is no longer present the fruit should still be perfectly alright. I have made the mistake of not checking thoroughly and can testify that the shield bug has a crunchy texture and lives up to its alternative name of 'stink bug'. Moulds and grubs are different matters and whilst the former is fairly obvious, the latter is not. It has been said that the larvae of the raspberry beetle account for a considerable number of flavour variations, if not the protein content.

Picking is done, as with other soft fruit, with 'soft fingers' – in other words, not gripping too tightly which can crush or smear the fruit. Use shallow containers or only half fill larger tubs, to stop the bottom fruits getting squashed. Don't hold the container: set it down and use both hands to pick and to move the stems to find the fruit. Some seasoned raspberristas have adapted containers to hang from their chests / abdomens. Just be careful – there are few things in life as disappointing as upending a full pot of raspberries onto the earth, weeds or gravel path.

It is important to keep testing the fruit for flavour and ripeness. Coupled with eating those fruits not worthy of keeping, you might not want any lunch. But that's ok: for doing all of the picking, you deserve a good helping of fresh fruit. It always tastes better straight from the plant, anyway.

Pruning

Pruning is usually carried out in the winter at any time from the moment the leaves have fallen off, to the time that new leaves or shoots appear. Some people prefer earlier rather than later, going as far as cutting out canes as soon as fruiting has ceased. It is probably better to let any energy / resources in the leaves and canes to travel back into the body of the plant (the root system) and wait for everything to settle down before snipping away. Others prefer to wait until late in the winter when you know exactly where you are: standing in a freezing raspberry patch with bits of you dropping off in the cold. Normally cuts made in pruning would be *to* something (a bud, branch, etc.). With raspberries just cut out the canes as low as you can without getting your secateurs in the soil: new shoots come off the root system.

Summer Varieties

Summer raspberries fruit on canes which were produced the previous year. The fruiting canes then die. Pruning therefore is exceptionally straightforward: remove any dead canes in the winter. They are identifiable amongst the new still-to-fruit canes in that they have long wispy laterals – the new canes have none. They are different colours: old canes are patchy grey; new canes are a plum-brown. Often the old canes can be bent sideways and they simply snap off. Once this has been completed consider pruning out some more.

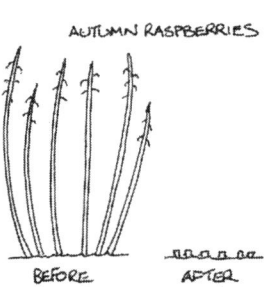
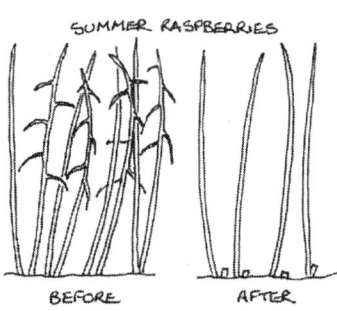

In fact, be strict with the thinning of the new canes – it is very easy to get a congested patch, making the fruit harder to pick and potentially increasing fungal diseases. It is extremely tempting to leave all of the new canes that have grown regardless of their position and number, especially when you know that they are to fruit in the coming summer. If you have girded your loins and got on with it, choose the weakest shoots and space out to 7.5-10cm / 3-4".

Occasionally, the new, non-fruiting canes actually fruit in the same year in which they grew, usually as the result of a warm, sunny autumn. This is very a) wonderful because you got a double crop in one year or b) tedious if you already have autumn varieties to fill that gap. The fruit will be right at the top of the cane so it's just a light crop, and it is this piece that is removed in the winter along with the normal old canes.

Autumn Varieties

If you thought the summer ones were easy, have a look at this lot. Autumn raspberries fruit on the growth that is produced in the same year. Because they are doing two things at once (growing and fruiting), they tend to be shorter, have a lighter crop and fruit later – hence the autumnness about them even though they actually start fruiting in late summer. The upshot of this approach is that the canes are not needed at the end of the year – the whole lot are removed.

If you only have autumn raspberries you can make the whole thing suddenly more complicated by getting some to fruit early and so extend your cropping season. Select a section of the row and instead of cutting the canes down to the ground just cut off the top bit that has fruited. They will produce a small crop in the summer, followed by the normal autumn raspberry crop from the rest of the row. Cut out completely these early-fruiting confusions once they have finished.

Weeding

Like a lot of soft fruit, but perhaps even more so with raspberries, perennial weeds need to be kept out. The roots of raspberry canes are shallow and easily damaged so it extremely difficult to extract weeds once they're in there. When planting raspberries it is recommended that a wide strip is thoroughly cleared first – at least a metre wide. This gives you a buffer zone and a fighting chance of stopping weeds spreading from beyond to the canes.

Once weeds have got in there, we are limited to a combination of repeated pulling / careful extraction and mulching. The mulch, unlike with the currants, can't really include a fabric or sheet material such as cardboard apart from along the edges of the strip. That leaves loose organic matter and persistent perennials will laugh at anything less than 10cm / 4". Deeper than that and they'll probably still have a gentle chuckle.

Raspberry problems

Yellowing of leaves

There are a number of reasons for this.

If the soil is too limey (pH greater than 7) then there can be yellowing between the veins of the youngest leaves caused by iron deficiency. It is hard for a plant to mobilise iron within its system so an absence at the root shows up first in the young, actively growing parts. The remedies include supplying iron (a seaweed foliar spray) and reducing the pH. The latter is not an easy proposition (it is far easier to raise it, by adding lime): add sulphur to the soil or an acidic mulch such as pine needles or bracken compost.

If too much of something like potassium has been used then it can cause yellowing between the veins of the oldest leaves – magnesium deficiency. Magnesium is a component of chlorophyll and is highly mobile in the plant, being moved to the young parts of a plant in times of shortage, hence the deficiency symptoms being in the older leaves. Apply doses of magnesium sulphate (Epsom salts).
Poor drainage can cause root rot and this may show initially as the yellowing of leaves. Conditions that are too dry can interfere with the uptake of the above nutrients as well as stress the plants – result? More yellowing of leaves.

Birds

Blackbirds are fond of a range of fruit and although raspberries might not be top of the menu, you can still lose a good percentage of the crop. Netting once again can be employed – it must be checked regularly to make sure nothing has got caught up in it: birds desperate for a berry or two may find a way in but not back out again. If you can bear a bit of a loss, as with strawberries, leave them uncovered: losing a small amount of fruit seems a fair payment for a blackbird's song (apart from at 4.30am). Other birds, particularly those arch scavengers the tits, will remove virus-carrying aphids and raspberry beetles, again suggesting that it might be best to leave off the netting.

NETS CAN ACCIDENTALLY TRAP WILDLIFE.

Raspberry beetles

These over-winter as adults in the soil, emerge in the spring, mate and the females go on to lay eggs in the flowers of blackberries, raspberries and hybrid berries in summer. The eggs hatch in about two weeks and the grubs feed for over a month on the developing fruit. This is where you get half collapsed fruits; rots may also take advantage of the damage. Eating damaged fruit may mean you consume the grub, not necessarily a disaster depending on your dietary preferences since it will have reduced the population by at least one. However, the flavour may be compromised.

There will be some natural predation of the pest in a diverse plot especially if the canes are left un-netted. Since the pest over-winters in the soil, developing from grub to adult in the process, it will be in the vicinity of the raspberry patch (there is a limit to how far a larva will be prepared to go for a late summer wriggle). The usual recommendation would be to disturb the soil around the canes in the winter so that it is easier for scavaging birds like robins to have a go at them. However, this can only be partially successful because of the shallowness of raspberry roots, plus beetles can fly in from anywhere in the surrounding area: there will be lots of other host plants keeping the population going – think how many clumps of blackberries there are around the place. Still if you are able to borrow a chicken to scratch around it might help. If the canes have been well-mulched for the summer, this could be (temporarily?) removed in the winter to expose the pests.

Autumn varieties are resistant, presumably because the later fruiting doesn't fit in with the pest's lifecycle.

Shield bugs
These are a range of sucking insects with broad flat bodies, typically the green shield bug. They cause damage to raspberry fruits and are often responsible for deflating some of the round, bobbly bits (drupelets) that make up a raspberry. Not a major pest but just occasionally annoying when you're not paying attention as you eat the fruit, as alluded to in 'picking', above.

Viruses
Where does one start? There are at least 10 different viruses or combinations of viruses that affect raspberries. They may not all have identifiable symptoms like raspberry leaf curl virus does (leaves curl, surprisingly), but most have the same end result: both yields and vigour decline. It is likely that, as with blackcurrants, the life of a raspberry plant will be curtailed by the acquisition of a virus and the most obvious symptoms will be a tailing-off of production and shorter canes. The lifespan is dictated by how soon a virus arrives and around 12 years is generally considered to be the limit as a result.

Two significant points to consider:
- Most viruses are spread by aphids of which there are at least three different species that feed on raspberry plants. Certain varieties may be resistant to one or even two aphid species but not more. Still, any resistance at all has to slow the arrival of viruses (and so prolong the life of the plants).
- Resistance to the viruses, or some of them, is possible. The variety 'Leo' does a pretty good job of being resistant to some of the worst viruses as well as two of the aphid species. Autumn varieties will be slower to acquire viruses depending on their mode of movement within the plant: canes are present for less than a year whereas summer variety canes are in leaf twice before being removed.

Other issues

Botrytis: the ubiquitous grey mould is very happy on fruit and simply requires a little care when picking, sorting and eating. Good air movement, facilitated by generous spacing of the canes, will help as will avoidance of damage to the fruit: tie in the canes to prevent abrasion and pick off pests such as shield bugs.

Blights and Spots: fungi of different flavours with varying degrees of seriousness. Most involve infections forming on the canes, with resulting lesions, dieback or cane death. If you see any canes shrivelling, any dark patches on the canes or any leaves dying, prune them out immediately and take away: it won't be a huge loss and could prevent a disease spreading.

Raspberry Varieties

There is a steady production of raspberry varieties meaning that it is worth checking recent availability rather than relying on a book like this. However, those listed in the 'Essentials' at the beginning of this chapter are reliable and likely to be around for a while yet.

Many old varieties have been well superseded: they are considerably less productive and don't (unlike apples for example) have a particularly better flavour. Still, I hope that Brogdale or the like is keeping them going for 'future reference'.

A good proportion of the varieties available to us have been bred at one of two research stations. The James Hutton Institute based in Dundee continues to develop and release varieties, helpfully with the prefix 'Glen', such as 'Glen Clova', 'Glen Lyon' and 'Glen Coe'.

Plenty of soft fruits, and of course a good range of tree (top) fruit, have been bred in Kent at East Malling Research Station, briefly Horticulture Research

International, now NIAB EMR. Strewth. That stands for the National Institute of Agricultural Botany East Malling Research. They have a similarly uplifting naming system: their releases are prefixed with 'Malling' such as 'Malling Jewel', 'Malling Admiral' and 'Malling Orion'.

Nowadays, any new variety will only be worth releasing if it improves on previous efforts in terms of flavour, yield and disease resistance to name just three. Nurseries breeding new varieties may be less scrupulous in their claims, relying on publicity rather than reputation. Quite often just one feature will be concentrated on making that variety's unique selling point (at the expense of the others) such as, say, pink flowers or large fruit. Still, we might get more interesting names from nurseries like the now obsolete(?) 'Chilliwack' and 'Dinkum'.

Raspberry 'Glen Coe'

This is a cross between two species: *Rubus idaeus* 'Glen Prosen' and the American black raspberry *Rubus occidentalis*. And it is very interesting in a number ways, not least because it displays 'hybrid vigour' (in the same way that Leylandii conifers do).

- It has an intense colour (purple) and flavour.
- It produces high yields.
- It is vigorous - too vigorous? There are reports of canes up to 4m / 13'. Plant 60cm / 2' apart in rows 3m / 10' apart.
- The canes are spine-free and are semi-erect.
- It is summer fruiting, early in the raspberry season.
- It is apparently more tolerant of limey soils.

So, all round this is a new superstar in the raspberry world – if you have the space and the nerve.

REDCURRANTS *Ribes sativum* or *R. rubrum*

(*Ribes*, from Arabic, acidic, *sativum*, cultivated, *rubrum*, red)
Family: GROSSULARIACEAE

Why we should grow redcurrants
High pectin perfect for setting jams and jellies, beautiful appearance when fruiting, they keep the birds off other fruit. Can be used in shady positions.

Redcurrant Essentials:
The redcurrant season runs for about 6 weeks starting in early July. Actual cropping time will vary depending on the weather, the variety and the position it is grown.

REDCURRANTS WINNING THE 'SHINIEST FRUIT' AWARD – AGAIN

Varieties:
'Laxton's No.1': upright / slightly spreading, early season, medium sized fruit with smaller seeds, heavy yields.
'Redstart': upright, moderately vigorous, mid-flowering, late fruiting, medium to large berries, heavy yielding.
'Red Lake': upright, moderately vigorous, mid season, very large berries on long trusses, good yields.
'White Versailles': early season, good yields, fruit can be eaten raw.

Site: Can be grown on a north facing wall or under other plants – shade tolerant. The fruit is sweeter and earlier in sunny positions (but not by much).

Size: Up to 2m / 6½ft.

Spacing: 1.2-1.5m / 4-5ft between plants, 1.5-1.8m / 5-6ft between rows.

Feeding: Mulch with compost in spring. Occasional doses of extra potassium – comfrey liquid?

Pruning: None at all or spur pruning or almost whatever you fancy.

Pollination: Self fertile.

Harvesting: Selective harvesting is possible, making at least a couple of pickings or wait until all berries are fully ripe (some will be over-ripe) and make a clean sweep.

Propagation: Hardwood cuttings or layering.

Weeding: Redcurrants seem to cope admirably being stuck in the middle of other plants and still cropping, though yields will be lower the greater the competition.

Redcurrant Origins
Natives of N.W. Europe (Holland and Germany) and brought over to the UK in the sixteenth century, but not particularly appreciated until more recent times. White currants are a sport of the redcurrant so are therefore the same species (though a pale imitation?).

Redcurrant Nutrition
Really good levels of minerals (Potassium 280mg/100g, Calcium 36mg/100g, Iron 1.2mg/100g) and not bad with Vitamin C at 40mg/100g.

Discussion / rambling / elaboration
Picking / Harvesting
The same recommendations for redcurrants are given under blackcurrants but to save you fumbling back through the book here is the same information with the words shifted around a bit. Redcurrantss can be picked (and it is probably easier to do so) as complete 'strigs'- they are sometimes sold like this. A strig is a little dangly stalk to which the berries are attached. If picked as such, the berries still have to be separated at some point to be able to use them. You may find this easier to do in the comfort of a well-upholstered, redcurrant juice-besmirched armchair or just get it out of the way by doing it as you pick.

You may choose to employ a picking device. No, not a small child, though they could probably reach the fruit more easily than a creaking adult and enjoy the experience, too. Imagine the pan part of a dustpan and brush. Then imagine the front edge of the pan being deeply indented so that the appearance is like a row of flattened fingers or a strange comb. The idea is that, by holding the handle and gently combing up through

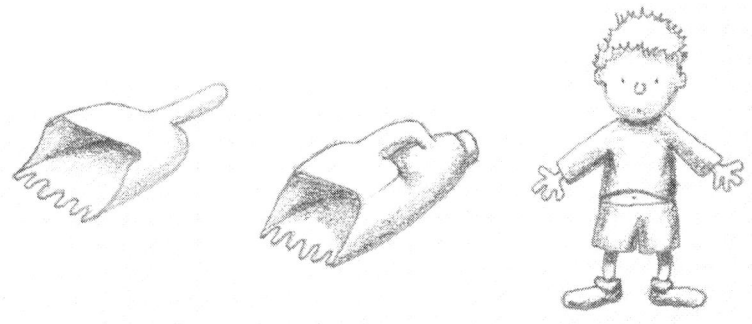

SOME POSSIBLE DIFFERENT BERRY - PICKERS

the plant, the berries are eased off the strigs and fall into the collecting part of the pan. Inevitably, a lot of extraneous matter is also collected, including rotten fruit, dead, yellowing and unfortunately-healthy leaves plus wildlife. The berry comber is particularly good at extracting snails. Empty into a bucket and continue combing; the contents can be sorted out later. You are asking 'Where can I lay my hands on such a cunning device?' and the answer is in the catalogues, though you could try adapting your own dustpan or a large plastic milk container complete with handle (those of you who buy plastic milk, that is).

Pruning

There is some discussion about whether pruning of currants, especially redcurrants, is necessary at all, especially when you see how much time and effort is spent: pruning twice a year with many cuts being made. After all, currants naturally produce fruit without all of that nonsense. In a forest garden, for example, they not only don't get pruned but they can go walkabout: old branches, where they drop and touch the ground, can root in and form a new plant.

What pruning does is give us control. Depending on your personality, this could be seen to be totally unnecessary or could be just what is required to distract you from invading a neighbouring country. Pruning is normally done to keep a plant open, get good air movement throughout, allow even light distribution and to stimulate the regular production of young vigorous wood, ensuring regular crops at the same time.

I can go both ways with this: where I have plants in a bed with allotted space, I will be bearing down on them, wielding secateurs and uttering blood-curdling cries. Where I have bushes nestled under apple trees, communing with herbs and, it has to be said, a few weeds, my main visits will be to pick the fruit.
Let us suggest three different regimes for you:

1) Do nothing.
2) Regulatory pruning. Occasionally, in winter, use some loppers to remove really old bits and any dead wood, shaping if possible, and then get back to a warm armchair (a warmchair?).
3) Spur pruning. Follow the ensuing procedure. Remove any dead wood. Identify major branches that emerge low in the crown of the plant and trace them upwards – there will be young sideshoots (laterals) growing out along its length and it should end in a strong piece of new growth. This is called the leader. You can have more then one leader per branch, usually when it forks low down and the side branch is in a suitable bit of space.

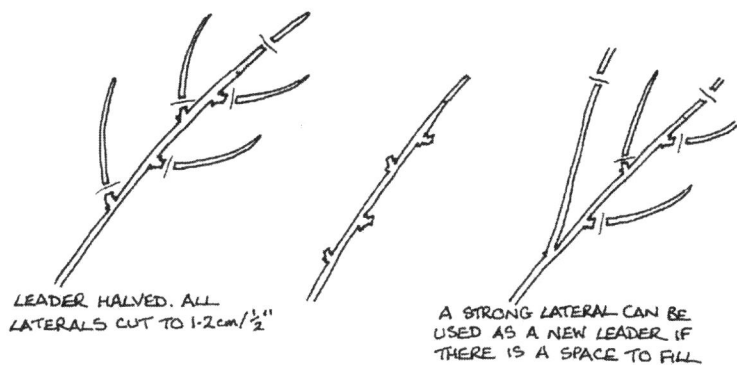

LEADER HALVED. ALL LATERALS CUT TO 1·2cm/½"

A STRONG LATERAL CAN BE USED AS A NEW LEADER IF THERE IS A SPACE TO FILL

Once a leader has been identified it is cut in half to an outward-facing bud – remember this is just the new growth at the end of a branch. Everything else on that branch (unless it has side branches) will be laterals and they should all be removed – but not completely. This is because fruit is formed at the base of these laterals so we want to leave about one to two centimetres / a couple of buds. Fruit is also formed on 'spurs' (short stubby shoots) on the older parts. In fact, the only part of the bush that won't fruit is the new growth: the laterals and the leaders.

You can make the third regime even more complicated by having a repeat pruning in the summer to just partially reduce the laterals. This is so that light and air can circulate when fruit is forming. And of course there is nothing else to do in July…

Numbers 1 and 2 give earlier fruit but it tends to be smaller, the opposite for number 3 which has larger, delayed fruit. The plants of number 3 tend to be stockier and it is also the pruning regime required to keep a plant on a 'leg'. This is where, right from propagation, a clear stem has been maintained (about 15cm / 6") holding aloft the ring of branches. It allows good air circulation underneath the bush. Regimes 1 and 2 lend themselves to the opposite, a thicket, otherwise known as a stooled bush, where the branches originate at or below ground level.

IMPROVISATION. A STRONG LATERAL USED TO REPLACE WEAKER LEADER

Redcurrant Problems

Amazingly free of issues though birds will take the lot in preference to other fruit. Perhaps they're less worried about getting the pips stuck in their teeth. Occasional, and usually minor, attacks of leaf blister aphid, mildew and grey mould can occur – see 'Blackcurrants', 'Gooseberries' and 'Grapes', in that order.

Poor pruning technique (in other words, not pruning to a bud) can lead to invasion of coral spot. Prune it out as soon as seen and be more careful in future.

Redcurrant Problems and Pips

Redcurrants are one of the least developed of the soft fruit, in that varieties of blackcurrants and the like are constantly being bred and trialled. Poor old redcurrants seem to be stuck with the same varieties that have been around for ages. One is tempted to ask the question 'Why?'. Alright, go on then: 'Why?'. Well, it's strange in a way because they are no more acid-tasting than blackcurrants and they are more attractive when in fruit than a lot of other species. They are also relatively problem-free, not like mildewed and sawflied gooseberries or reverted, big-budded blackcurrants.

One major drawback for me is how to use them: there are various puddings and other dishes to which they can be added but if those little granite pips are still there then I'm not interested. They wedge themselves between teeth, inviting you to spend many a happy hour trying to prise them out again, occasionally popping out the odd filling in the process. I am told that they also insinuate themselves under a dental plate or dentures.

PIP REMOVAL

There is the great stand-by of redcurrant jelly which generously excludes the pips but takes ages to make, particularly the straining part. The pectin in the juice is still very valuable for helping other jams set, but does this justify having more then one plant?

RHUBARB *Rheum x hybridum*

(*Rheum* from Rha the Russian name for the Volga where rhubarb was found, x *hybrida*, hybrid)

Family: POLYGONACEAE

Why we should grow rhubarb
It is available in spring when there is little else. Rhubarb crumble is hard to surpass with any other cooked dessert (subject to personal taste).

Rhubarb Essentials
Varieties: '**Timperley Early**' (early), '**Valentine**' (mid), '**Victoria**' (late), '**Livingstone**' (autumn). Some more recent selections such as '**German Wine**' and '**Raspberry Red**' have concentrated on sweeter stems. '**Valentine**', also sweet, holds its shape well on cooking.

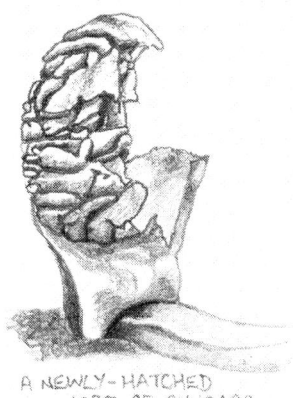

A NEWLY-HATCHED LEAF OF RHUBARB

Size: Up to 1m high x 2m spread / 3ft x 6½ft.

Spacing: 90cm / 3'.

Position: Sunny, perhaps a little shade, but not dry.

Feeding: Lots, a regular mulch of manure or compost in the spring.

Harvesting: Usually March to June. Pick when stalks are between 30cm / 12" and 45cm / 18" long – too small and there will be a reduced overall yield, too large and they're not very tender.

Propagation: Can be from seed in spring or by division in the autumn.

Weeding: Keep perennial weeds well at bay. Annual weeds should get shaded out.

Rhubarb Origins
Siberia, apparently, though some reckon China was the starting point. Cultivation in Europe began in the 17th century.

Rhubarb Nutrition
Surprisingly, not bad; surprising because a stick of rhubarb is not, botanically, a fruit which we would expect to be particularly good for us. Vitamins A and C are 102 International Units and 8mg, respectively and the main minerals are Potassium 288mg/100g, Calcium 86mg/100g and Iron 0.22mg/100g.

Rhubarb Botany
Rhubarb is an herbaceous perennial meaning that it doesn't have a woody framework and dies down to the ground in the autumn to re-shoot again in the spring. The stem is a compact 'block' partly below ground. The bit we eat is the leaf stalk, technically called the petiole. A flowering stem can appear at any stage in its life.

Discussion / rambling / elaboration
A Fruit or not a Fruit
Despite not remotely satisfying the botanical criteria for 'fruit', rhubarb has been included purely on account of its culinary applications. That is, we most often eat it sweet. If vegetable books can claim tomatoes (very much a fruit) then I'm happy to even it up by having a look at rhubarb.

RHUBARB TRIANGLE

Apparently, it hails from Siberia which is quite good news, since it is likely to tolerate cold conditions (making it suitable for the Yorkshire rhubarb triangle – what other plant would be suitable for the Yorkshire rhubarb triangle?). If anything, it might get too hot and dry.

Uses of Rhubarb
Rhubarb is in an elite group, possibly shared only by quinces: it is completely inedible. That is, it is not normally eaten raw. Yes, I'm sure there are some people of a curious disposition who may like to crunch away on a large stick provided it is dipped in sugar or the like. But all by itself?

Rhubarb is also poisonous. Just a bit, and not all of it, though those of us with particular issues such as osteoporosis and joint problems might want to minimise the intake. Note: don't exclude it completely (unless advised to do so) just don't have it for pudding at every meal. The poisonous bit is something called oxalic acid and is what makes your teeth go all furry after a bowl of stewed rhubarb. It binds up iron and calcium making it hard for the body to absorb those essentials

– that is not a major problem unless you are in particular need of them, but it is still wise to go easy.

Oxalic acid builds up as the season continues which is one reason harvesting doesn't normally continue beyond midsummer. 'Glaskin's Perpetual' has lower oxalic acid levels so can be eaten for longer. Before cooking, cut the stalks into chunks and soak in a kettle-full of boiling water for 20 minutes. Pour that away before continuing as though nothing had happened (it actually gets rid of a lot of oxalic acid).

The really poisonous bit is the leaf. There the oxalic acid is in impressive quantities and, should you wish to shuffle off this mortal coil prematurely, try a good helping of rhubarb leaves – about 6kg should do it. You'll probably die from boredom before getting through all of that, or excrete your entire digestive system (rhubarb is also a laxative). Instead of yourself, you can try killing other things by boiling up rhubarb leaves. Recipes differ but if you insist, try a pound of leaves in two pints of water boiled for 30 minutes before straining and bottling. Just before use, add a squirt of soap to make it stick and aphids are at your mercy. Just remember that it will kill the larvae of beneficial insects like hoverflies, lacewings and ladybirds, too…

It is often recommended that pieces of rhubarb stem are put in the holes when planting brassicas to stop attacks by cabbage root fly. This recommendation was probably given by someone who didn't actually like the stuff and was trying to find another way of getting rid of it.

Chilled Rhubarb
I admit to being a little perplexed (it doesn't take much nowadays) by rhubarb. We are told that, to break dormancy i.e. to start into growth in the spring, the plant needs to have had a cold spell in the winter. The length of this cold spell – a certain number of days below a certain temperature – that is required, depends on the variety. For example, an early type like 'Timperley Early' needs less of a chilling to get it in to growth, so it produces shoots sooner in the year (around the end of March / beginning of April). There are varieties that produce stems later; the later they produce, the longer the cold spell that they will have needed. Another example: 'Victoria' (to be distinguished from 'Early Victoria') is a lot later and therefore has a requirement for longer exposure to cold during the winter.
So far so good.

I can understand that a later variety, should it not get all of its necessary chilling, will not grow well. But the bit I have trouble with is, if the cold is necessary to break dormancy and a plant doesn't get it, does that mean it doesn't grow at all? Clearly not, because it has actually produced some growth, albeit poorly. So what is the cold really doing? I think we ought to be told.

Incidentally, all of this tells you why it is the northern climes of this country that provide the best crops of rhubarb: there is a reliable supply of perishing winter weather to ensure the best crops, particularly of the later, superior, varieties. In the balmy (barmy?) south, in some years it will be fine, but in other winters with our apparently warming climate, performance may be well below par.

The properties of different varieties of rhubarb are surprisingly diverse:

- Earliness / Lateness
- Oxalic Acid content
- Length of stalk
- Sweetness
- Colour: dull green, sparkling pink and everything in between

Planting

It is a good idea, when planting up a new rhubarb bed, to get hold of clean, virus-free plants. This, unfortunately, may preclude getting a lump from the clump of an ancient plant on someone else's plot. A certified plant will be more vigorous and will last longer so, as with other plants like blackcurrants and strawberries, start with fresh stock. They will last over twelve years. Plants raised from seed will be virus-free (hurrah) but you will have to wait longer to get your first harvest (boo).

If you are planting a rhubarb crown (a piece from an established plant that has been divided), make sure that each piece has at least one good bud. Plant it at the end of the year (November to December) in ground which is well prepared and loosened, with compost incorporated - lots. If the soil is quite light (sandy) bury the crown just below the surface, but if it is heavier (high clay content) then plant it with the buds showing above the surface.

Rhubarb, slightly surprisingly since it is quite a different plant to other soft fruits, is easily invaded by perennial weeds. Couch grass for example can run straight through a crown. It is quite important to not only be scrupulous when preparing the planting site in terms of the removal of bits of pernicious weeds, but to establish a no-grow zone, a buffer, around the plants that is kept clean at all times. If a perennial weed starts moving in, this zone gives you time to deal with it before it reaches the crown when there is a chance you will be unable to remove it at all without lifting the whole plant.

Seed-raised or container-grown plants can be put in at any time of year as long as soil conditions are good. They need a fair amount of sun but will still crop well with some shade: not one for planting under fruit trees but possible at the edge of an area.

It is sometimes recommended that a clump of rhubarb is lifted every five or six years to get rid of the pooped middle, older part and start again with fresh vigorous pieces from around the outside. Other growers have had a patch going in the same place since their ancestors were still clad in animal skins. Well, quite a long time, anyway.

Feeding

I remember my father's rhubarb patch being, like many others on that site, alongside the allotment access track. This wasn't because he needed vehicular access to take away the vast loads of rhubarb (though actually the yields were very good). It was because the manure lorry defaecated at the front of the plot in winter and although he had to be careful with muck re-distribution, it ensured that the rhubarb underneath benefited enormously from the nutrients and water retention. This was particularly important since his soil was distinctly on the light side and prone to impoverishment.

The lesson from this is: feed and water your plants – they are hungry and demand regular inputs. Exactly what you use is up to you and what you have available. The aforementioned manure is usually put on rhubarb but well-made compost is also popular. Personally, I prefer custard.

Harvesting

The first year after planting restrain yourself and pick no stalks. You may need to wait a further year if the plants went in quite small. Thereafter, pick just a few stalks stopping earlier in the year than you'll be able to do later. By building up to full harvest after three years, stopping will be May to mid June for the early varieties, with some others continuing as late as August. When plants are in full flow, up to a total of half of all the stems will be removed. That is not easy to work out especially as they are removed gradually and new stems are growing at the same time.

Stalks are pulled off by levering outwards. They should not be cut, which would leave a small piece to rot, but removed cleanly. Straightaway, remove the leaves and compost them and, yes, they are fine on the heap. It is the same principle as not buying bunched carrots – water continues to be lost from the leaves, depleting the stalk (or carrot) which then becomes wilted and tougher. This is a shame since the carrots particularly look great with the foliage still attached. Rhubarb with the leaves still on is actually just a nuisance – it is hard enough to find a plastic bag big enough to put the stalks in to get them home as it is. Bin liner, anyone?

Forcing

George Glenny in 'The Culture of Fruits and Vegetables' says 'The aim we should have in the culture of rhubarb is… earliness, because as it can be produced when there is no fruit for tarts, every day that the production can be hastened is an object'. It makes sense therefore, in order to avoid fruit-less tarts, to try forcing.

The idea behind forcing, as the name suggests, is making a plant do something it wouldn't normally want to do. It perhaps sounds more aggressive than it is, though there are degrees of forcing. The type most of us practice – comparable with a verbal threat and a slightly menacing leer – is the old chimney pot / plant pot / bucket / expensive-but-rather-handsome terracotta forcing pot placed over chosen plants in the winter. As long as all gaps, drainage holes etcetera are covered over, the stalks will be produced around three weeks earlier than uncovered plants. The leaves are small and yellow and the stalks are long,

FORCING RHUBARB

thinner, sweeter and more succulent. After harvest, the plant is fed up and it is best to take few or no more stalks from it that year.

The forcing more equivalent to an arm held behind one's back or being prodded with a sharp stick is that practiced by the great commercial growers in Northern England and other selected sites devoted to plant torture. Crowns are lifted in November or December and left in the open to get a good frosting. To produce a sequence of pale, sweeter and more tender stalks, they are gradually brought indoors and potted up. Kept in a dark and, crucially, a warmer place, they respond with these more succulent shoots a lot sooner than those forced outside in situ. The reward for the crowns at the end of cropping is to be composted – they are too exhausted to be of any further use.

Rhubarb Problems

Surprisingly free of problems. The aforementioned viruses can gradually build up without you realising and the plants don't crop quite so well or the stalks are a bit shorter.

Slugs and snails can have a go at the leaves, particularly the older ones and on young plants, which is always a bit of a surprise because of the high levels of oxalic acid. It just shows that slugs don't have much taste. They may also choose to use the plant for accommodation which makes it advisable to have your rhubarb patch away from vulnerable plants on the vegetable plot.

Sometimes the crowns can rot out which isn't really preventable, apart from detaching the stalks properly rather than breaking or cutting them. In which case, there isn't really an option other than starting a new patch elsewhere. It may be that, like many herbaceous plants, the centre becomes tired, less productive and less able to resist rots.

Probably most issues with rhubarb come about because of poor management: too shady, too dry or not enough food. Remember that forcing is quite a stress on a plant, too.

STRAWBERRIES *Fragaria x ananassa*
(*Fragaria*, L. fragrant, *ananassa*, pineapple-like)
Family: ROSACEAE

A COUPLE OF PRE-STRAWBERRIES

Why we should grow strawberries
A sun-warmed, fully ripe, rich, sweet strawberry is hard to surpass, making a mockery of the hard, tasteless out-of-season supermarket specimens we are tempted with. They also have excellent levels of vitamin C, considerably better than most citrus fruit.

Strawberry Essentials
Varieties: A small selection in order of ripening – '**Gariguette**': a new early variety with an apparently splendid flavour. '**Honeoye**': early-mid season, a more established early strawberry (1979), vigorous. '**Sonata**': mid season, resistance to rain damage and hot, dry spells, Dutch 1998. '**Alice**': mid season, sweet and juicy conical fruit, good disease resistance. '**Cambridge Favourite**': mid season, established variety, heavy yields, good flavour, rounded fruit. '**Florence**': late season (late June), needs leaving until it is quite dark red for the best flavour, resistance to powdery mildew, wilt, crown rot and some tolerance of vine weevil, result of at least four crosses, 1997. '**Rhapsody**': late season, very heavy yields of conical fruit of excellent flavour, upright leaves make picking easy, good resistance. '**Finesse**': a 'perpetual' variety, meaning it crops lightly from June to September – to get a decent yield at any one harvest, more plants are required than the summer varieties.

Size: Up to 30cm / 1' high and 45cm / 18" spread.

Spacing: 45cm x 45cm (18" x 18") depending on variety.

Feeding: An annual dollop of compost at the beginning of the season (April), otherwise known as a thick mulch, 5-7.5cm / 2-3". Additional feeding with comfrey and other high potassium feeds is beneficial during flowering and fruiting and never allow water stress at the same time. Watering can be daily.

Pruning: Removal of old and diseased leaves at the end of the season. Not really pruning but I felt I had to write something.

Pollination: By insects – no real issues apart from late frosts.

Harvesting: One of the joys of home-grown fruit is being able to pick and eat it when it is fully ripe. No more so than with strawberries. Get used to the shade of red that your variety turns when it is ripe and leave them until then.

Propagation: By runners from two-year old plants in August to September.

Weeding: Weeding is essential for strawberries. They are quite needy plants and are resentful if they have to share resources with weeds: an annual thick mulch of organic matter is helpful.

Strawberry Origins
There have of course been wild strawberries in this country for millennia, but strawberries as we know them – huge, juicy things – are the result of the happy marriage of North and South America. It is interesting that the marriage and honeymoon took place in Europe (France and England). *Fragaria chiloensis* was crossed with *Fragaria virginiana* (the names give it away) to produce the slightly curiously named *Fragaria x ananassa*, curious in that the name relates this hybrid to pineapples – pineapples are in the genus *Ananas*. The similarity is not particularly obvious: flavour? Not really, though *F. chiloensis* is apparently a little pineappley. A fruit with a little tuft of green at the top? Pushing it. Anyway, ignoring that, there have been other crosses since to give us a huge range of varieties, in terms of fruiting times, flavour and appearance.

Strawberry Nutrition
Strawberries have an unexceptional range of minerals and vitamins apart from Vitamin C which, at 60-80mg/100g, is second only to blackcurrants and kiwis: wonderful, and they're very easy to eat fresh too.

Strawberry Botany
The fruit itself is not a true fruit. It makes sense therefore to call it a false fruit. The red flesh of a strawberry originates from the top of the flower stalk, the receptacle. To confuse matters further the true fruits with a strawberry are the little pips that look like seeds embedded in the surface of the 'berry'; they are technically called achenes, also known as single-seeded fruits. Other achenes of note are sunflower 'seeds' and the woody seed-like structures in rose hips.

Strawberries are short-lived herbaceous (non-woody) perennials, cropping well for 3, possibly 4, years only. The plants die back in early winter. They spread and perpetuate via overground stems, technically called stolons but more often referred to as runners, which go bounding over the soil, the plant equivalent of a kangaroo. These runners will naturally produce new plants at nodes, typically two in total but can be more. The number of runners produced per plant depends on the variety.

Discussion / rambling / elaboration
How to get strawberries from your patch for as long as possible
The first stopping off place to give you strawberries for a longer period is, of course, a selection of varieties – standard, summer varieties with early, mid or late fruiting. For example. An early variety could be the bizarrely-named 'Honeoye' from the US of A (Honey eye? Hone Oi? Ho-knee-oh-yee?) which has a good flavour and is ripe from late May. Whereas 'Sonata' is ready in early-mid June and 'Florence' is ready in late June.

Also available is a type of strawberry, very similar to the usual summer kind, but one that produces small quantities of fruit sporadically over quite a few weeks later in the year (July to September). These are ever-bearing or perpetual strawberries e.g. 'Finesse', 'Aromel' and 'Mara de Bois' and are great for grazing (the allotmenteer's reward). Because of the lightness of cropping, to get a good helping in one pick, extra plants are needed.

Next is where they are grown. Traditionally they would be outside in beds but nowadays a lot of commercial production is in polytunnels or versions thereof. So protection of some kind will advance the fruiting. We could use a cloche or put up a hanging basket in a greenhouse.

Another recent method of extending the season is the use of cold-stored runners which, for some peculiar reason give you fruit about 60 days after planting. As the name suggests, you plant runners that have been in a fridge for months. Again developed for commercial purposes, it is a method designed to give fruit almost whenever you want it within the confines of the growing season. A common planting time of cold-stored runners is April / May so that fruiting, about two months later, is after the usual maincrop strawberries. Unfortunately, some reports are not great: if the runners are under-sized then they may not fruit well when intended. Also, they can run out of steam and not give a full three years cropping.

For us, we might be tempted to say forget all of this nonsense and just enjoy the thrill and anticipation of the usual strawberry season and then don't have them for the rest of the year. Different varieties certainly, maybe even growing a few with protection to bring them on more quickly – but buying specially chilled plants to push it even further? Hmmm.

Where to grow strawberries

Unlike virtually any other commonly grown fruit, strawberry plants are short-lived perennial herbaceous plants so can't be accommodated in the same way that a woody bush or tree can be. Ideally, the best spot is the vegetable plot where a series of smaller patches can be grown in succession, as opposed to the surprisingly common permanent strawberry bed. The latter is very tempting basically because it seems to work – fruit is produced year after year. However, after three years an individual strawberry plant is a bit fed up and cropping rapidly declines. We don't notice this though because it has sent out runners during its life which are now bearing fruit. In response to this you may say 'Great – that's just what I was after' but there is a build up of pests and diseases and the plants become far too congested. Yes, fruit will be produced but not nearly so well as if you had followed the regime coming up now (patent pending).

Year 0 - Planting
This is the starting point and if bare-root plants are used (your own or bought-in) they are best planted in early autumn. They should become established in time to fruit the following summer.

Year 1 - A light crop
So, these are fruiting in the region of nine months after planting. Remove any runners that try to form as soon as you see them so that as much energy goes into establishment and fruiting as possible.

Year 2 - A heavy crop
If you are propagating your own plants, then allow one, maybe two, runners to form this year and start a new bed (Year 0) in a different site.

Year 3 - A heavyish crop
Once the fruiting has finished, grit your teeth, exhume the plants and compost them.

As mentioned, depending on the time of year there will be two beds of strawberries. *Either*
a newly planted bed (Year 0) plus Year 2 plants. If you have propagated your own strawberry plants for the newly planted bed they will have come from these Year 2 plants. *Or*:
(the following year) Year 1 and Year 3 plants.

After year 3, the plants are removed and something different is planted there (preferably not potatoes with which strawberries share root pests).
Runners are taken from Year 2 plants only, because Year 1 plants are still really establishing and Year 3 plants are more likely to have a build up of diseases. This sequence can continue indefinitely, providing you with strawberries every year.

Accepting that, at some point, home-propagated material will become infected, it might be worth using bought-in runners to start again. Some growers wait ten years before doing this.

It is possible, by buying runners for the first two (successive) years, to have plants of all ages at the same time. This also gives an opportunity to have different varieties:

Year 0: plant 'Honeoye' for example. One bed needed.
Year 1: plant 'Cambridge Favourite' for example. 'Honeoye' provides a light crop. Two beds needed.
Year 2: 'Cambridge Favourite' provides a light crop, 'Honeoye' has a heavy crop and provides runners for a new Year 0. Three beds needed.
Year 3: 'Cambridge Favourite' has a heavy crop and provides runners for a new Year 0, original 'Honeoye' has a reasonable crop and is removed and the new bed of 'Honeoye' has a light crop. Three beds needed (a new one planted and one emptied). And so on, with a new bed needed each year and one made vacant. That's why it is best to have them slotted into the vegetable area.

If all of that talk about beds and years has left you wanting to find a bus to step in front of, just buy some strawberry plants, stick them in the ground, get rid of them after three years of cropping then buy some more to start off a new bed.

Propagation

Propagating your own strawberry plants is very straightforward since they are very keen to populate an entire garden or allotment by themselves. It is as much an exercise in restraining them as spreading them.

PROPAGATION

In the second year of cropping (Year 2 plants if you've been paying attention), collect the runners, no more than two per plant. Pinch off any others that try to form. Position the ones you are saving into an appropriate gap and the first plantlet that forms on a runner should be pegged down using a little hoop of thick wire or a stone placed on the runner just behind the plantlet. If the soil has been loosened before doing this it should root in very happily. An alternative is to sink a pot filled with potting compost into the ground and the plantlet is pegged in to that; this makes it easier to transplant but requires more care (watering) until it has rooted in. If the runner tries to continue its travels beyond your pegged-down plantlet, pinch it off. Show no mercy.

September is a good month to move the new strawberry plants so that they have time to establish well and start cropping the next summer. September has the potential to be quite hot and stressful: watering is essential and possibly shading, too. They should be moved to a new bed which is in good heart. In other words, the soil should be loose with reasonable levels of organic matter – those two go together. Fertility isn't a major issue at this stage since there will be some residual fertility in their new patch with which to establish. After planting, your shocked little plantlets would appreciate a good mulch of compost – there is a lot of blank space between them.

Planting

Spacing is variable depending on the vigour of the variety but 45cm (18") in all directions is one recommendation. If the foliage of your variety joins up so that there is no soil visible, perhaps try a wider spacing next time when you come to propagate them. On a typical 1.20m / 4 foot bed the above spacing will give you following pattern:

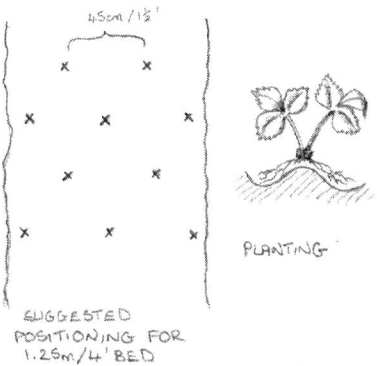

If your soil is particularly heavy – a high level of clay – it is worth spending a little more time with the planting procedure: dig a comparatively large hole, 15cm / 6", and spread the roots out. It might be worth making a little mound in the bottom of the hole to help with this, but it can get slightly fiddly.

Strawberries in Containers

Commercially, strawberries are nowadays grown in containers: grow-bag-like things on benches, or hydroponics (growing in water). They are also normally in covered structures such as polytunnels and have automated feeding and watering. Picking strawberries from endless rows in a field is a miserable job, unless you are young and have a flexible back, so having them raised up is an advantage in that respect as well as giving higher yields, but it is a shame not to have the traditional strawberry fields anymore.

The potential of growing them organically is much reduced: the resources being used must be considered including the origins of nutrients that are being supplied. Chris Bowers and Sons (Nursery) is quite clear about this: "Potting compost makes the fruits a little 'sharp' and lacking in the rosy roundness of well-flavoured fruits [grown in the natural soil]."

Always when growing in containers we are faced by these issues. The much under-studied relationships that plants form with the micro biota in soil is lost when plants are put in a receptacle filled with partially sterile compost (even less of a connection if growing them in a hydroponic system). Still, we can use recycled containers and organically-certified compost and, if there is no opportunity for open ground growing, it is a vital way of producing food and staying sane.

There are strange containers available for growing strawberries, looking like small dustbins with planting holes down the sides. There are also things to hang up with pockets attached, a kind of room-tidy, but instead of shoes the pockets are filled with compost. And there are large plant pots. It doesn't really matter about the container as long as it is big enough. As ever it is the care that is given to the plants in the containers that counts. The container should be placed in a sunny spot – if it has been planted around the sides, then it should be re-positioned frequently so that all sides get a good amount of light. Containers in sunny positions need extra care and not just when they are cropping – the plants need regular supplies of both water and nutrients for the whole growing season.

Strawberry Maintenance
As mentioned earlier one of the first jobs in the spring, just before growth starts, is to apply a mulch. As usual, compost would be the preferred choice to improve the soil, maintain friendly organisms and feed the plants.

When the fruit is forming it can get splashed by soil and it is particularly vulnerable to slugs. For these reasons you could raise it up by resting it on a good helping of straw. Unfortunately, it is not always that easy to come by. Maybe you can get hold of the stuff from a local friendly farmer (I have met several), but for many of us it would involve the relatively expensive trip to a pet shop. You could make your own by cutting and drying long grass, popularly known as hay, but it is inferior and if you have the time to do this on top of everything else I hope you are enjoying your retirement.

Alternatives include specially purchased strawberry mats, growing through polythene or, my favourite for financial reasons, cutting pieces of thick cardboard or even bits of old carpet. The latter two would have to be checked occasionally to make sure they aren't harbouring pests.

Part of the ongoing care of strawberries involves the removal of the older leaves late in the season. This is not a bad idea since the old decaying leaves can pass on diseases to the newly developing ones next year. From mid August, the plants take a break from the everyday strawberry activities and it is then onwards that foliage destruction is recommended. The excellently named H.G. Witham Fogg in 'Fruit Growing' 1963 recommends that the leaves are cut off using a scythe (perhaps for the majority of us a pair of secateurs or strong scissors would be easier) followed by setting fire to the straw that has been pulled away from the crowns a little. Now this all sounds a trifle alarming but old Foggy, as we like to call him, explains that tests (at East Malling Research Station, as was) have shown burning to not only 'clean up' the bed but give an increased yield the following year. How does it do this? you are keen to know.

I am not a fan of burning anything on the plot nowadays: prunings, weeds, witches, anything – there is always another solution. So if we can get the same results as an incinerated patch of strawberries without the carcinogenic, anti-social, CO_2-producing smoke, maybe it is worth investigating. The fire destroys the diseased leaves – answer? Take them away instead and hot compost them somewhere. The fire deals with a certain number of pests including slugs (and unfortunately beneficial predators like beetles). Answer? Don't provide slug-friendly conditions in the first place – there are alternatives to straw. The burnt straw and leaves provides a dressing of fruit-promoting ash since it is high in potassium – answer? Perhaps apply an extra dose of potassium-rich fertiliser such as comfrey liquid, the occasional slosh of diluted urine or even ash from a wood burner.

Forcing Strawberries

Forcing means getting plants or parts of them to grow out of season. Forcing strawberries to fruit earlier then normal is a bit of a hit and miss affair. The fruit we get that is grown in polytunnels (most UK production) is often advanced: the higher temperatures bring on early growth and ripen the fruit so that we can buy bright red shiny strawberries in, for example, April. Unfortunately, what the polytunnel or greenhouse can't provide, unless there is the unlikely event

ALTERNATIVES IN FORCING STRAWBERRIES

of supplementary lighting, is additional sunlight. The sun, for photosynthesis, decides how much sugar is formed and how sweet the strawbs are: out of season fruit is often incredibly disappointing. They look good (some imported ones don't even do that – they're a pale orange) but taste awful. Part of that is down to the way that they are grown but also down to the amount of sun. You may be lucky in that your early indoor strawberries get lots of spring sunshine and are lovely. You may be unlucky and your main outdoor crop has a rubbish season and the fruit is pretty tasteless / 'unsweet'. However, in most years, I reckon it'll be the other way round.

My recommendations therefore are as you might expect: grow your own organically, outside, and eat them as fresh from the plant as you can. Revel in the arrival of this joyous moment and accept it as a sad but inevitable day when the cropping for that year finishes. If you have to pre-empt the season with early, forced fruit, accept that it is a different product altogether and don't be too disappointed.

Strawberry Problems

Vine Weevils: In no particular order of preference, the grubs delight in feeding upon the roots of primulas, heucheras, strawberries plus many plants in containers. It is quite easy to see that strawberries in containers might as well have a neon sign overhead advertising all day breakfast and light lunches for vine weevils. The adults (nearly all female) lay unfertilised eggs around favoured plants. When they hatch, the grubs feed on the roots – for ages. Affected plants may, first of all, wilt in hot weather despite being well watered and shortly afterwards simply lift out of the soil / compost. The grubs, technically the larvae, will pupate and unusually the adults emerge in the autumn. Most insects pass the winter as the pupa or eggs.

The adults themselves do little damage apart perhaps from a little leaf-nibbling. Quite often, once their presence has been detected, it is too late. Maybe if one plant has been nobbled and the blighters identified as the cause then a biological control can be applied to the others: this is a parasitic nematode and it will invade the larvae stopping them in their tracks. Other controls include using a vaguely resistant variety such as 'Florence' and, if they are to grow in containers, use a soil-based compost.

See 'Blueberries' for a handsome picture of a vine weevil.

Grey Mould: Starting discoloured, then soft and brown and then finally an attractive grey fur coating on the fruit; not as pleasant to stroke as a mole. The spores of this fungus find their way to the strawberry by first infecting the flower or by entering a wound in the fruit. Prompt removal is recommended as is making sure that the plant isn't wetted when watering.

Viruses: Yellowing, stunted, and / or dying plants. Remove and dispose of rapidly. Viruses are often spread by aphids so control of those may help, too.

Leaf Spot: Reddish spots form on the leaf with a grey centre. They can increase and coalesce or 'join up' as I might have said before reading a Thesaurus. Because it tends to happen late in the season, vigour of the plant may not be affected unduly. Still, as part of the annual clean up, old leaves should be removed from the plant at the end of the summer anyway.

Red Core: Plants are stunted: the central leaves are reddish and the outer leaves are brown and stiff. The roots have a, yes, central red core as well as rotting. Spores are released into the soil from the roots where they can remain for over ten years, sitting waiting to pounce on the next batch of strawberry plants to be put there. Control, therefore, is not to do that: use a long rotation.

Because it can only move around on plants or contaminated soil, make sure that when you are buying runners they come from certified stock. If you are using home-produced runners be strict with which plants you collect from or their proximity to other dodgy-looking plants. Don't shift soil around, either. No-dig?

Powdery Mildew: An old favourite on fruit or just plants in general brought on by stress, particularly dryness at the root and dampness at the leaf. Such conditions are surprisingly common such as poor watering – too little, all over the plant – or a light shower in otherwise hot dry weather. A white coating appears on the leaf which can become discoloured and pucker. Keep well-watered, mulch and feed well and use resistant varieties such as 'Florence', all as prevention. Remove infected leaves.

Straw Berry

The name 'strawberry' incidentally doesn't refer to the straw that is used to put around the plants. It is most likely from the Anglo-Saxon *Streabariye* meaning straying berry in reference to the runners. It is unlikely to have come from the occasionally-cited practice of threading wild fruits on grass stalks or straws. Children still collect tiny strawberries using this fine method particularly in Scandinavia, though, as pointed out by a Norwegian friend, they call the fruit 'earthberry' in Norway in Norwegian, not 'strawberry'.

OTHER FRUIT

A random selection of fruiting plants possibly of some interest.

Cape Gooseberry *Physalis peruviana*

Now here's a dilemma. It seems that the plants in this book are dessert fruits, meaning it excludes fruit like tomatoes and squash. And then along comes *Physalis*. If we were being strict it should only refer to *P. peruviana* or the Cape Gooseberry. Others include *P. alkekengi var. franchettii* (the ornamental Chinese Lantern) and *P. ixocarpa* (tomatilloes, definitely in the tomato-camp of savoury).

The Cape Gooseberry has a single berry in a papery, lantern-like husk as do they all, but this one is great in fruit salads or as jam. They are treated as annuals: sow the seed in April, two seeds per module, thinning to one later. They can be grown inside or out or in containers – plant in a prepared area or a 5-7.5l pot towards the end of May, or in June if you are in a cooler region.

Treat them like tomatoes including plenty of water. Less water is required when the fruit starts ripening which is before outside tomatoes ripen. Indoors they can reach 1.8m / 6' but outdoors and in pots it is more like 1.2m / 4'. Some support, perhaps a stake, may be required.

Low temperatures stop the ripening process but any fruits that have started to ripen (the husks have just begun to dry) can be brought indoors to finish, just like a tomato that has started to change from a dark green colour. If they have been grown in pots then the whole thing can be brought indoors to finish ripening.

Extract the fruit, a marble-sized thing, when the husk is completely dry which is the indicator that it is fully ripe to eat.

The variety 'Pineapple' really does have a pineapple taste – combined with custard. Who could decline any fruit tasting of pineapple custard?

Chokeberries *Aronia x prunifolia*

Reasons to grow chokeberries: Not many other people grow them – the constant striving for individuality could start here. The berries have high levels of antioxidants and Vitamin C and can be eaten fresh or cooked. The bush is intermediate in size: 1-2m/3-6' and will tolerate some shade and dry conditions. The berries are ripe in September followed by lovely autumn leaf colour. The easily-available variety 'Viking' is self fertile.

Reasons not to grow chokeberries: The flavour is 'acquired'. The yield is low compared to the mainstream soft fruits. Though generally pest and disease-free, birds are attracted to the fruit.

Elderberries *Sambucus nigra*
Reasons to grow elderberries: The flowers and fruit, separately, make two of the best homemade wines. You can also make elderflower fritters, which seems to me just a good excuse for having lots of deep-fried batter, and the berries can be included in other-fruit jam. The twigs are angled and branching making them okay for pea sticks despite being a little brittle.

Reasons not to grow elderberries: Apart perhaps from when they are in flower, the tree itself is pretty ungainly. The wood is fairly useless having a hollow, pithy core. In fact we are warned against even burning it for fear of something to do with evil spirits / the Conservative Party.

Hazelnuts *Corylus avellana* and *C. maxima*
Perhaps not the most common fruit tree, but a fruit tree it is. The strange thing is that the name seems to change depending on the stage of production. We eat the nuts as 'hazelnuts' yet we would buy plants for their superior fruiting qualities known as 'cobnuts' or 'filberts'. That doesn't mean, of course, that we wouldn't harvest nuts from wild hazelnut trees just that the squirrels will probably have got there first. In fact Martin Crawford in 'Creating a Forest Garden' quite rightly states that there is no point growing any nuts apart from sweet chestnuts if uncontrolled squirrels are in the locality.

The hazelnut is a true nut which is defined as a singled-seeded fruit in a woody coat. Our ancestors relied heavily on hazelnuts as a storable form of protein and healthy fats as indicated, for example, by the great stashes of shells found at Neolithic sites in the Western Isles of Scotland. This also indicated, incidentally, that there was wonderful tree cover once instead of the bald, over-grazed or grouse moor landscape of today.

Cobnuts are planted at about 2.5m / 8' apart and if there are no wild / hedgerow hazelnuts nearby, then more than one variety is needed for cross pollination. The positioning is quite important because they cross pollinate using wind; the male flowers are very familiar being the long dangly catkins we see in early spring, throwing out pollen in the hope that it drifts to a nearby female flower on a different plant. The female flower often goes unnoticed – it is close to stems and has red structures called stigmas protruding. The pollen can be effective for over 50m / 160' but it makes sense that pollination will be more reliable the closer the plants are. It is important to choose varieties that coincide in terms of pollen release and receptive flowers. 'Cosford Cob' for example is an excellent pollinator for, say, 'Kentish Cob', according to Bob Flowerdew. The RHS Encyclopaedia of Gardening, however, states that 'Kentish Cob' is actually self fertile.

They are propagated by using cuttings, removing rooted suckers or layering (see 'Propagation') not grafting since they are suckering shrubs / trees. In fact wild hazels, used for hedging or free-standing plants, can be coppiced (cut to just above ground level) as a great supply of poles. Often in commercial orchards the trees are limited to single stems and grown in a more traditional tree shape. This is supposed to maximise production with good light distribution.

To increase production of female flowers (and hence nuts), any strong upright stems are snapped in half in the summer. Going by the terrific name of 'brutting', the brutted shoots in the following winter are cut all the way back to three or four buds from their origin, building up a spur system as with so many other fruits.

To store hazelnuts (cool and dry) they need to be fully ripe and de-husked. For the uninitiated, the husk is a little shaggy jacket which the nut wears, particularly evident on the version of hazel called a filbert.

Melons *Cucumis melo*

From Africa, the melon is the only fruit in this book to have originated there and, as a result, needs particular attention. Development has been widespread including Europe (hence the cantaloupe melon named after Cantalupo near Rome). They were grown in England in the late 16th century with the advent of glass and hot beds.

There is a wide range of melon derivatives of which we are concerned with:
Cantaloup / summer muskmelons – medium-sized, netted or scaly skin, flesh is orange with a sweet scent.
Honeydew / winter melons – large size, smooth or wrinkled skin, flesh is white or green with less of a scent.

One of the few fruits covered here that is grown afresh each year. There are plenty of others we could include, of course, since technically they are all fruit, but we are being sensible. Besides, tomatoes, squash, peas and beans, etc are all covered in another volume of possible interest entitled 'Good Earth Gardening – Vegetables'.

Melons are sweet and unless you are a TV chef trying to impress somebody they would normally be eaten as a dessert or starter. In some respects they are more straightforward to grow in that, if something goes wrong, you can always start afresh next year. In other respects – blimey, what a faff – principally because of the need for protection. This is protection from the elements not particularly from melon-stealing ne'er-do-wells and is likely to involve a greenhouse, polytunnel or conservatory. That doesn't mean that something else couldn't be rigged up outside – where would an allotment site be without lots of plastic flapping in the wind? For good light levels and distribution melons are normally trained upwards on a framework, but that doesn't rule out cloches and coldframes.

Apart from light, the other main requirement is warmth, so to reliably achieve this we need at least a sheet of glass or piece of polythene between the plant and the cruel outside world. Passive heating is enough, plus of course the vital protection from wind, though a heated structure using lots of fossil fuels will give the most consistent results. Melons are closely related to cucumbers and are treated in a very similar way which isn't much help if you know nothing about cucumbers.

Let us summarise. The plants are started in heat early in the year to ensure a long growing season. For most of us this means sowing (two seeds in a small pot) at home where the temperature will be approaching the ideal around 20°C for seed germination. A propagator is more reliable if you live in a cave or other poorly heated abode.

Once germination has taken place, light plus the continuing warmth becomes important. A south-facing window would be the minimum though in many houses this isn't enough. At this time of year a south-facing window means sunrise and sunset are opposite each other and your seedlings could have natural light for the whole day. In practice, something will get in the way. Thin seedlings to one per pot, grow on for five or six weeks before hardening off and planting out.

The easiest way of growing is to allow a plant to sprawl in, say, a coldframe where it can spread out. Remove flowers to leave one per branch and as the fruit starts to form cut off the end of the branch two leaves beyond the fruit. Water, feed. There are methods of growing in greenhouses involving training and lots of pruning, not to mention supporting the fruit as it increases in weight – an ideal use for that reject bra.

Sea Buckthorn *Hippophae rhamnoides* Family: ELEAGNACEAE
Reasons to grow sea buckthorn: Huge amounts of vitamin C. Heavy yields of attractive orange berries. Silvery foliage. The plants fix their own nitrogen.

Reasons not to grow sea buckthorn: They can sucker until you find yourself living in a sea buckthorn thicket. They have lots of flesh-hungry thorns. The flavour is quite sour, as with blackcurrants – the pay-off for all that Vit. C. You need a male plant to pollinate the female plants – the male is non-fruiting and takes up, potentially, valuable room – who said males are a waste of space?

Walnuts *Juglans regia*
This may come as a bit of a blow, but a walnut isn't a nut, it's a drupe like a plum. It is just that we eat the seed instead of the flesh. This little brain of a seed is quite nutritious containing healthy unsaturated fats, high levels of antioxidants, and a high vitamin content. It has also been cited as a help to overcome arthritis. Some key features of growing walnuts: They make quite large trees (9-12m / 30-40'). They should be bought as grafted trees of a known variety (taking 4-8 years to start fruiting) not trees grown from seeds (taking over 20 years to fruit). They are normally grafted onto black walnut, *Juglans nigra*. They are wind-pollinated, with separate male and female flowers on the same tree, like hazelnuts. They are often self-fertile – normally self sterility is brought about by the male and female flowers ripening at different times. The trees live for ages with peak fruiting reached in 20 years.

Blight resistant varieties (except 'Broadview'):
'**Lara**' – early-season, new French variety, large fruit, good yields.
'**Broadview**' – mid-season, well adapted to the UK climate, partially self-fertile.
'**Buccaneer**' – mid-season, good in UK conditions, moderate yields of moderate-sized nuts, partially self-fertile.
'**Fernette**' – late season, French variety, large high quality nuts, excellent yields.
'**Franquette**' – late-season, thin shell, partially self-fertile, good-sized nuts, heavy cropping.
'**Rita**' – self-fertile, large fruit, good yields, relatively small (6-8m / 20-25').

Even if partially self-fertile, it is advisable to have a pollinating partner: any combination of the above varieties will work. A fun technique to try if your single tree happens to be not self-fertile is to collect male catkins on a dry day when they are open, store them for a week in the cool and dry and then, by popping them in a mesh bag on the end of stick, shake them amongst the branches where the female flowers will now be ripe and receptive.

Walnuts are a little like grapes when it comes to frosts: it is not so much the flowers that are affected by late frosts but the new, tender growth which blackens and effectively has to start again. Later leafing varieties avoid this problem but it is still best to avoid a frost-prone area.

No pruning is necessary once a little formative pruning is out of the way. This would be to ensure a clear trunk and raised canopy (making it easier to deter squirrels).

Walnut blight is a major problem especially in wetter areas of the country. It is a bacterial disease which, apart from creating spots on leaves, can spread to the fruit which blackens and drops. Resistant varieties are essential in the west of the UK.

Squirrels are enormous fans of walnuts and will swipe the lot before they are ripe. Smooth guards wrapped around the trunks to prevent assault from ground level are the starting point followed by wide spacing: the canopies should be at least 3m / 10' apart to stop a little menace from jumping between trees. It is probably not a bad idea to have that spacing anyway to reduce blight. Try 15m / 50'.

Because the trees are so tall, harvesting is mostly by picking off the ground. Watch out for those pesky squirrels again. The trees can be shaken in late September to October with a long pole when you notice the green husks starting to split open. After collecting, the nuts are 'shucked' from the husks and dried (airing cupboard?).

For pickled walnuts, which are harvested immature, you will have to clamber around a bit. This is at the end of June and they are tested for readiness by being able to push a thick needle through the fruit.

Beating the trunk of a walnut is supposed to a) improve fruiting b) cause it to produce interesting patterns in the wood, presumably in anticipation of your prize walnut tree being cut down and logged. Unripe fruit was used as a hair dye (dark) and stained hands are still an attractive feature of walnut harvesters if they have forgotten gloves.

GROWING SYSTEMS

In short this refers to where to put the plants, and can be summarised by the following:

1) Fruit garden
2) Orchard
3) Hedges
4) Forest garden
5) Mixed fruit and vegetables
6) Two-dimensional training
7) Containers

Whatever the arrangement, consideration should be made of a fruit's preferences, particularly requirements for sun and shelter.
Shade tolerance (including a north-facing wall): redcurrants, gooseberries, acid cherries, rhubarb (light shade).
Sun-worshippers (including south-facing walls): figs, peaches, apricots, grapes, kiwis.

All the others would prefer a good half day's sun, give or take.

1) Fruit garden
This is pretty much what most people do. All the fruit plants are put together in one area, making it easier to protect from birds. It may therefore involve a fruit cage. The plants are grouped together according to type, so that the apples will be next to each other, separate from the plums / pears / whatever, the currants will be in rows and cane fruit also trained in rows using a post and wire system.

Advantages
- You know where you are.
- It is possible to protect the entire fruit garden in one cage.
- If there are pollination issues, fruit types are right next to each other.

Disadvantages
- It is a missed opportunity to use the plants in other situations i.e. ornamental, protection.
- A bit formulaic?

2) Orchard
Not that dissimilar to the fruit garden but on a larger scale and consisting mainly of trees. It gives the opportunity to have larger specimens. How many trees does it take to make an 'orchard'? At the risk of taking away the fun of you trying to guess that one yourselves, I reckon a minimum of half a dozen, though am happy to be persuaded otherwise.

Advantages
- What a wonderful sight is the orchard in full flower or full fruiting.
- An orchard with half standards or even standards ('normal trees') has an atmosphere all of its own, combining the feeling of a woodland with shade and dappled sunlight, mixed ground cover and enhanced wildlife opportunities, plus spectacular productivity and beauty.

Disadvantages
- Just how big is your garden?
- Most commercial orchards have dwarf trees, herbicided strips and no atmosphere. This is to maximise yields of very high quality fruit and, crucially, enable easy maintenance and picking. We don't have to grow trees like that if we don't want to.

3) Hedges

Instead of a fence or a privet hedge, why not plant a row of fruit trees / shrubs? A low hedge could be closely planted gooseberries, for example, and something more substantial could be trees on appropriate rootstocks. The range of fruit that could be used is paradoxically expanded and contracted: traditional hedgerow plants like sloe, bullace, wild rose, etc. can be included in this situation whereas we wouldn't normally include them in our fruit area. On the other hand, yields on traditional fruit trees subjected to hedge-cutting / pruning regimes combined with close planting may be reduced to the point of negligibility.

Advantages
- Combined functions are always worth considering. A mixed fruiting hedgerow provides a boundary barrier and a productive strip.
- Space-saving.
- Looks really interesting compared to the usual hedges.

Disadvantages
- Not so easy to take a hedgetrimmer or shears to – may need selective pruning. So this is not such good news if the hedge was the main function. If fruit production is uppermost, well, you would have had to prune carefully anyway.
- Yields may not be the highest.
- Passers-by may swipe fruit as they pass by.

4) Forest garden

A slightly more complicated affair but, in a nutshell, all the fruit plants are mixed up together. 'Advanced' forest gardens have a huge range of plants, all of them productive, filling in all of the niche habitats that are available. It would include plants for fibres and fuel, some for salad leaves and tubers, some to promote the fertility of the garden and, perhaps most of all, plants for nuts and fruit.

If we are hoping to grow just the commonly cultivated fruits described in this book, we can make a simple version by having trees with bare stems (half standards or standards) with fruit bushes underneath and even a ground cover of productive plants such as alpine strawberries, arctic raspberries, etc. We could include here a few herbs which we would normally be growing elsewhere on our plot or plants with other purposes that are essential somewhere on an organic plot such as comfrey.

A simple plan is given here.

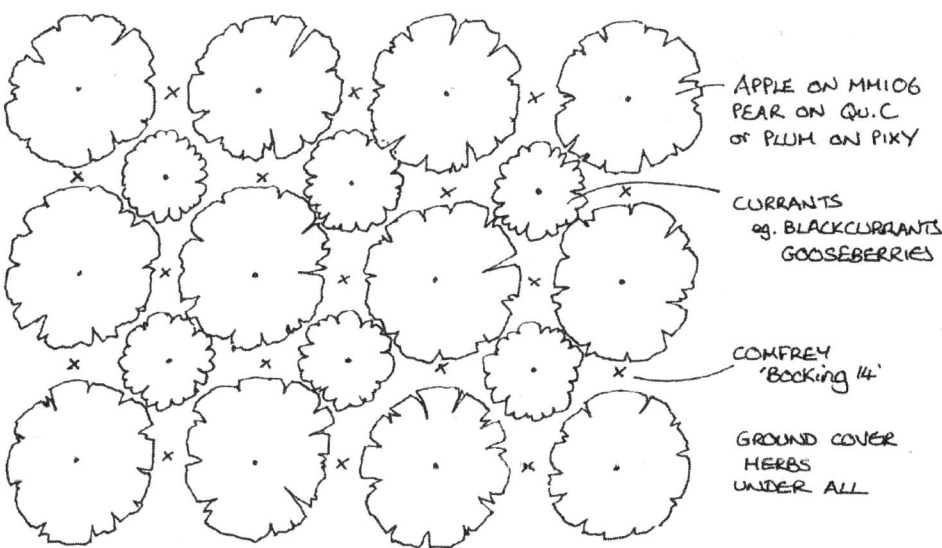

Using apples on the smallest rootstocks will give a planting which is simply fruit plants in a grid mixed up – the trees and bushes will be the same size. That's ok but it loses some of the benefits of the forest garden canopy system. Slightly larger rootstocks would also be fine but the low branches end up making it trickier to get around. Medium rootstocks seem to give the best of all worlds – see 'Rootstocks'. Apples on the medium MM106 might be the best compromise, for example.

If you were feeling bold you could take the decision to not prune anything, apart from perhaps the initial formative pruning. After all, the ancestors of these plants were never pruned twice a year or whatever.

Advantages
- Really rather exciting.
- Plants can be positioned exactly where they would have the optimum conditions, especially in terms of shade / sun.
- It looks and feels 'natural'.
- Low maintenance.
- Almost self-sustaining: a little light mulching, especially to start with, plus perhaps a bit of ash or urine or comfrey.
- Pest and disease control is often not required: birds, particularly, seem less inclined to strip plants.

Disadvantages
- Requires careful planning.
- Some fruit types don't fit in as easily, such as raspberries, certainly not if we want to grow them in the traditional way of regimented rows on supports. They can, of course, be left to wander through a forest garden which is how they would normally grow. They will congregate in the areas they find most suitable but you might still have to seek out the berries.

5) Mixed fruit and vegetables

This arrangement is perhaps more typical in continental gardens where you might see a large central fruit tree with vegetables grown almost to the trunk. The tree in that case is being used for shade as much as anything else. There is nothing remotely wrong with having fruit plants dotted throughout a vegetable plot, as long as the requirements of all of the participants are considered.

Advantages
- Everything just, well… 'fits in'.
- Looks more natural.
- Strawberries should be part of the vegetable area anyway.

Disadvantages
- Competition – very dwarf trees don't tolerate much competition and larger trees mean that the vegetables can suffer.
- The fruit is less easy to protect. Individual nets may be required, for example.
- Roots can get damaged with nearby soil cultivation.
- Rotations can be compromised: a tree may take up space in one block of a rotation but not in the next; rotation blocks should be the same size.

6) Mixed everything

This is quite complicated, so pay attention: plant your fruit in the garden.
Yes, it is quite acceptable to mix up all of your plants: ornamentals, fruit, vegetables, herbs. Someone has come up with a name for it – the Cottage

Garden. The blossom on fruit trees can be as attractive as any ornamental flowering plant.

Advantages
- Beautiful.
- Like the forest garden but possibly more so, there is natural pest and disease control with many predators attracted. The ripe fruit can be harder for pests to find.

Disadvantages
- Access – can you find the gooseberries if they have been submerged under a wave of geraniums? How easy is it to reach the plum tree?
- More complicated when it comes to pruning and shaping plants: there may be more importance placed on the appearance than the functioning of the plants.
- Not usually applicable to an allotment.

7) Two-dimensional training

This is particularly for those of us with very limited space or who are keen to squeeze in another plant where there isn't really the room. It is a combination of climbing plants, such as kiwis, vines, tayberries and other cane fruit, being held on a wall or fence and trees and shrubs pruned to a two-dimensional shape against the same structures.

Advantages
- Vertical surfaces are a great opportunity and should be used.
- Can look terrific, especially espaliers and fans.
- Easy to protect plants.
- Very productive given the space occupied.
- A wide range of plants can be grown this way including redcurrants and gooseberries.

Disadvantages
- Hard to maintain the fence or wall with a plant growing on it. But then it's a horrible job anyway so you have a good excuse not to do it.
- Not suitable for particular plants e.g. black currants.
- The conditions at the base of a wall may not be very favourable, with dryness and old lime mortar being possible problems.
- A certain amount of knowledge is required regarding pruning.

8) Containers
Advantages
- You can take your plants with you when you move house or get thrown off your allotment.
- Plants can be put in different locations according to the time of year.
- Probably the only way of growing some plants if your garden soil isn't appropriate: blueberries.
- Some plants benefit from being confined: figs.

Disadvantages
- Maintenance – very time consuming.
- Cost: containers, potting compost, fertilisers. You can of course make all of those yourself, you don't have to buy them. But most of us do.
- Limited range of plants and / success: most fruit trees are too big for containers unless you are exceptionally good at keeping on top of the feeding and watering. Other plants simply find containers too hostile with respect to water. For that reason, both blackcurrants and raspberries (suckering plants) don't enjoy it for too long.

TOOLS

A general note about cutting tools is that, as with quite a few things in life, you get what you pay for. If you have only a couple of fruit bushes, for example, then a cheap pair of secateurs may be all you need. For regular, plentiful work get the best you can afford – for durability, longevity, servicing and joy.

Pruning saws

One of the key differences between a pruning saw and a woodworking saw (e.g. a tenon saw) is that the latter has a straight edge to the blade with smaller teeth whilst the former frequently has a curved, tapering blade, with big teeth.

The shape of a pruning saw lends itself to squeezing between close branches and in awkward angles. The teeth, being a good size, enable very rapid cutting – a negative aspect of big teeth, apart from being spotted by Little Red Riding Hood, is that the cut may not be the smoothest: don't rush it and don't force it when coming towards the end of a cut.

It can sometimes be hard to start a cut too, with the blade bouncing over the bark. This is not disastrous if the bark affected is on the piece being removed; it is less than desirable if you wound the piece remaining or get it to skip merrily over the back of your hand. Maybe there is a case to be made for wearing gloves, here. And starting gently.

There is nothing to stop you using a wood-working saw except it is more cumbersome to use and takes longer since the teeth are small. Folding saws are

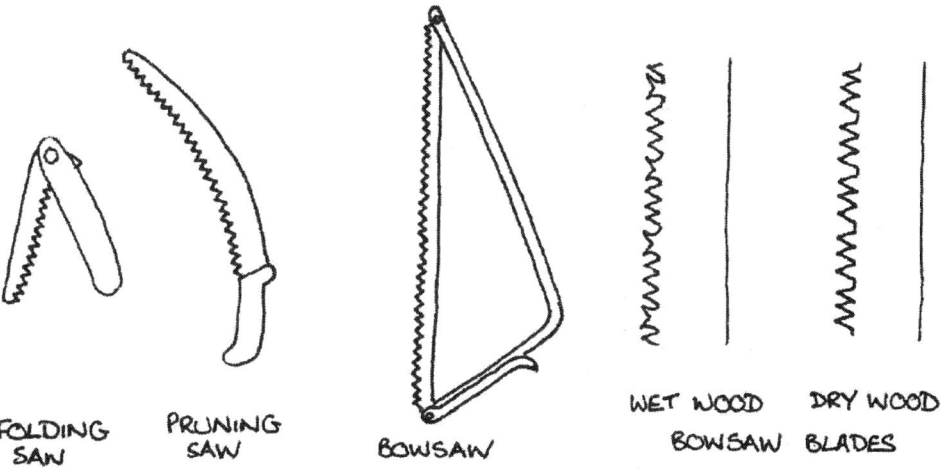

exceptionally useful particularly when it comes to transporting and protecting the blade (and you from the blade).

Many pruning saws cut 'on the pull' – in other words, they only cut in one direction, when pulling towards you. This is because, when cutting at a stretch or above your head, it is easier to cut when pulling than it is when pushing.

Bow Saws

Not as easy to fit in to those little gaps, but considerably cheaper, is the bow saw. The best bow saw for pruning is the pointed type, rather than the less versatile capital-D shape, which is better for the biggest pieces, cutting logs and, heaven forbid, felling.

Don't waste a good pruning saw on thick branches and easily accessibly parts – use a bow saw: the blade of a bow saw can be replaced easily and comparatively cheaply when they start getting blunt. To complicate matters, there are different bow saw blades for different occasions: for wet / live wood (pruning), for dry wood (firewood) or for family gatherings (disagreeable uncles). The pictures show the best blade to look for.

When carrying a bow saw. Put it over your shoulder with the handle at the front – just make sure no-one tries to pat you on the back.

Secateurs

These are mentioned in pruning but here is some extra information at no additional cost. There are two main types of secateurs: **anvil** and **by-pass**.

Anvil types are less common, the blade often having a straight edge and when closed that edge meets a metal pad – there are curved blade versions. They are very useful with thick branches but, unless they are kept extra sharp, they tend to squash / crush smaller and softer pieces. They

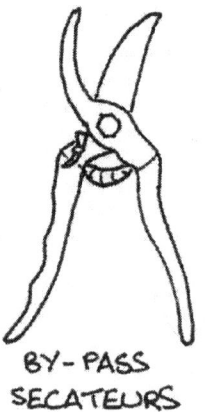
BY-PASS SECATEURS

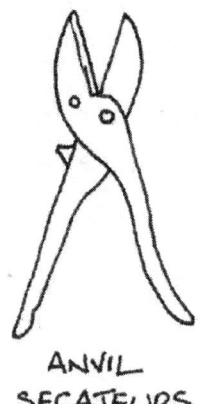
ANVIL SECATEURS

also cut more efficiently when the stem being pruned is at right angles to the blade. Anvil secateurs usually have a 'bull-nose' appearance making them harder to squeeze in a narrow space just to snip off a fine piece.

By-pass secateurs act more like scissors, with the curved blade running past the curved metal block. It is easy to see that if block and blade are not tightly fitting, it will be a messy cut with whiskery bits at the edge. They can usually be adjusted.

Other features / alternatives of mild interest.

- Very small blades for snipping / easy cutting.
- Left-handed models.
- Ratchet secateurs for less than strong hands: 'pumping' the handles gradually works the blade through the stem.
- Rotating handle for the professional: it rotates in your hand as the secateurs are closed up, with the idea that it reduces the strain on your wrist if you've got loads to do. Expensive.
- Colourful handles: it sounds daft but the gaudier the handles the easier it will be for you to find your secateurs again once you have put them down. When concentrating on a plant (as one should) it is surprisingly easy to lay down an implement without looking and then be amazed when it is 'no longer there' when you look round again. They are usually red for this reason. It might be best to avoid green: if it is too late, personalise them with your own colourful tape. Some brands have one handle red and the other white especially for the extra incompetent of us – I have two pairs.

Other things to look for, a.k.a. why is this pair so much more expensive than this other pair?:
- **The weight of them**. A light pair might be easier to wield and carry, but are they strong enough? Light would be around 120g, heavy would be over 250g.
- Comfort. Shape of the handles, size of the handles and how wide they naturally open.
- **Robustness**. Quality and strength of materials both the handles and the blade, the latter being better quality if it has a high carbon content in the hardened steel.
- **Ease of maintenance.** When you need to clean thoroughly it helps to be able to dismantle and re-assemble the secateurs so that they still function and you don't have several parts left over. Personally, the fewer little cogs there are, the better it feels.

THE EASE OF SECATEUR MAINTENANCE

- **Size of blade.** Coupled with how far they open and the robustness, this dictates how well they cope with large cuts.
- **Back up**. When you have made a complete mess of them, the company that has benefited from your hard-earned may step in and retrieve the situation. Replacement blades save you from having to buy a complete new pair.
- **The spring**. You need a Goldilocks sort of spring: one that is strong enough to open the handles easily but not too powerful so that you have repetitive strain injury after five minutes. Something in-between.
- **Safety catch**. This holds the secateurs closed when not in use and can be surprisingly irritating. Either they don't hold and the things pop open at a most inconvenient moment or it is the opposite and they require two hands to try to open them again.
- **Guarantee**. It is a bit of an indicator if a manufacturer is prepared to say, 'If this thing falls apart from normal usage within your lifetime, we'll replace it.' Of course, they might only allow sales to 85 year-olds with arthritic wrists.

Maintenance involves regular wiping down and oiling both the spring and the pivot joint. 'Regular' should mean 'after every use', but in practice means 'whenever you think about it'. A few snips aren't going to warrant washing with soapy water and a mild abrasive followed by oiling, but after a week of occasional use or an intensive pruning session, it might be advisable.

The cutting parts can gradually get a build up of dried sap which blackens. To clean this off use wire wool or a scouring pad. The wire wool should be kept away from the cutting edge. Another remedy for this has been suggested that involves daubing the blade with tomato ketchup, leaving overnight and then wiping everything off. It has been stipulated that this should be Heinz tomato ketchup on the principal that this brand is non-acidic so won't create pits in the aluminium parts. I would like to thank Heinz Ltd. (Advertising Dept.) for help with this useful information.

All blades should be kept sharp by gently running a small steel or a sharpening stone along the edge two or three times at the same angle as the existing bevel

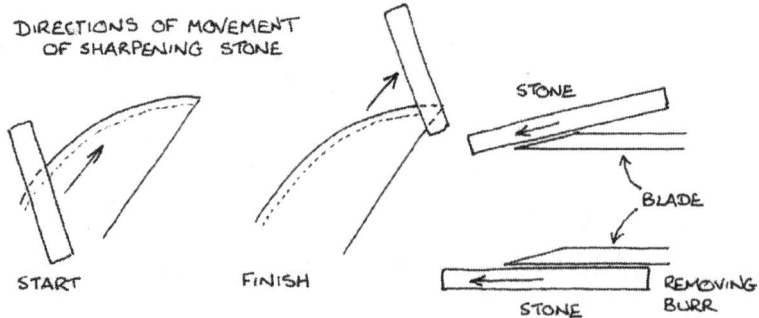

The bevel is the slope of the blade leading to the cutting edge. Then run the stone once along the back of the blade to remove the burr – a small curl of metal that is formed during sharpening. This last burr-removing swipe should be done with the steel / stone flat against the underneath of the blade, not at an angle. When a blade is truly pooped, either from constant use or from not spotting that piece of wire hidden behind the shoot, it should be possible to get a replacement (expensive models only).

The best quality blades are hardened steel and are more difficult to sharpen, but then they are more difficult to foul up in the first place (also known as 'lasting longer').

Averuncator / Long Arm Pruner
Secateurs on a stick, operated using a rope or thick wire from ground level. It is less accurate than being up close, but may be valuable for cutting small(ish) pieces off the ends of branches, like dead, diseased or damaged twigs. It is a useful tool for using on ornamentals which need shaping, like bay trees, rather than fruit trees which are best pruned lower in the canopy, making larger cuts with a saw.

Loppers
The cutting parts of loppers have the same action and options as secateurs except that anvil types are more common. With thicker branches it is to loppers or a saw that we should turn – a very common sight is someone squeezing secateurs, often with both hands, and wiggling them to and fro to try to get through a too-thick branch. This action is often accompanied by very strange facial expressions.

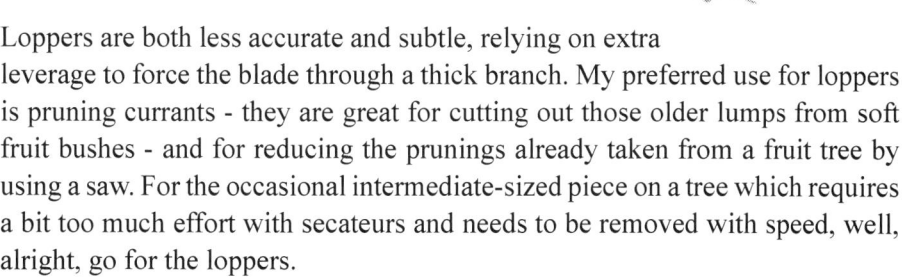

Loppers are both less accurate and subtle, relying on extra
leverage to force the blade through a thick branch. My preferred use for loppers is pruning currants - they are great for cutting out those older lumps from soft fruit bushes - and for reducing the prunings already taken from a fruit tree by using a saw. For the occasional intermediate-sized piece on a tree which requires a bit too much effort with secateurs and needs to be removed with speed, well, alright, go for the loppers.

An adaptation to loppers, making them considerably more interesting, is the telescopic handles. With these, the handles of the loppers, when they are in their short mode, are rotated to unlock them, pulled out to extend them and then turned again to lock them back. It is extremely easy to get mixed up with directions of turning.

Also worthy of note is that, in the extended form, the sponge / rubber handle ends are now considerably further apart.

To use loppers well, they should be closed close to the body, elbows out: it is far harder to operate them at a stretch. It's all physics, you know. A reason for not using loppers: when up a ladder or clambering about in a tree canopy, you shouldn't have both hands operating the tool – again, use either a saw or secateurs depending on size of cut and use your spare hand for holding on.

Knife

A knife is an exceptionally useful tool, though I have yet to use one when pruning. Pruning knives are broad, strong and curved. They are recommended for removing the rough edges of a saw cut but that suggests that the saw cut was not done well enough in the first place.

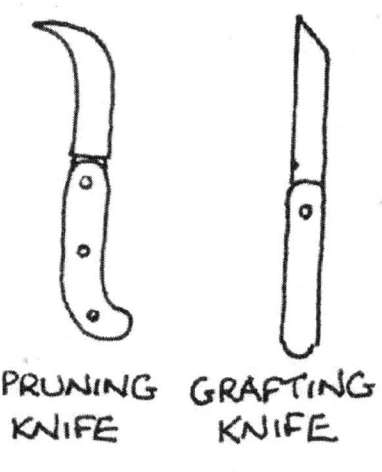

PRUNING KNIFE   GRAFTING KNIFE

They are used to snick off thin shoots quickly, a process I have far more success with by either pulling off the shoot or by using secateurs. But don't be put off by my incompetence – try pruning with a knife.

Apart from pruning knives, there are a thousand and one other shapes and sizes. Of these, the other one worth considering is thinner both in terms of width of blade and thickness of blade. It is a grafting knife and has a completely straight cutting edge.

As with all of the cutting tools mentioned here, the key to making a pleasing cut is the sharpness.

Carrying tools

Bow saws, as mentioned, if carried any distance, should be over the shoulder with the blade facing backwards. All the other tools can be attached to the

person in some way so that, with a full complement, you too can look and sound like an itinerant ironmonger.

The secateurs often slot point down in a holster made from the skin of some animal or from yellow plastic; personally, I find that the back pocket suffices, though they should be the other way up.

Pruning saws can also come with a sheath which attaches to a belt or, if a folding type, can drop in a multi-pocket pouch belt thing along with a knife. Even loppers can dangle from your trousers with the arms pointing down: the business end is held in a device best(?) described as small leather underpants.

When working in a tree canopy, it is often recommended to detach tools from oneself (they tend to catch on branches) and to hook them on small branches within reach. It is probably best to keep secateurs on you. However, only marginally less distressing than dropping one's glasses having climbed to some dizzy height is dislodging a saw (for example) and seeing it freefall into the undergrowth back at ground level. Of course, if you have just lost your glasses then you won't have the dismay of seeing the saw go, too.

PLANTING

Preparing

If your new tree is to be planted in a lawn or grassland, the turf can be placed upside down in the bottom of the hole and chopped up. Clear an area of grass at least one metre square. The hole itself need only be twice the diameter of the root ball – apparently square holes are better at getting the roots to grow out into the surrounding soil than round ones. If planting in bare ground, carry on as though nobody had said anything.

The Hole

Apart from recycled turf, tree roots and a stake, nothing else should go in to the hole. It used to be that we were encouraged (especially by garden centres) to pile in organic matter and fertiliser, to make it as welcoming to roots as possible. Well, it appears we were making it too welcoming and the roots weren't bothering to leave the hole, so now we just say 'Be thankful you're in the ground, now get on with it and spread your roots out'. Talking to your plants is essential even if it means being a little stern now and again.

There is an exception to not putting anything in the hole and that is, if the soil is poor, mycorrhizal fungi can be added. It has to be an appropriate type that will associate with a tree (or fruit bush). You might choose to add the fungi anyway especially if there are no woody plants nearby; the association between fungus and plant is vital and it might be worthwhile to get it to happen earlier rather than waiting for it to happen naturally.

When digging a hole, the soil should be loosened up at the bottom and sides roughed up a little to encourage root penetration. The depth should be just enough so that the surrounding soil is level with the depth the tree has been grown until now.

Only if the location is a very wet one should the tree be planted higher than this (on a mound) and, if water supply is an issue as in hot climates, it should be planted in a slight dip, like a shallow bowl or satellite dish. One of the main aims is to make sure that the graft union is well above the soil level. When very dwarfing trees have been planted too deeply, the part of the tree above the graft has managed to produce roots and a huge specimen has resulted. Let that be a lesson.

Container-grown Trees

These are more expensive because a nursery has had to maintain them more intensively with feeding and watering, on top of the additional cost of a pot and the growing medium. However, they can be planted throughout the year, except in extreme conditions like drought or frost / freezing / snow. The level of the compost / growing medium in the pot is the indicator for the depth of planting.

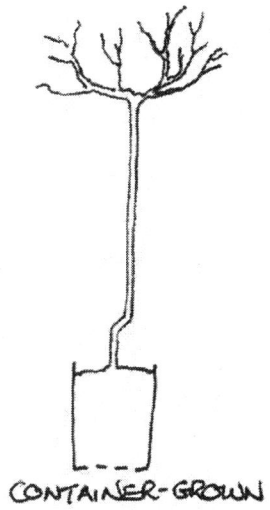

CONTAINER-GROWN

If there is a cane supporting the tree in its pot, remove it and save it for the vegetable patch.

Bare-root Trees

A bare-root tree is grown in open ground in a nursery, periodically having its roots undercut, usually by machine. This stops it getting too established and promotes a denser mat of roots closer to the stem, ensuring good survival when it is finally dug up and sold to us. Its planting time is, ideally, late autumn–early winter when the soil is still warmish and encouraging for root growth, though any time in the dormant season is possible.

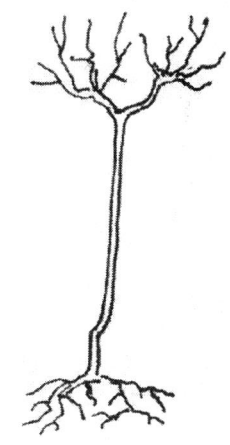

BARE ROOT

It is worthwhile quoting a major authority on the subject to back up this theory, namely Beeton's Shilling Gardening Book of 1873: Dr. Lindley recommends, and we quite agree with him, on the early transplanting of different trees that "They cannot be removed from the nursery too soon after the wood has become ripe and the leaves have fallen off, for between this time and the winter many of them will make fresh roots, and be prepared to push forth their young shoots with more vigour in the spring than those whose transplanting has been deferred to a late period of the season".

It is the same for both bare-root and container-grown trees in terms of getting the levels right, though it is slightly trickier with bare-root trees. Look for the 'soil mark' on the stem, indicating the depth it was planted at the nursery – there will be a change in colour – and plant at the same level as that.

Stakes

The purpose of the stake isn't necessarily to support the stem of the tree. It is to anchor the roots. Therefore you don't have to buy a full length stake: usually it is enough to use a stake of about one metre.

This stake has to be close enough to the stem at some point to use a tie (see below). The bare-root tree will be planted with the stake hammered in vertically before the tree is planted, the tie being fitted about 3-5cm (1-2") from the top of the stake.

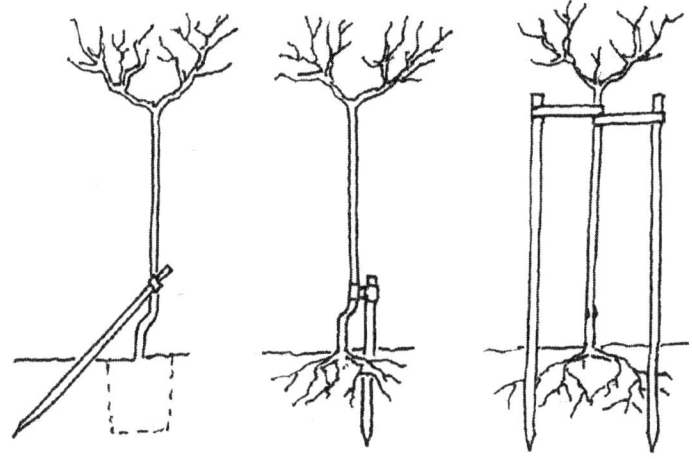

The stake is knocked in at an angle after planting a container-grown tree to avoid it going through the rootball in an unruly and damaging fashion. This creates a small triangle near the base just big enough to fit a wellie boot and crosses the stem at a single point where the tie is affixed.

Exceptions: a misshapen or floppy stem might need supporting and straightening along its entire length. Generally (and easily said) we should ensure that the tree we buy is in a better condition than that so it shouldn't need it. If the tree is in a vulnerable location as found with street trees it may be necessary to protect the stem with at least one full length stake and a cylinder of weldmesh – a robust version of chicken wire – stapled to it. The deluxe version of staking consists of two vertical stakes, one either side of the tree, and a loop of strapping from the top of each around the tree, tensioning it in between.

Tying

Whatever tie is used, the aim is the same. That is, to create a figure of eight where the tree is in one loop and the stake in the other. The mid-point of the 'eight' (the waist) is thickened out to make sure that tree and stake are not only kept apart but so that the part of the stake above it also doesn't come in contact with the tree. It is easier to ensure this doesn't happen if the tie is near the top of the stake. A bought tie should consist of a strap and a 'spacer'. The latter is a plastic block that sits at the waist of the '8'.

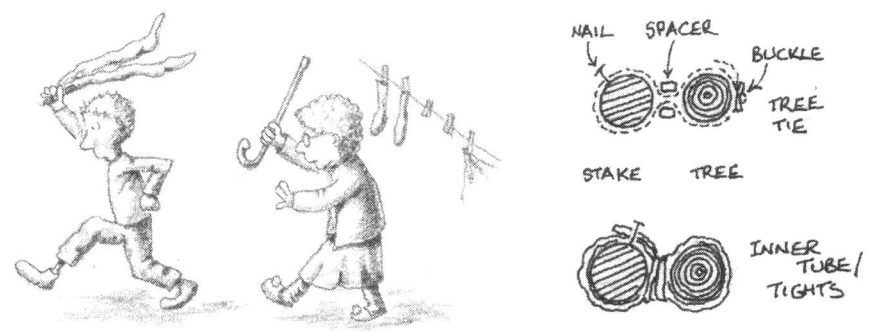

Perhaps, to minimise our intimate relationship with plastic, we can improvise with something else that is flexible and strong. Bicycle inner tube is a favourite though a pair of stockings comes in a close second. The inner tube is easy to obtain – ask at any bike shop and they will be thrilled to unload any number of punctured specimens on you. Stockings can be obtained from most elderly relatives though it is perhaps best to wait until they have got out of them first (and have agreed to the change in use).

After running the inner tube around the stake and tree in your figure of eight, finish off by going round and round the waist several times to strengthen it as a spacer. Then stabilise the whole thing by putting a small tack through the end of the tie into the stake (not the tree).

Mulching

For the first three years it is reckoned that the soil around a tree should not have plants growing in it. That is either weeds or plants we've put in to jolly it all up. In practice, the first year is the most important, thereafter it depends on the vigour of the tree. Very dwarf specimens will need to be kept clear for their entire life. The reason why the tree is dwarfing in the first place is because the root system is so poor, hence it won't cope with the competition. More vigorous trees will need help to establish initially, but can then cope with surrounding vegetation.

One of the best ways of preventing weed growth is to cover the soil with some form of material, ranging from an organic matter to black plastic or landscape material. Obviously, it would be terrific to reduce the amount of plastic we are chucking around the place but organic matter isn't so effective by itself. The recommendation therefore is to combine a good sheet of thick, brown cardboard with some loose material like compost or woodchip.

The next decision is should the cardboard go down first or on top of the organic matter? It looks better if it goes down first and the compost etc. will hold it down. However, the cardboard will break down more quickly, and hence become less effective, if it is covered in lovely damp, nutrient-rich material. Is there no end to our dilemmas? Here are some options:

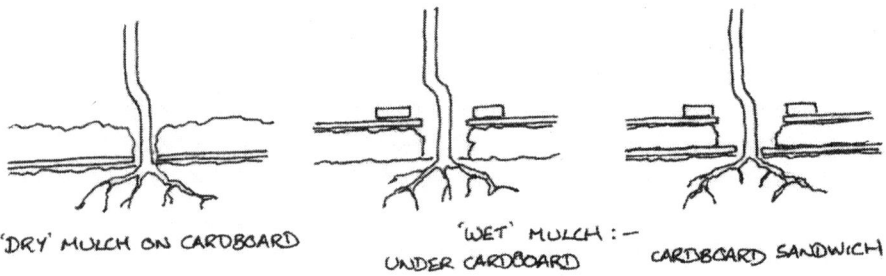

'DRY' MULCH ON CARDBOARD   'WET' MULCH :— UNDER CARDBOARD   CARDBOARD SANDWICH

A wet, mulch-like compost or manure should not be spread right up to the stem. It would be the same as planting it too deeply and the bark may rot or the top of the tree could root in over the graft. A gap of about 10cm (4") should be left all the way round the stem. A 'dry' mulch like woodchip or bark can go right up to the trunk.

FEEDING

The way we use fruit trees and bushes means they lose nutrients. These need replacing.

It's a not unreasonable question to ask what happens in nature, since animals are running off with fruit all the time. The possible answers include the fact that in nature, plants don't produce such big fruits so require fewer nutrients; feeding is more necessary for our (unnatural) selected and bred specimens. Also, in nature, some nutrients are returned to a plant by birds etcetera; it is fair to assume they will occasionally vacate their digestive systems around the time they are plundering a bush: manuring.

There is something else which is quite exciting that might provide an answer and that is mycorrhizal fungi. In any healthy soil, it has been said that most nutrients are in plentiful supply but just not necessarily in a form for plants to take up. These fungi, however, will be present in a natural situation, plugged into the root system of the plants to benefit from their sugars. In return, they supply nutrients, water and protection. For it to work, you need undisturbed healthy soil and no chemicals: in other words, a no-dig, organic system.

This is eminently achievable with a fruit area. For that reason, when it comes to the section 'Feeding' in the essentials of each of the fruits there is rarely a recommendation for large applications of nutrients. It is a different matter with fruit growing in containers where root systems are restricted and mycorrhizal fungi are likely to be absent.

The nutrients taken up by plants are as follows:
Nitrogen, Phosphorus, Potassium – lots.
Magnesium, Calcium, Sulphur – reasonable amounts.
Iron, Copper, Boron, Manganese, Molybdenum, Zinc, Chlorine – small amounts.

The top three are needed throughout the plant but also have particular roles: nitrogen promotes leaves and shoots, phosphorus promotes root growth and potassium encourages flowers, fruit and hardiness. We could use slightly more of one over the others to emphasise specific growth – it is common to use elevated levels of potassium on fruit plants simply because... we want fruit. Their chemical symbols, commonly found on the side of a box or bottle of fertiliser, are N:P:K in that order, with percentages following. For example, the fertiliser fish, blood and bone has the biblically amusing NPK analysis of 6:6:6 - the mark of the (ex-)beast.

The last seven nutrients are called trace or minor elements and despite being required in only tiny amounts, they are as essential as the others. If any of these nutrients are missing or levels in the soil are low then the plants will be vulnerable in the same way as we are to ailments if we don't have the right nutrition. Our food has gradually been depleted of vitamins and minerals over the past 60 or 70 years because we have concentrated on supplying only N, P and K through chemical fertilisers like Gromore, and destroying mycorrhizal associations. Hence the nutritional content in our fruit and vegetables have declined over the years.

To make our food healthy again, it is vital to ensure we supply all of the nutrients above, or enable them to be supplied, and the most obvious source for us is the compost heap. Compost, consisting mainly of decayed plant matter, should contain everything required: a complete range of nutrients.

Compost is the stuff of dreams – when well made it is the best organic matter available, providing much more than the nutrients. It contains beneficial fungi and bacteria that help plants in a number of ways. It is produced on site, though some of the ingredients may have come from elsewhere, and involves principally waste material. Recycling, soil inoculation, slow release nutrients, minimal transport: sustainability heaven.

COMPOST IS VERY VALUABLE

Other bulky organic matters such as manure, green waste (municipal) compost and fresh seaweed will come from off-site. As soon as that happens then there starts to be 'issues', not least because of the lack of control you have over their origins.

Manure is also decayed / processed plant matter like compost but it has added complications. These are:

- It is unlikely that we will generate any of our own in a back garden or allotment so it has to be bought in, involving cost and transport to your plot plus the barrowing involved with moving it.
- It will have been mixed with other material – bedding, like straw, woodchip or sawdust.
- It can be contaminated – it can contain chemicals, such as wormers in horse manure, which should be stacked and composted for at least six months before using. Farmyard manure may contain herbicides like aminopyralid despite first having passed through an animal: it can seriously affect your crops – beans and tomatoes seem especially sensitive.
- It might not have been broken down thoroughly: always ask for well-rotted manure and reject it – before it has been unloaded – if it isn't. You shouldn't be able to clearly identify the bedding material.

Green waste compost is, in some ways, an ideal product: lots of material previously destined to landfill is processed via a huge aerobic compost heap. Aerobic composting confers even more microbial properties than our anaerobic heaps chugging along in the back garden. Unfortunately, it is often contaminated. People have trouble distinguishing a rotten satsuma from a plastic bag when they are sorting out their recycling. Still, I'd happily settle for this than chemically contaminated manure.

Seaweed is a wonderful waste product. It has been broken away from its mooring by storms etc. and washed up on the beach. Remember to check with owners of the beach, often the local council, that it is acceptable to stroll down there and load up umpteen bin bags. Often they are pleased for you to help with the clean-up but sometimes some has to be left for little beach critters to feed on.

There is a significant difference between bulky organic matter and fertilisers. The latter are a concentrated source of nutrients providing little else other than that, whereas, as with composts, there are far greater benefits to using organic matter.

It might be, however, that on certain soils, an extra boost may be required from that concentrated form. Where fertilisers come from is one of the defining features of organic growing, and a simple guide is to only use one that originates from something that was once living. There are exceptions.

Sources of Nutrients from Fertilisers (in order of splendidity)
- Comfrey
- Wormery liquid
- Bodily wastes e.g. urine
- Nettles
- Wood ash
- Bought stuff

The reason for the top five being the top five is purely on sustainability grounds: they can (should?) be available on site and may involve recycling.

Comfrey and nettles can be cut and used fresh around plants or 'melted down' to produce a tea or a concentrate. Again, they provide a range of nutrients but are particularly useful for supplying nitrogen and potassium. What is exciting for those of us who get excited about such things is that you can grow these in amongst your fruit plants. Comfrey, specifically Russian comfrey *Symphytum x uplandicum* 'Bocking 14', is by far the better of the two since it brings up nutrients from way below the rooting zone of most fruit plants and has an excellent analysis: some nitrogen and elevated levels of potassium which encourages flowering and fruiting.

A **wormery**, being effectively a closed-in compost heap, leaks nutrient-rich liquid which can be collected. It is often, unfortunately, referred to as worm wee. The liquid from a 'normal' compost heap can also be collected but it is physically more awkward to do so. It is more of a general fertiliser and should be diluted by between ten to one and twenty to one.

Wood ash, from a woodburner or from a bonfire night conflagration, has lost some nutrients such as nitrogen and sulphur to the atmosphere (as well as a lot of carbon dioxide) but still has valuable levels of potassium (up to 12%). However, it also has lots of calcium (25-40%) which could raise the pH of the soil too much, so never use wood ash around blueberries and be careful using it on raspberries. The potassium itself can also cause deficiencies by displacing other nutrients from the soil, such as magnesium. Maybe it is safest to add wood ash 1) very sparingly, 2) only occasionally or 3) via a 'buffering' intermediary such as mixing it into the compost heap.

Our **bodies' wastes** are eminently suitable for fruit growing but worry a lot of people. Urine is the easiest and most acceptable but even that gets some folk worked up, it being variously termed 'disgusting', 'unnecessary' and 'smelly'. There is no denying the last one there, but that only indicates its potency: we can smell ammonia which just tells us that there is lots of nitrogen in wee (up to 11%).

With a fairly constant supply, whether we want there to be or not, it is a distinct case of changing a product requiring waste disposal into a valuable resource. Collect it, store it if necessary, dilute it to anything between 1:3 and 1:8, urine to water, and pour it on. Don't use it too frequently in the same place: how often depends on how much salt you have in your diet (the more you have, the less you should put on), how much rainfall there is (the more there is the more can be put on), soil type (heavier soils can take more urine solution), presence of a mulch, etc.

A compost toilet which allows you to collect everything would be ideal: the composting process neutralises any 'issues' and when it is applied as a mulch it is not in contact with any part that we eat. Most of us, especially in cities, are going to find it difficult to install and operate compost toilets, but we can at least widdle into a bucket or bottle and take it to the allotment.

Bought stuff is multitudinous and most of it fairly nasty – chemical, artificial and uses lots of energy in its manufacture. Chemical fertilisers also give the soil microbes a good bashing, but what does that matter?– if bacteria or fungi aren't able to help your plants anymore just bung a bit more fertiliser on the soil and spray pesticides on the plants because they are no longer protected… We have just described conventional agriculture in this country.

Some fertilisers you might want to buy include the following:
Seaweed meal or liquid – for centuries we have deposited our nutrient-rich sewage into the sea. Perhaps if we can recoup some of those nutrients sustainably it might reduce algal blooms and provide us with a terrific source of trace elements, much needed for our depleted food crops. The meal (dried, powdered seaweed) can be applied by sprinkling over the soil surface, a top dressing, perhaps in combination with a relatively low nutrient organic matter such as leaf mould. Seaweed liquid can be watered around a plant or sprayed over the whole thing when it is in leaf for a more instant effect. Nutrients in foliar feed, as the name suggests, can be absorbed via the leaves. Analysis: 2:0.3:2.7

Sewage pellets – cut out the middle seaweed and go straight for the origin of sea pollution. They are produced by water companies and are hard to get hold of. On top of that, they are not allowed in a certified organic system which I reckon is a big mistake; using sewage in a safe form completes a nutrient cycle of sorts: nutrients into plants, plants into us, nutrients out of us, nutrients into soil, nutrients into plants, etc. Analysis: 3.5:4.1:0.3

Rock dust – derived from quarry waste which is high in a wide range of minerals. This is one of the few fertilisers acceptable in a certified organic system which doesn't originate (directly) from living organisms. There are question marks over the speed of release, the quantities needed to have an effect and the cost to us and the environment of shifting such a heavy material. Still, if you live next door to a suitable quarry and your bike panniers are empty… Analysis varies enormously depending on the rock, but usually contains a wide range of micronurients.

Other rock products that are allowed include **rock phosphate** which is about as sustainable as the M4. It is quarried from islands and mainland South America leaving a devastated landscape and then shipped halfway round the world. Analysis: 'high phosphorus'.

Chicken pellets – made from the bedding and manure. So potent is the manure that it is applied in the small quantities defined as a fertiliser. Are you sure those pellets have come from an organic, free-range system or are you not quite so fastidious when it comes to that sort of thing if you're not actually eating the eggs or the chickens?

Animal fertilisers – various mixtures and combinations of animal body parts, dried and ground up: by-products of the meat industry. Depending on which bit has been reclaimed from the abattoir there will be a variety of nutrients supplied. For example, bonemeal analysis: 1.4:29:0.2 showing very high levels of phosphorus and hoof and horn analysis: 13:2:Trace, showing high nitrogen. There is fish, blood and bone and various other fish emulsions but, interestingly, dried blood by itself and in quantity is not allowed under organic certification because of the speed of release of nitrogen. This is one of the big reasons why artificial fertilisers should be avoided, unless one of your main aims in life is to cause stream eutrophication and fish genocide.

An interesting question for those choosing to grow organically who are also fine with using animal products is: like the chicken pellets, from what system of farming has that fish, blood and bone come? Is it certified organic or are you unwittingly supporting intensive, industrial animal farming?

There are commercial brands of organic fertiliser available, quite often mixtures of different materials, for example, chicken manure combined with sugar beet waste. The main thing is not to be blinded by the word 'organic' emblazoned on the front of the packet. Firstly, check the origin of the ingredients especially if you have concerns about the use of animals. Next, ensure that 'organic' means 'organic' – look for the symbol of a certifying body such as the Soil Association or Organic Farmers and Growers. Finally, look at the analysis, the letters N:P:K, as explained above. You need to know the concentration of the fertiliser – if the figures are very low, are you being cheated? You need to know the relative proportions, remembering that higher levels of one particular nutrient will promote particular growth in a plant – see at the beginning of the chapter if you've forgotten already. You need to know what else is in there, specifically if there are micronutrients / trace elements.

Gromore is a chemical fertiliser (really, don't use it) with a balanced N:P:K analysis of 7:7:7 but hardly anything else. Seaweed meal has a low N:P:K analysis yet is extremely valuable for all of the trace elements.

So, apart from avoiding the soil-unfriendly chemical fertilisers and choosing ones that are suitable in an organic system, perhaps, for the same reason that there is a strong movement away from the exploitation of animals for food, we should also avoid fertilisers derived from the meat and dairy industries.

Not all of your fruit plants need feeding. To help you decide whether to feed them, here are some questions (and answers) to clarify things:

Is it cropping?
Yes: it might be wise to replace the nutrients that have been used to nourish you.
No: perhaps ease up – one reason for some plants failing to produce fruit is that they've had too much fertiliser and are extremely happy just to grow big and not bother reproducing.

Do you prune it?
Yes: fruit wood, like the fruits themselves, contains some nutrients which might need replacing, particularly nitrogen. For example, raspberry canes are replaced each year.

Are there other plants growing close to the main stem(s)?
Yes: competition for the nutrients and water that are present can reduce cropping. This would include nearby trees, other fruit plants a trifle too close, ground cover plants and weeds. To compensate, higher levels of nutrients could be supplied.

Is it a strong-growing plant?

A vigorous plant may need little help searching for nutrients. For example, a fully-grown standard apple tree can have grass growing underneath or be in amongst other trees and shrubs in a border or forest garden, and require no inputs. A dwarfing apple tree (rootstock M27 or M9 perhaps) will not tolerate any competition – see previous question.

Is it a greedy plant?

Some plants thrive better in a rich soil which should be maintained as such.

How much should be applied?

It depends on the system of growing that you have chosen – see 'Growing Systems' for some rather wonderful alternatives. For example, it is essential to feed fruit plants in containers whereas you can get a way with just the occasional urination in a forest garden arrangement.

PRUNING AND TRAINING – TREE / TOP FRUIT
(for soft fruit, see individual fruit chapters)

1) Formative pruning (general)
2) Formative pruning of an open centre bush tree
3) Formative pruning of cordons
4) Formative pruning of espaliers
5) Formative pruning of fans
6) Maintenance or regulatory pruning (general)
7) Pruning established espaliers and cordons
8) Pruning established fans
9) Pruning dwarf pyramids
10) Pruning cuts
11) Climbing trees
12) Disposal of prunings
13) Festooning
14) Root Pruning and Bark-Ringing and Worse

The two main types of pruning are **formative pruning**, when the tree is young and it is being shaped and **regulatory** or **maintenance pruning**, when the tree is older and hopefully cropping.

Formative Pruning

Formative pruning means the pruning required at the beginning of a tree's life to form a particular shape and produce a strong framework. The framework is the key to a successful fruiting tree. You are setting up the structure and from it growth will be produced that bears the fruit. The formative pruning that is carried out is principally to stimulate strong vegetative growth so no flowers or fruit should be allowed during this period. There are a myriad of shapes to consider – some are here.

What happens if fruit is allowed to form during the formative stage? It is extremely tempting to allow the occasional fruit to grow 'just to see what it's like'. Or you just didn't notice it. There is a school of thought (one that perhaps should be in special measures or at least visited more frequently by Ofsted) that says this is great – this tiny tree is already producing, let's get what we can as soon as possible. Just be aware that the energy trapped by a tree by photosynthesis is divided up and developing fruit will demand a good proportion. In the formative pruning phase it might be more prudent to allow all of that energy to go into the production of shoots and get it established as soon as possible before cropping.

Formative Pruning of an Open Centre Bush Tree

The most common shape, perhaps because it is the most pleasing, is the wineglass shape: a stem of a particular length topped by a crown of branches forming a ring or cup. The middle is open. The size of this wineglass depends on the rootstock, so a vigorous rootstock would generate a tree with a longer stem and a bigger crown. Usually, the strongest rootstocks would give a standard tree and the technical definition of a standard tree is one that has a clear stem of 2m / about 7 feet. These rootstocks and slightly smaller ones could be formed into a half standard (clear stem of 1.5m / 5 feet) but many of us will be using the smallest rootstocks. In which case, the description is 'an open centre bush tree'. Whichever of these you choose, the formative pruning to create them is the same, it is just over a longer period for the bigger trees.

The basic principles are to halve new growth to an outward-facing bud and remove growth forming in the wrong place / direction. That's it.
Here it is in more detail:

In **Winter 1**, a one-year old tree (or 'maiden') is decapitated at the height where the crown is to form. For the open centre bush tree this will be in the region of 65-70cm / 27".

In **Winter 2**, the growth that has resulted from this topping is hopefully three or four even, strong shoots. Each of these is halved to an outward-facing bud. In practice, the shoots won't be even or there will only be two or five or whatever. Cut off a bit more than half of any shoots you need to include in the framework that you think are a little weak. More than 4? Remove the excess (usually the lowest). Only one? Start again. Only two? Halve as usual and pretend it is exactly how you wanted it.

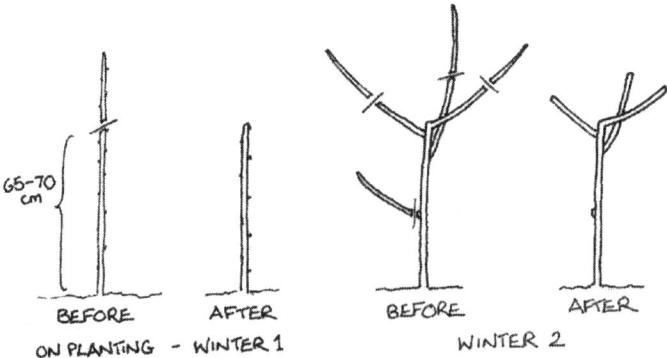

In **Winter 3**, repeat the process. For a very dwarf tree (one on apple rootstock M27 for example), this might be the last time you do any formative pruning because the tree will want to get on with fruiting. The more vigorous the rootstock the more formative pruning years there will be, up to six or eight years for an apple on MM111. Plums on 'Pixy' and pears on 'Quince C' should have three years, give or take.

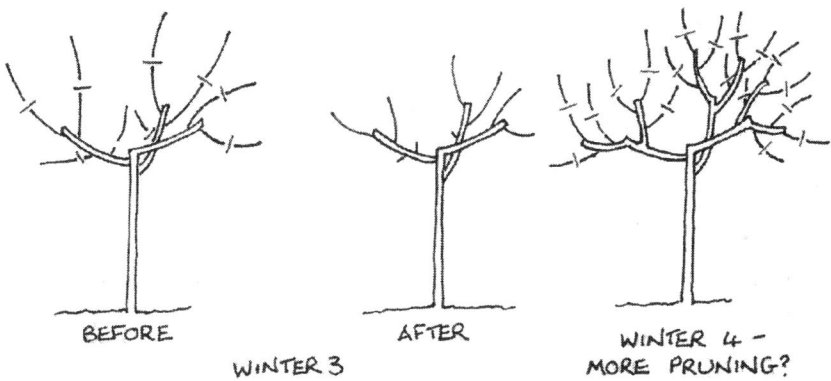

During formative pruning, young shoots will arise which are not required: either there are too many of them or they are in the wrong place. For example, they may point into the middle of a newly-shaped open centre bush tree. If they are left they will continue to grow and fill the space you are at pains to keep open. However, if they are simply pruned away, it will stimulate more growth in their place. The dilemma then is how to get rid of them without re-growth.

1) Leave it another year. Always a popular solution. An errant shoot will extend in length (curses) but fruit buds will develop towards the base of the shoot. When they have, the shoot can then be safely removed back to these buds which theoretically won't respond by sending out more vegetative growth but will settle down and produce flowers and fruit. In other words, you've got rid of the shoot and generated fruit spurs. The possible downside of this is the unreliability of fruit buds: will they form low down the shoot or be spread out or indeed appear at all?
2) Pull yourself together and take control: prune the shoot to three or four buds. As expected, this will stimulate re-growth (curses again) from the outer one or two of these buds. However, fruit buds should develop at the lowest one or two. A year after the first cut, return and remove the vegetative re-growth back to the fruit buds and, hurrah, we have a fruit spur system started and the young shoot has gone. If the tree is being awkward and no fruit buds have formed, prune off the whole thing and start again.
3) A combination of 1) and 2) is taken from Beeton's Shilling Book of Gardening pub.1873 '... break the young shoot near the third bud from the

main branch, leaving the broken part hanging down… middle of March. The broken part, while it droops, nevertheless draws up a portion of the wood sap. The following winter, when the buds are turned into blossom-buds and become fruitful, the hanging shoot should be neatly pruned away…'

4) Getting ever more apparently brutal, rip them off. This pulls off the shoot with its basal buds so it 'shouldn't' re-grow. This is a missed opportunity to form fruit spurs and can rip bark. It is a terrific technique for dealing with re-growth when established trees have limbs removed and when young shoots appear along the main trunk (water shoots), but is less friendly on a very young tree.

Formative Pruning of Cordon Trees

Cordons are trees planted and trained at 45 degrees against a wall, fence or on wires between posts. They are used for pears and apples and consist of a branchless stem clothed in fruiting spurs (wrinkled, knobbly bits). A cordon has to be one of the easiest shapes to create and maintain, easier than a free-standing tree in a way because we don't get so stressed by having to make decisions. Plus it's all done with secateurs. The aim is to prevent branches developing and, at the same time, promote fruiting spurs. This is done by removing any shoots already there (a 'feathered' tree) at planting by cutting back to three buds from the base of each shoot. From then onwards all pruning will be done around the end of August.

If you start by planting a maiden / whip / one-year-old tree / branchless stem, whatever you want to call it, then you don't even have this initial work, you simply start pruning in August.

New shoots that develop directly from the stem are cut back to three buds above the basal cluster – the basal cluster, not always present, are a few simple leaves, yes, clustered at the junction of new shoot and main stem.

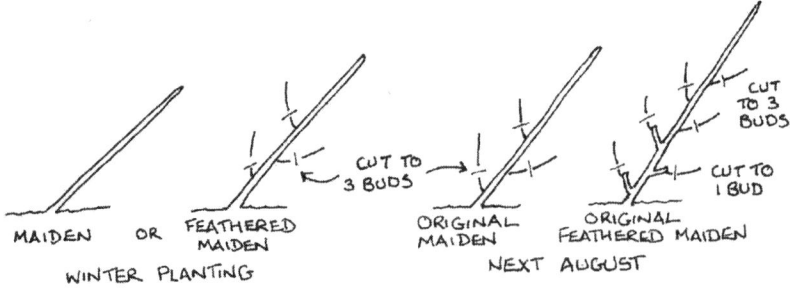

New shoots that develop from previously pruned shoots, not the main stem, are cut back to just one bud above the basal cluster. There would be none present in the first August starting with a maiden.

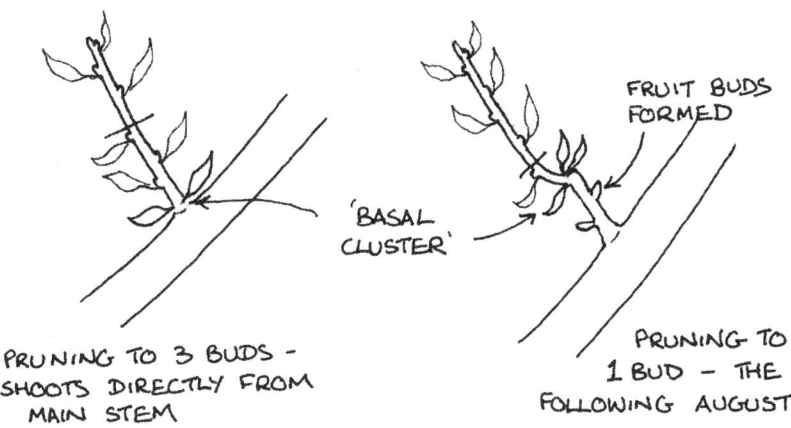

Leave the end of the main stem to grow unchecked, just tie it down to the cane as it extends. Now go to 'Pruning Established Espaliers and Cordons'.

Formative Pruning of Espalier Trees

For espaliers, the wires against a fence or wall, or between posts, are spaced about 45cm / 18" apart. Each wire will be used to train a tier of the espalier. Our newly planted tree, again hopefully a maiden if only because it is cheaper, will be cut to a bud at or just above the lowest wire.

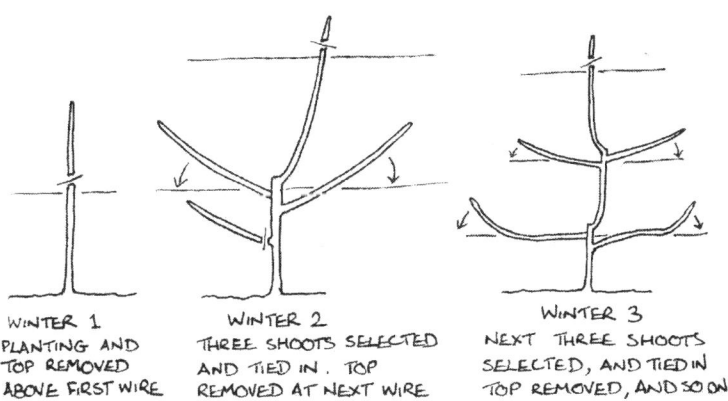

The response, ideally, is the growth of three strong shoots. More than this should be removed, to leave the top three. If these new shoots are already angled then the lower two can be tied down to the wire. If they are fairly upright they can be tied to a cane fixed at 45 degrees to be lowered further at a later date. You can also play around a bit with balancing the tree: if one of the two branches making up this first tier is a little weaker than the other then it can be held up at greater than 45 degrees for longer with the other, stronger arm being lower.

The third shoot is usually the top one and in the first winter after planting it would be pruned at or just above the next wire (presuming it has grown about 45cm / 18"). And the whole procedure starts again.

Following this annual routine, you'll see that one tier takes one year to create and if your espalier is to consist of four tiers, it'll take four years. Incidentally, four is a good number for a standard 1.8m / 6' wall or fence and it is easy to manage.

The final tier will be created as before and the third (uppermost) shoot removed. While all this framework formation has been happening, shoots have been trying to grow on the lower tiers, and these you deal with in exactly the same way as those that appear on cordons: cut to three buds above the basal cluster if they are growing directly from the main branches or to one bud if they growing from previous years' shortened shoots.

Formative Pruning of Fan Trees

Fans are used particularly for stone fruit (plums, cherries, etc.) and it is an opportunity to grow trees of a sensitive nature against a wall and so benefit from the protection and warmth, as with peaches, sweet cherries and apricots. The beginning of formative pruning is done in the early spring.

The starting point is as for espaliers, with a maiden tree being pruned back to a bud about 45cm / 18" above the ground or a feathered maiden cut back to two strong low branches, the lowest about 30cm / 1' above the ground.

The branches that grow from a maiden and the two chosen from a feathered maiden are tied to canes and pruned to 45cm / 18": the canes themselves are fixed to wires at 45 degrees. If there is an imbalance in the strength between the two shoots, the weaker one can be tied in slightly closer to vertical than 45° and the stronger one can be lower towards the horizontal.

The growth resulting from these two cuts will be thinned the following early

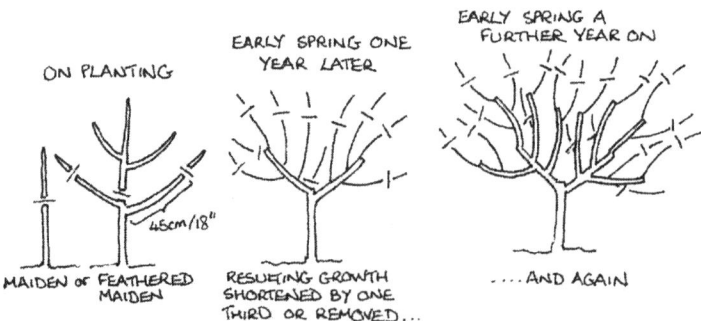

spring to leave two well-placed shoots on the upper side and one on the lower side of each shoot. Any other growth is removed. The new chosen pieces are also shortened by about a third. Once again there will be a reaction and new growth formed: select and tie in shoots to fill in as part of the framework and pinch out other growth (early summer).

The following early spring – this is the third year of formative pruning and hopefully the last – do the same again: shorten the newest framework shoots by a third. This time the shoots stimulated to grow as a result of this will be left to fruit, though they still need thinning: leave a spacing of 10-15cm / 4-6" between shoots and tie them in. Do this thinning by selecting misplaced shoots – those growing directly out from the framework or straight towards the wall / fence – and any crowded ones.

Maintenance or Regulatory Pruning
Introduction
Depending on the book (not this one), we are told that after pruning an established tree a pigeon ought to be able to fly straight through the canopy. Alternatively you should be able to throw your hat through it. It is extremely rare to see a pruned tree that would enable either of these momentous events to occur, but then we're not told about the type and size of hat (or pigeon). Maybe it is referring to the formative pruning stage when there are few branches. Or maybe it is simply trying to make us pay more attention and get those branches nicely spaced out. Maybe it is also saying we ought to practice throwing hats.

Regulatory or maintenance pruning usually involves a saw of some description. In fact there used to be a saying 'If you can prune it with secateurs you shouldn't be pruning it'. Maybe it was said by someone without secateurs or, even worse, someone who has coughed up £5 for an amazing pair of red-handled secateurs with lots of little cogs and nuts to play with: these will be fine to start with but will pack up at the first sign of serious use or when used on branches that really ought to be cut with a saw. It is a common sight to find a gardener with both hands on the secateurs, wiggling them backwards and forwards to force them through a too-thick branch. The cheap secateurs will resent this kind of abuse more than a more expensive 'professional' pair.

Before pruning an established, cropping tree an answer should be given to the question 'Why do I need to prune this tree?' Too often the answer is simply 'Because I'm supposed to'.

Here are some good (and less than good) reasons to prune a mature fruit tree:
1) To remove dead, diseased or damaged branches.
2) To maintain the shape created in formative pruning.
3) To give branches more space, air and light.
4) To remove crossing, touching or rubbing branches.
5) To stimulate new vegetative growth.
6) To renovate a tree.
7) To promote flowers and fruit.
8) To reduce the size of the tree.

Sorry about this but we need to look at these more closely, mainly because the starting point should perhaps be IF AT ALL POSSIBLE, DON'T PRUNE. If your tree is healthy and cropping well, year after year, why do anything? Most pruning will do Number 5 and as already discussed there is limited energy in a tree: too much pruning gives too much re-growth and this will be at the expense of the crop. Emphasis on the 'too much': moderate pruning has been shown in some varieties to increase the proportion of good-sized fruits, if not increase the total yield.

Let's go through the reasons in detail.
1) Dead and damaged branches are a natural thing to find in any tree and it should be able to cope with them. They are entry sites for diseases but then so is the cut surface you generate by pruning out these pieces. They are unsightly (good point) and may add to congestion. Your choice.

Diseased branches are a different matter – it depends on the type and extent of the disease. For example, it is probably best to remove a few shoots on an apple tree with canker to stop it being a source of further infection.

If there are lots of shoots on an apple with canker then the options are a) if it is still cropping, leave it, perhaps occasionally removing a large branch to keep it thinned out or b) remove the tree. The last option sounds a bit devastating and there are very few times when I'd recommend removing a tree but, really, what is the point of keeping a disease-ridden, infective tree that doesn't produce any fruit?

2), 3) and 4) are all different sides of the same coin, if, that is, coins had three sides. If branches in their intended position as part of a shape are evenly spaced they should have plenty of air and light and won't be touching.

5) This is the principle behind formative pruning. With a mature tree we don't want to stimulate a lot of new vegetative growth. However, as with 6), a tree

may become 'moribund' – it is old, congested and needs re-invigorating; the fruit may be poor quality and small. The idea in this case is simply a slightly more extreme version of 2, 3 and 4 again. If done well and sensitively this older tree can continue cropping and still become more active.

7) Pruning for fruit is a contradiction in terms for most trees since, as with 5), the opposite effect is normally achieved. However, it is possible to prune to give the opportunity for fruit to develop well. Only with trained trees like espaliers and cordons, and removal of misplaced shoots in formative pruning, is pruning carried out specifically to generate fruit spurs.

8) Pruning to restrict the size of a tree is the worst of all reasons since the size is dictated by rootstock and pruning to confine it is effectively an admission that the wrong choice was made initially. The difficulty with reducing the size of a tree is 5). The most common (and disastrous) approach is to shorten all of the branches: the end result is lots of new growth being stimulated at the ends of these branches. The overall impression is of a hedge on a stick, a suspended thicket, with no fruit and a lot of work to come to deal with it.

Reasons why your fruit tree might be the wrong size:
1) You inherited it from the previous, possibly incompetent, owners.
2) You planted a 'special offer' that didn't indicate either size or rootstock.
3) It specified the size but didn't say that this was reached in five years, with another 75 years of growth after that.
4) You got feet and metres mixed up.
5) You thought that M25 referred to a motorway.
6) Changes were made to the garden which meant that the tree was now too big for its position (sorry, that one is a bit sensible).

Whatever the reason, pruning a tree to restrict its size is not a good idea. This is because the tree will always want to be the too-large size, necessitating an annual cycle of the removal of much of the strong vegetative growth produced. The question that usually follows this explanation is something along the lines of 'So, what do I do about it, smarty pants?' Well, this is the exciting bit, because it involves something called judgement and imagination.

Standing well back from the tree, note the highest point. Follow it down into the crown of the tree and imagine what it would look like without the whole of that branch. Usually, if removed, it would open up the tree and take away several tall pieces in the process. Do it by following the directions of 'how to remove a large branch'. Look at the tree again and see if the next highest piece can be treated in the same way; sometimes it will be next to the branch just removed and it might therefore be best to leave it to avoid making too big a gap in the crown. Repeat the process taking out at least 3 large pieces, possibly more depending on the specimen – remember not to cut out more than 25-33% of the tree.

Reasons why this is a rather splendid technique are multitudinous. You would be making only three to, say, six cuts as opposed to the dozens / hundreds of little cuts made at the periphery. Because the cuts are made low down in the crown, the reaction from the tree should be less than at the ends, and any re-growth that does appear can be removed easily i.e. pulled off the following year. You also get usable timber – apple wood is especially good for both carving and firewood.

Possible downsides to this approach include the size of the cuts – they will take longer to heal – and the fact that you can't get the tree to the desired height in one pruning: it will possibly take three years or more. But then the technique scoffed at above, of cutting off all of the re-growth, would be every year anyway.

Some trees produce fruit at the ends of young growth – these are called 'tip bearers' – and if the above approach is used they will be unaffected. If you have a pruning system which involves snipping off all of the young growth then there will be a problem. For that reason, perhaps don't grow tip bearers as espaliers or cordons.

Pruning Established Espaliers and Cordons

This is a continuation of the formative pruning since it begins when the first tier of an espalier has been formed and the lower part of a cordon has developed. It is worth repeating:

Any brand new shoots coming directly off the framework are cut back, at the end of August, to three buds.

Any brand new shoots coming off the three-bud stumps created the previous year(s) are cut back at the same time to one bud.

When the frameworks are complete nearly all pruning will be the one-bud version. The ends of horizontal branches (espaliers) or the main stem (cordons) are cut back to one of these developing spur systems at around the desired length.

When an established trained tree has been producing for a few years, the gaps between the tiers of an espalier and between the trunks of adjacent cordons get filled in: the fruit spurs have built up gradually year on year.

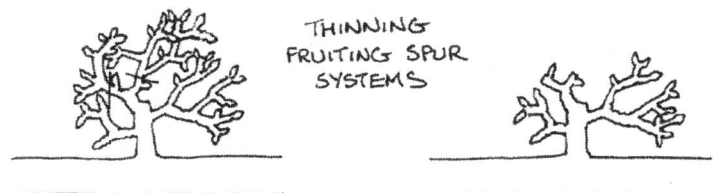

This is to be expected since, each year, with pruning that always leaves a short stub, miniature branching shrub-like structures of fruit spurs – spur systems – will develop. The usual recommendation is to reduce this spur system in the winter to maintain the spacing between framework branches. This will, of course, reduce the number of fruits that form but this is partly the aim, since too many apples, pears etc. on a highly restricted framework will mean that they will usually be smaller. There will also be a reduced air flow between the branches, already a potential issue if the plant is growing against a wall or fence.

All formative pruning will have finished ages ago so no other winter pruning will be taking place with these trees. There is therefore a case to be made for reducing non-fruiting spur systems at the same time – or instead of – the usual one-bud pruning at the end of summer. Why carry out the usual snipping in August and then cut again in winter, removing parts already pruned?

Pruning Established Fans

Most fans are stone fruit but it is not all plain sailing: in one port are plums, apricots and sweet cherries and in another are peaches and acid cherries. They are so divided because the former produce fruit on the older wood and at the base of new wood, so requiring only a gradual renewal of branches. Let's call these '**Group A**'.

Peaches and acid cherries fruit on new growth produced the same year; it makes sense to use a regime that promotes plenty of new growth each year. Perhaps we ought to call these '**Group B**'.

Group A – If fruit is produced on old wood and at the base of new growth, pruning focuses on i) keeping plenty of space between fixed branches, ii) controlling the amount of growth left to grow fully as replacement branches for the existing framework (not much), iii) removal of most of the new growth (subject to ii) to leave the fruiting part at the base of each shoot.

In practice this can be pretty complicated and time consuming. Let's see if we can understand it then decide whether it's worth doing.

Looking at just part of a branch of the fan framework, let's suppose eight new shoots appear. None of them are needed to replace that branch soon. There are too many for the space so, for the sake of argument, four are removed completely as soon as they appear in spring (they can be pinched out) – choose those that are badly placed including close to existing shoots, each other or heading towards the fence or wall. The remaining four should be nicely spaced at no closer than 10cm / 4".

Fruit is going to be produced at the base of these four shoots (and on older branches) but they can be too long, causing crowding, so pruning number two is done in June, shortening them to six leaves. As soon as the fruit has been picked, the shoots are cut back further to three buds (= pruning number three). We are left with a neat, open framework ready to start again next year.

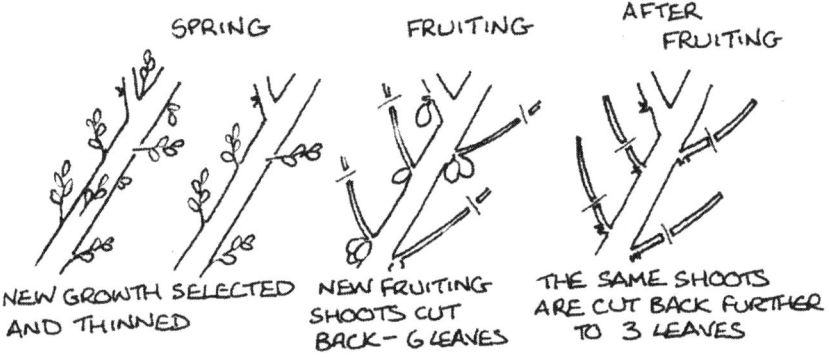

But it has taken three visits to prune.

An alternative is to leave all of the new growth until after fruiting when four are removed completely and the remainder are reduced to three buds. The compromise is that, up until then, there has been lots of congestion, the fruit was perhaps hidden and there has been lots of energy put into growth not required. Still, it was just one uncomplicated visit.....

Group B – These species, peaches and acid cherries, fruit only on the growth produced the previous summer. It's a good idea therefore not to (try to) prune away the this growth as with group A otherwise there will be no fruit next year, but to have a more regular turnover of branches ensuring new growth is stimulated.

That doesn't mean everything is left to grow and then big lumps cut out with new growth at their base tied in to replace them. Though it's not far off. In spring, there will be last year's shoots ready to flower (and fruit) and new growth starting at its base. Thin this new growth to one shoot using the fingers. The remaining shoot will be left until its older neighbour has finished fruiting (late summer?) when the latter will be pruned out and the former tied into its place. That's it.

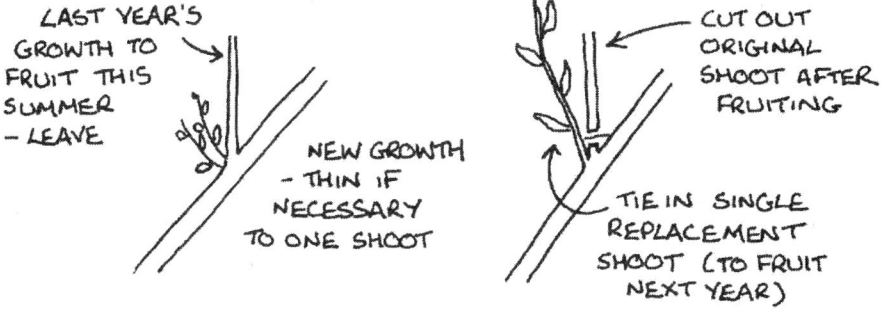

Pruning Established Dwarf Pyramids
This a narrow tree with close-to-horizontal branches, allowing closer planting than with other forms. The good news is that it can be considered in exactly the same way as espaliers and cordons with just late summer new shoot pruning with perhaps some winter spur pruning later.

Pruning Cuts
The first technique doesn't actually involve a cut but is the way to dispose of young shoots known as water shoots. These have arisen on main branches often as the result of letting in more light or they grow around a large pruning wound. It simply involves a quick tug and removes the shoot complete with basal buds, helping to prevent re-growth. Some are easier to pull away than others but it should be done only with the most recent growth.

All of the following should be accompanied by the chanting of the mantra 'Always prune to something'. When formatively pruning, the cut will be mainly made to a bud. Other pruning will be done back to a main branch or to a side shoot. Whatever it is, it is still to something. The only time when it doesn't seem to matter is when pruning raspberries.

Secateur Cuts
Formative pruning requires secateurs work. Cuts are made at a slight angle / straight across, immediately above a bud. It used to be said that pruning cuts should be made at an angle (30-45°?) down back away from the bud so that

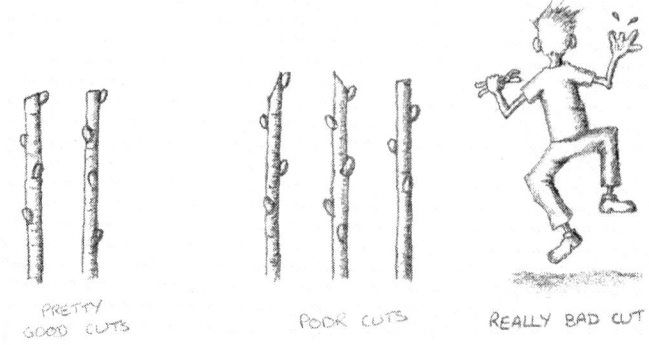

water doesn't stay on the cut end or gather behind the bud and rot it. Since it has been shown that less than 5% of shoots on a plant are close to vertical, it becomes more important to make a cut with the smallest surface area: most shoots will naturally shed the water.

So why have any angle at all? A slight tilt enables you to get closer to the bud without damaging it. In practice, with lots of cuts to make, it is more of a case of doing as best as possible as quickly as possible. With formative pruning and the preparation of cuttings, it is worth spending a little more time. The first cut to be made to a maiden tree at the beginning of shaping, is to remove the top off a vertical stem, so it should be done at an angle.

The removal of larger pieces

This is when it gets exciting.

Firstly, let's cover what you're supposed to do. You should make four cuts to remove a branch. The first is an undercut 30-60cm away from the final position, about a quarter of the way through. The second cut is made just 'upstream' of this so that the branch drops off – you have just removed the weight. You don't need to worry about the quality of these cuts. Cuts three and four are the same except they are at the desired point of removal and will be better quality in that the fourth (down) cut should meet the third (undercut). The undercuts are done to stop any ripping downwards under the weight of a piece of wood. The biggest problem is getting cuts three and four to meet up cleanly. For that reason it might be worth employing a little improvisation.

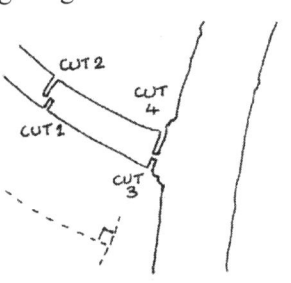

CUTS 1 + 2 REMOVE WEIGHT
CUTS 3 + 4 ARE OUTSIDE THE COLLAR (WRINKLED BIT) AND AT RIGHT ANGLES TO THE BRANCH

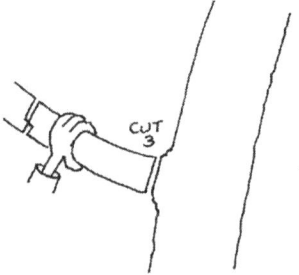

IMPROVISED VERSION – ONE FINAL CLEAN CUT MADE WITH BRANCH SUPPORTED

It is best to still carry out cuts one and two but a smoother finish to the final cut is a lot easier if it is done in one operation. In other words miss out cut three, the second undercut. We can only do this if we are supporting the stump with the non-saw hand. In fact, we can cut off some branches with just one cut if we are able to support the branch – this is definitely quicker and takes less work.

The only possible problem with this lazy approach is if you are in the canopy of a tree (see 'Climbing', below) when, momentarily, your non-saw hand will no longer be supporting you – it will be clutching a detached lump of wood.

When emerging from the final cut, especially if it is being done in one go, slow down and gently move the saw to finish off so that a rough edge or ripped bark is not left on exit.

The position of the final cut is slightly tricky. It should be made, not flush with the trunk as one feels it should be, but approximately at right angles to the line of the piece being removed. Often there are lines circling the branch, helpfully provided by the tree to guide us. The cut should be on the outside of the wrinkled collar often (but not always) found at the base of the branch: this is where healing tissue will regenerate and eventually cover the cut.

A narrowly-forked branch may mean that even a very thin, tapering pruning saw can't fit in to make that final downward cut, so everything has to be done from a single upward cut. If so, the piece being removed should be eased upwards to stop it closing on the blade as you cut.

Climbing Trees
The climbing of trees is essential for all children up to retirement age. Beyond that, only do it if you feel comfortable and your creaking joints allow. My creaking joints aren't given much choice, but the reasons for immersing oneself in the deep end of a pool of foliage are manifold.

First and foremost is the view; rarely does one have the opportunity to see neighbouring gardens, streets and beyond from this angle. If it is shady at ground level, it may be beautifully sunny high up in the canopy. It is on a par with giving a trunk a good hug, and gives such a feeling of elation that I'm surprised tree houses aren't mainstream accommodation. Climbing trees also enables you to prune a tree better than by using cutting equipment attached to the end of a pole.

The key piece of advice is to maintain a three-point linkage at all times. This normally refers to implements attached to the back of a tractor but applies equally well here. It means that we have (normally) two feet and two hands and only one of those four is allowed to not be in firm contact with the tree at any one time. Therefore, one hand – it is usually a hand, feet having poorer gripping skills – is available to hold and use a saw. When climbing, feet will successively leave their anchorage but each time the hands will be completing the three-point connection, as when climbing a ladder. It is for this reason that loppers (requiring two hands) are to be discouraged, apart from usually not being big enough for the branches needing removing.

Disposal of Prunings

The following are some options of what to do with all of the prunings generated, some of them more useful than others.

Re-use Them: Pea sticks, plant supports. Branching pieces interlock and give lots of twining tendril options. Stick them in before the plants have emerged, whether they be pea seedlings or the new shoots of an herbaceous plant. Short sturdy pieces are essential as row markers.

Make Something With Them: Small forked pieces can be fashioned as pegs to hold down netting, larger pieces for whittling. Don't know how to whittle? Large sheet of plastic or newspapers on the lounge floor and a very sharp knife. Pop on some rather lovely music and arrange for some stimulating company and you have the most perfect evening possible still keeping your clothes on. Making spoons seems to be the most popular woodcarving – easier than a fork.

Wildlife Habitat: Make a distinct heap – there is nothing more annoying than coming across loose twigs hidden in the long grass that you're trying to cut with shears. Actually, that's not true: there are many things more annoying – I meet some on a regular basis. The habitat heap will gradually decay but that will simply increase the range of creatures attracted to it. Hedgehogs love to hibernate in piles of branches, hence the November the fifth pleas to avoid construction until the last moment: it wouldn't be roast hedgehog, it would be incinerated hedgehog. Slowworms and a variety of beetles, all using slugs as a major food source, would be encouraged.

Recycle Them: In very small pieces, they make a good compost additive – long term compost, that is. It has been recommended that the size of individual pieces should be no larger than 7.5cm (3"). However, it depends on the thickness of the prunings: maybe a very general rule of thumb should be that this covers pieces that can be cut comfortably with a pair of secateurs. That then brings into play the quality of your secateurs and hand and arm muscles. Maybe we're getting a little bogged down here: use pieces as small as possible. Shredders of course do the trick but we're in the realm of expensive, rarely-used machinery and fossil fuels, but then if you have a car and drive regularly, you're not going to be worried by a little more noise and pollution.

Burn Them: Not on the archetypal, carcinogenic-smoke-producing, neighbour-annoying allotment bonfire, but the now-very-popular double or triple burn wood burning stove. The double / triple bit means the stove is more efficient and produces fewer emissions. Indeed it is the only legal type to use in cities. Result? You are warmer. You have wood ash still with some nutrients – they haven't all disappeared up the chimney. You have disposed of the prunings. A triumph.

Festooning

Simply put, which makes a change, vertical branches tend to dominate. They receive an unrestricted flow of sap from the roots and will continue to grow vigorously upwards given the chance. Probably unconsciously, we carry out the principles behind festooning in lots of trees: when we train them, whether it is against a wall / on wires or free-standing, we tend to select and prune for branches that are angled and even horizontal. These lowered branches have the sap restricted and this, apparently, puts them under a slight stress, enough to encourage the forming of fruit buds. It also makes it easier to reach the fruit. This is why espalier, fan and cordon trees are so productive.

Festooning is the rather lovely name given to the same process on free-standing trees but without pruning. In other words, vigorous upright shoots are brought towards the horizontal by being lassoed and tied down. If these shoots were cut off, they would simply re-grow replacing the original with umpteen more vigorous vertical shoots. Between 30° and 45° to the horizontal is nice. Another benefit of festooning is that the shoot can be eased into a particular position in the canopy, filling a gap or balancing a tree.

THE PERILS OF FESTOONING

The rope / strong string strung from a branch should have a bit of padding (more recycled bicycle inner tube?) on the branch to stop it digging in and would normally be attached at the other end to a small angled stake in the ground. An alternative, one that perhaps lends itself more to the name of festooning ('decorated', 'draped with', etc.) is to hang a weight from the branch. The easiest version is a small net bag filled with stones; they can be gradually added to the bag to achieve the desired bending. Or a plastic bottle topped up with water. This also makes the grower more 'present' or mindful when moving amongst the trees – a faceful of rocks is an instant remedy to a reverie. Whichever method is used, it will be necessary to adjust the position of the string on the branch and to check that it won't move. It is easy for the branch to bend too far or not enough. Check it regularly especially after windy weather – one season should be long enough to set a branch in its new position.

Occasionally, particularly if the festooning works and fruit is produced, the weight of the fruit will take the branch down even further and you end up putting a prop underneath the branch.

Root Pruning and Bark-Ringing and Worse

There is a hint of desperation when it comes to root pruning. It indicates that a tree is either too vigorous or not cropping or both. This is usually the result of too vigorous a rootstock – the tree is out-growing its space and, as described above, pruning the branches can make the matter worse. It can also be caused by the fertility of the soil, in particular high nitrogen levels which stimulate leaf and shoot growth over reproductive growth.

THE EFFORT OF ROOT PRUNING

THE WORRY OF BARK-RINGING

In the dormant season, a circle around the tree is marked out at the periphery of the canopy and a trench, 30-45cm/1-1½' wide by 60cm/2' deep, dug outside this limit. That's a lot of work. Any thick roots are cut through in the process

If we have to go to the trouble of digging trenches and hacking through roots to get the message over to an uncooperative tree then it feels as though something went wrong somewhere along the way.

It seems that in the past, root pruning was a matter of course. In the 'Gardener's Chronicle' 13th October 1881, E.W. asks "I have a splendid young Apple tree which has made a wonderful lot of wood. When is the proper time to prune the roots? and how?" The answer was [Lift the tree carefully; then cut back to at least half their length all the strong roots. Be careful not to injure the fibrous roots. Plant again at once.]

I don't want to contradict our ancestors but if a young tree needed pushing into fruit production, perhaps try festooning first.

Not for stone fruit, another way of stressing a plant into fruiting is to perform 'bark-ringing', which is as worrying as root-pruning.

A narrow strip of bark is removed from the reluctant tree about 3mm/1/8" for small trees, 1.5cm / ½" wide for large trees. It is at waist high, around the trunk and is normally a complete circle. If you are too stressed by this either don't do it or cut two staggered semi circles in the bark instead (*see picture*). Cover the wounds with tape until they heal. If this bark removal is excessive or you are just unlucky, it won't heal and resources travelling down the tree, from the leaves to the roots, will be interrupted for too long and the roots will die followed rapidly by the tree itself. That'll teach it not to fruit when it's asked.

There is yet a third way to force a tree to fruit, possibly even more brutal than the previous methods. It is illustrated by a little story:

There was once a row of apple trees. They were growing in some lovely soil and were very happy. But the gardener was not so happy: they had never fruited. He'd given them a chance and they were way past the age when they should have fruited and he had grown impatient. Growing grass underneath, supplying no extra food and even talking to them – nothing worked. The gardener borrowed a tractor and using some chains lassoed, one by one, the main branches. He pulled on each branch until they cracked and lay more horizontal. To the visitor, this was nightmarish and they were wondering when the tornado had passed through. The end result, the following year, was a full crop of fruit.
See, a happy(ish) ending.

The moving of the branches, despite being of a good size, towards the horizontal – as with festooning – combined with the partial breaking, forced the trees to reconsider their lax lifestyle and desperately shift into reproductive mode. On top of that, no infection has got into the breaks so far which, presumably, trees are more adapted to than neat pruning cuts.

I'm not saying anything.

POLLINATION

Most soft fruit and a small number of top (tree) fruit varieties are self fertile. See individual fruits. This is great for us since we don't need to consider mixing varieties. Pollination of a raspberry flower, for example, could be by an insect moving between flowers on the same plant, on other plants in the same row or between flowers on nearby rows of raspberries. It doesn't matter to us unless we wanted to grow raspberries from seed, which not many of us with a full complement of grey matter will ever do. The top fruit that are self fertile will produce fruit all by themselves, which is also splendid if you only have room for one tree and there aren't others nearby. However, the yield is lower than if you had a different variety nearby (see under pollination solutions below). Most top fruit requires cross pollination. This is significant to us for the following reasons:

We need two *different* varieties of the same fruit. For example, Apple 'Sunset' and Apple 'James Grieve'. A crab apple may work but a pear would be no use. A pear pollinates a pear and so on. Emphasis there is on 'different': every Apple 'Cox's Orange Pippin', for example, is effectively the same tree – it has been cloned ever since the original tree was grown from a pip. If a tree rejects its own pollen then it will reject the pollen from other clones of itself.

The two varieties should flower as close to the same time as possible. See 'Flowering Groups' below.

The two varieties should not be too closely related. If they are, they may be incompatible, meaning their pollen is useless to each other. Unless you are fairly familiar with fruit tree genealogy you are unlikely to know this. However, each type of fruit has 'incompatibility groups' which should be quoted on a label. For more on this (it's incredibly fascinating) have a look at 'Incompatibility' later in the chapter.

If one of your trees (and you only have two) is biennial – it only produces fruit every other year – it may mean that there is no pollen for the other tree on the 'off' year, so that won't produce any fruit either.

Be aware if one of your two trees is a *triploid*. This is a genetic thing and is just a bit irritating. If a fruit tree is a triploid (it should say in the books or at least on the labels) then it won't pollinate any other tree.

A Diversion into Diversity
Plants reproduce sexually by transferring genetic material between individuals in the form of pollen. Pollen is analogous to sperm in animals, though has added features to allow for the fact that it is blown by wind or carried by creatures. Sexual reproduction is a way of mixing up genetic material so ensuring that there is a greater chance of survival when environmental changes occur. A good example of this is the elm and the ash. The elm had far reduced genetic diversity – many trees in hedgerows were clones of each other via suckers – meaning it was less able to resist Dutch elm disease. The end result is that there are virtually no mature elms left in the UK. Ash dieback is currently sweeping the country but because ash produces seed readily, by sexual reproduction, of course, there is great hope for resistant versions to be present in the existing population. This doesn't mean that there won't be carnage in the meantime, but does mean there is hope.

For plants that are self-fertile there is reduced genetic mixing: not good news for them in the long term, but good news for us since that is one less thing to have to worry about with our fruit. Those that require cross pollination are very sensible but, blimey, it can get complicated for us. Here is some more detail:

The Botany of Pollination
Unless a plant is self-fertile when the pollen may drop from the anthers to the stigma in the same flower, the pollen has to move from a flower on one plant to the stigma in a flower of a different plant. There is a wonderful range of insects prepared to help themselves to pollen and nectar so transferring pollen between plants. It includes beetles, hoverflies, flies and even wasps. By far the most useful are bees and of them it is the solitary bees and bumble bees which are the most efficient, mainly because they work harder. They operate in colder weather meaning they are more active throughout the year and they get out of bed earlier in the day. Apparently, bumble bees are not the cold-blooded creatures that insects are classified as: they are able to raise their own body temperature. Hence they are able to operate in quite chilly conditions.

Bumble bees will also range indiscriminately through an orchard. Honey bees may make up for their slack attitude by increased numbers – a colony may consist of thousands of individuals, and as long as that hive isn't too far away…

A bee can travel for over 6 miles / 10km according to Dave Goulson in his excellent book 'A Sting in the Tail', but this is to reach a tree, for example, and it is not wise to expect the poor thing to go backwards and forwards between two such widely-spaced specimens just because you need them pollinated. Two miles / 3km is pushing it for to-ing and fro-ing. It follows therefore, that to get the best cross-pollination, the two plants should be as close as possible without competing with each other for resources like water, nutrients and light.

Pollen is transferred, by accident as far as our insect is concerned, to the stigma – the receptive, sticky top part of the female flower part called the carpel or pistil – in a flower on another tree. Pollen can go from this flower in the reverse direction.

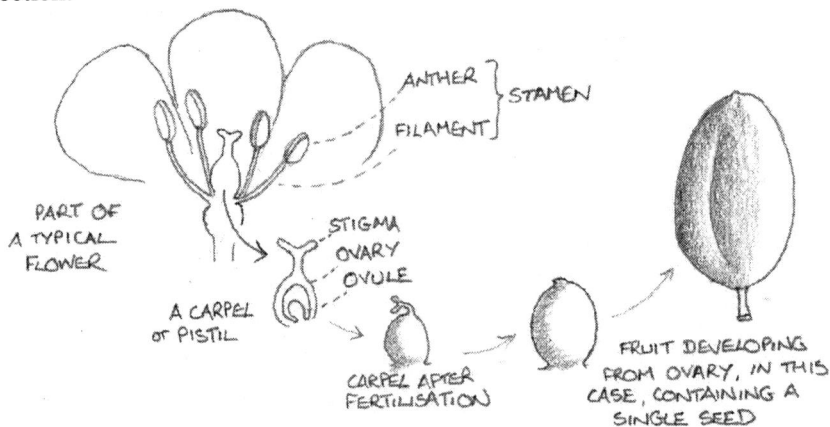

The pollen germinates and grows down towards the egg cell housed in a structure called the ovule. The ovule, following fertilisation, will become the seed and the housing (the ovary) becomes the fruit. The pictures above suggest a fruit like a plum – a single-seeded true fruit called, technically, a drupe. There may be more than one ovule in an ovary so producing a multi-seeded fruit such as a kiwi (a 'berry') – each ovule will need a separate pollen grain. There may be more than one carpel, each with an ovary, in a flower so producing a collection of little fruits ('drupelets') such as with the compound fruit of a blackberry.

There are lots of other variations.

Attracting Pollinators

The best way to ensure you have enough pollinating insects is to follow the three step approach:

1) **Provide food** for them as much of the year as possible, not just around the time you want them there to cross-pollinate your plants. The types of plant to use are early (e.g. goat willow) and late-flowering (e.g. ivy) plants plus some to fill the summer dearth. Avoid 'double' flowers (complicated, pom pom –like things which are often sterile and produce no pollen or nectar). Clovers are very valuable because the pollen has a high protein content: if you weren't aware,

bees collect both nectar and pollen to eat, and plants are okay about this as long as some of the pollen makes it to the right place – the stigma.

There is a conflict of opinion regarding providing bee-friendly plants that flower *at the same time* as the fruit trees. Some will say that this brings in more insects, some of which will also do the fruit tree pollinating – as mentioned, bumble bees, defying the laws of physics, seem to bumble around the place and are indiscriminate. Other authorities on the subject suggest the opposite, saying that the trees themselves will be the attraction and other flowering plants will simply divert the insects away. For example, MAFF as was, in 1980 recommended that 'flowering weeds such as dandelions should be mown off as bees may work them rather than the fruit blossom'. It would be a great shame to turn an orchard into a fruit-blossom 'monoculture'.

2) **Provide housing**. This will vary depending on the pollinating insects. Bumbles bees and many solitary bees for example nest in the ground and are partial to an undisturbed bank or hedgerow with leaf litter around. Bee hotels, consisting of boxes with a collection of hollow tubes inserted, can be used. A bee may lay a series of eggs in separate chambers within a single tube, cleverly sequenced so that that those laid last (nearest the exit) will be the first to leave. Before doing so, they will have of course first hatched, fed as a larva (grub) on their store of pollen provided by mum before pupating as an adult. Those emerging first are males.

3) **Don't kill them**. Insecticides kill insects – it is their raison d'etre. If you use insecticides, expect to kill insects which you didn't intend to kill. It is important in the timing as it can be done directly when the pollinating insects 'get in the way'. Some books recommend spraying pesticides in the evening when pollinators are less active – except that, on hot days, bumble bees will choose evenings to be active. Or it is cumulative where they pick up traces as they go about their business, enough to affect their functioning or even kill them. The execrable neonicotinoids of the early 21st century were the DDT of their time causing untold collateral damage to bees. They can disrupt bumble bee flight patterns, navigation and reproduction in incredibly tiny doses. Thanks to Dave Goulson, among many others, for his experimenting and campaigning.

Anybody still using these chemicals, or wanting to, after all of the damning evidence should be removed from public office and strapped, clad only in their underwear, to a honey bee hive. On second thoughts, they'd probably enjoy it.

Apart from ensuring that we have the vectors of transfer (a posh / unnecessary way of saying pollinating insects) we need to examine all the techniques that enable it to go swimmingly.

Pollination Solutions

1) Plant another tree; a different variety that flowers at the same time, as mentioned above. This is a rather splendid idea, a stage better than planting just one tree in the first place.
2) See if there is a neighbouring tree already there that flowers at the same time. Often, in built up areas, there is no need to worry about cross pollination since there are likely to be dozens of nearby fruit trees in back gardens.
3) Get a self-fertile tree – there are some quite famous trees: Pear 'Conference', Cherry 'Morello' and Plum 'Victoria' for example. There are very few self-fertile apples but there are one or two that purport to, like a version of 'Cox's Orange Pippin', cunningly called 'Self Fertile Cox'. There is a reasonable number that are 'partially' self-fertile. All of these produce fruit just by themselves but will still actually crop better if there is a pollinator tree nearby.
4) A family tree. Virtually all fruit trees are grafted (See 'Propagation') – the chosen variety is fused onto a chosen rootstock. Well, why not graft more than one variety on a single rootstock? The different varieties can pollinate each other providing, as before, they flower at the same time. Result? A single tree pollinating within itself and producing more than one variety of fruit. When these are bought, they often have three varieties together and are called a family tree.
5) Graft a pollinator on to a branch of an existing tree. This is a cobbled together version of a family tree but is worth giving it a go if you're desperate. When it has been clearly shown that the absence of a nearby pollinating tree is responsible for the lack of fruit, and there is no room to plant one, a new variety can be selected and a piece stuck on a clearly labelled and well-positioned branch, a.k.a. carefully grafted.

Flowering Groups

A big point has been made of the fact that, for cross pollination to take place, the participants must flower at the same time. To help you with this, varieties are grouped according to their flowering time. Depending on the source to which you refer, for apples there may be six or seven flowering groups.

Flowering continues for anything between one and three weeks with the peak / full flowering around the middle of that range. An apple example might be 'Discovery' with an average start date of the 6th of May, peak flower at the 11th of May and the end of flowering on the 18th of May; the actual times depend on the particular season and can vary year to year by as much as a month.

Group 1 would normally start flowering in April. There will always be an overlap between adjacent groups so you could choose one tree from Group 2, for example, to go with a tree from Group 3. Of course, best of all would be from the same group where flowering of both trees will be pretty much at exactly the same time.

Apples (for example)
Group 1 (early):   'Gravenstein'
Group 2:   'Egremont Russet', 'Idared', 'Lord Lamborne'
Group 3:   'Bramley's Seedling', 'Falstaff', 'Fiesta', 'James Grieve', 'Sunset', 'Worcester Pearmain'
Group 4:   'Ashmead's Kernal', 'Ellison's Orange', 'Winston'
Group 5:   'King of the Pippins', 'Newton Wonder', 'Suntan'
Group 6:   'Laxton's Royalty'
Group 7 (late):   'Crawley Beauty'

Pears, Plums and Cherries, in most literature, have been divided into five groups: 1 = early, 5 = late. In practice, nearly all varieties are in groups 2, 3 or 4, perhaps unhelpfully referred to as 'mid-season', unhelpfully since a '2' won't exchange pollen with a '4'.

Another point worthy of note is the length of time a flower 'lasts': how long from the moment of opening that it is receptive to pollen and a fruitlet will result. For many apples it is five to six days whilst for Pear 'Doyenné du Comice' it is only a couple of days at most. This means that some fruit trees could be affected by a spell of bad weather more than others. Fruit set also depends on other factors including the resistance of the blossom to cold, wet, etcetera, the variety itself and the amount of blossom.

Oh dear. There are a number of other issues to deal with involving pollination as promised at the beginning.

Incompatibility
Strangely, this seems to be more of a problem with pears, plums and cherries than

apples and others. Let us take the example of Pears: we could have Pear 'Doyenné du Comice' and Pear 'Onward' growing side by side. If there are no other pears around, there will be no fruit on either tree despite them flowering at the same time. These are termed 'incompatible' and will be in the same Incompatibility Group along with 'Packham's Triumph' and several others. Incompatibility groups exist for plums and cherries, too (see lists at the end of this bit).

The question lingering like an unfortunate odour is 'why?'. Let us open a horticultural window. The reason 'D.D.Comice' doesn't pollinate itself is because it has a chemical mechanism to reject its own pollen. If a variety has been bred from 'Comice' (as 'Onward' has) that same mechanism may have been inherited and they will therefore reject each other's pollen – they are too closely related. Exchanging sex cells with a close relative is never a good idea. So now you have to look out for varieties that not only flower at the same time but are compatible. It is a little mystery why apples don't join in with this complication in a major way: the many offspring of 'Cox's Orange Pippin' for example still seem to cross pollinate. The best known exemption to this is Apple 'Kidds Orange Red' which, being a parent of Apple 'Cox's Orange Pippin', means they won't pollinate each other.

Here are some useful incompatibility groups. There are plenty more varieties which can fit into these groups but they will be quite unusual / rare:

Pears:
Incompatibility Group 1	'Williams' Bon Chrétien', 'Louise Bonne of Jersey'
Incompatibility Group 2	'Onward', 'Easter Beurré', 'Doyenné du Comice'

Plums:
Incompatible varieties	'Blue Rock', 'Cambridge Gage', 'Jefferson', 'Golden Transparent', Early Rivers.

Cherries:
Incompatibility Group 1	'Early Rivers', 'Noir de Guben'
Incompatibility Group 2	'Waterloo', 'Merton Bigarreau', 'Merton Favourite'

An example. 'Cambridge Gage' won't cross-pollinate with 'Jefferson' because it is in the same incompatibility group, but also won't cross-pollinate with 'Avalon' for a different reason: they don't flower at the same time.

Triploids

There are a few significant varieties that won't pollinate anything regardless of all other conditions being in place. These are varieties that have, in their formation, mutated so that every live cell in the tree contains three sets of genetic information (chromosomes), making that variety a 'triploid'. Normally, fruit trees have just two sets – diploid. In fact, we are diploid, though I'm sure I've met some people where 'diploid' seemed to be a very generous estimate.

The positive outcome of being triploid is having increased vigour, with large fruit and strong-growing frameworks. The best example is probably Apple 'Bramley's Seedling'. The down side is that it doesn't produce viable pollen for the other tree that is being used as its mate. You need another (third) tree to pollinate the pollinator. In a way, a triploid tree is pretty selfish – it accepts pollen but doesn't reciprocate. Other notable triploids include the apples 'Suntan', 'Blenheim Orange', 'Jupiter' and 'Ribston Pippin' and the pear 'Jargonelle'.

Biennial Bearing

As mentioned at the beginning, occasionally a variety decides it can't be bothered to produce fruit every year. It has one year on and the next year off, and so on. It may be a natural phenomenon whereby particular varieties are simply prone to this couldn't-care-less attitude. Some relatively well known varieties that are biennial bearers can be found in the lists in 'Apples'. Biennial-ness can be stimulated by pruning a tree too heavily, forcing it to have an 'off' year and then it gets in to the habit. This is mildly irritating at the best of times but if that biennial cropper is a key pollinator then another tree's production may be affected since on its 'off' year it will produce little blossom / pollen.

Weather

Frosts are considered to be a major consideration with pollination in that, if an air frost is of a sufficient intensity, duration and repetition, a tree in full bloom may have the flowers or reproductive parts killed. Result – no fruit. Often, however, some but not all of the blossoms may be affected: even a tree in full bloom will have a few buds unopened and so unaffected. Result – a poor crop but at least some fruit.

An equal issue is if the blossom is damaged by winds, or the pollen is washed off by prolonged heavy rain – in other words, it's a rotten spring. Wet, windy weather, possibly combined with low temperatures – though not necessarily frosts – will discourage pollinating insects, reducing fruit set.

Age of Tree

Young trees, particularly those undergoing formative pruning, shouldn't be flowering and fruiting. They'll either simply not do it, putting all of their energy into building a framework of strong branches, or you should be picking off flowers and fruitlets to help the tree concentrate on the task in hand. Old trees can have a number of issues if they haven't been looked after well but even in their dotage can still be flowering (and pollinating). There is hope for us all.

Pruning

Pruning of young trees as above or pruning an established tree too heavily can promote a reaction consisting of lots of new shoots. Too many will mean the tree can't sustain both all of this vegetative growth and the flowers and fruiting. In effect, a tree can be shocked out of fruiting.

Pests and Diseases

There are few P & D that completely stop a tree from producing flowers. One is canker (see 'Apples') which, if severe enough, will have an effect similar to over-pruning: shoots are killed so promoting lots of new vegetative growth at the expense of reproductive growth. Often this new growth succumbs to the canker, too, continuing the process and making us question whether it is worth persevering with the tree at all.

Bullfinches used to be more of a problem, with an unfortunate habit of pecking off buds in the winter. Since we have developed, via agricultural policy, a strong persecution of birdlife in this country, bullfinches are currently not a major problem.

Other pests and diseases can reduce the energy of a tree e.g. aphids, mildew, scab so affecting the amount of flowering and fruiting but usually not totally stopping it.

THINNING
(Tree or Top Fruit)

It is often recommended, when there has been a good fruit set on a tree, that we start taking them off. The immediate worry is 'But if I take off young fruits the remaining ones might not make it or they could get damaged'. This is insecurity with a side-helping of paranoia: in some cases thinning is essential.

The practice is fiddly and time-consuming; which ones to remove and how to reach them? With a large tree it is almost impossible to do it accurately, it being confined to waving a long stick around in the upper branches.

However, there are some sound reasons for doing it, and there has to be an element of faith that the remaining fruits will survive intact to harvest. One such reason is if you desire large, high quality fruit. By thinning, the total number of fruits is reduced meaning that the tree's resources are divided between the remaining fruits. The result is fewer, but larger, fruits.

A second reason is, if thinning by hand as opposed to the big stick method, it gives an opportunity to have the first go at removing infested, infected or damaged fruit. Anything showing blemishes, holes or unusual colouring at such an early stage can be removed.

Thirdly, by thinning out clusters of fruitlets the remaining ones aren't touching so if there is any rot in a fruit later on it isn't passed on to its neighbours.

Fourthly, there is the very serious issue of tree damage. There have been reports of plum trees, notably 'Victoria' completely self-destructing. This is possibly

TREE: FRUIT THINNED

TREE: FRUIT NOT THINNED

because it is the most commonly-planted plum but also possibly because it is so vulnerable. The weight of a lot of fruit, coupled with leaves, wind and rain may mean whole branches rip off.

A fifth reason is to reduce 'biennial bearing'. This is where a tree, commonly apples, gets into the unfortunate habit of cropping one year and then having a year off. By reducing the amount of fruit considerably in the cropping year (thinning) and by pruning in the winter prior to the 'on year', and by not pruning prior to the 'off year', you can encourage a tree to get back to the sensible approach of cropping every year.

The last reason for thinning is not so much thinning as complete crop removal. A very young tree that is still in the process of being pruned and shaped (formative pruning) should be putting its energy into shoot growth and building a strong framework, not into fruit production no matter how much you'd love to get 'just one or two apples to see what they're like'.

The time to do thinning is in the region of early July but rather than pick a month, judge it according to the tree's own reaction to the amount of fruit it has set. If there has been good pollination and fruit set in the spring, the tree may decide to limit the number of fruits itself. Effectively, it will say 'I can only support this number to maturity; I'm going to get rid of the others'. This is called June drop and the clue to when it normally happens is in the name. So it is perfectly natural to have lots of little fruitlets drop off around this time. However, the tree is still keen to produce as many fruits as it can sustain, which is where we come in.

Apple fruitlets, incidentally, are terrific for chucking at one's brother without the worry one has regarding the removal of eyeballs as is attached to hurling stones.

In the fine city of Hull, an inspired teacher got the children to do a little nature study and maths at the same time. They threw down a couple of metre-square frames underneath a cherry tree. They counted the number of naturally-dropped cherries in each square then multiplied it up to represent the total area under the tree and so estimate the number shed. Two fascinating pieces of information emerged. One, this single cherry tree had naturally dropped in the region of 76,000 fruitlets. Two, there was still a wonderful crop of cherries. I'm pleased to say that due to the size of the fruit and (usually) the inaccessibility, we don't bother thinning cherries.

An interesting question is how much fruit should be removed and the less-then-satisfactory answer is 'It depends'. It depends on the amount of fruit set. Various tomes try to quantify the procedure e.g. leave apples one every 10-15cm (4-6"). However, this should be taken as an average – plants have a knack of doing exactly what they like and, inevitably, the fruit won't be evenly distributed along a branch. For example, if a branch is bare except for a single, large cluster then the fruit should be thinned to give an average spacing for that branch according to the figures below. That means there will still be a cluster, albeit a thinned one: this is less than desirable because fruits growing close to each other, like workers in a crowded office, pass on diseases. Normally, if the distribution allows, thin a cluster down to a single fruit – this will be the largest one and is called the 'king fruit'.

Spacings

Apples and Pears: 10-15cm (4-6") apart for dessert, 15-22cm (6-9") for culinary.

Plums: One every 5-8cm (2-3") or a pair every 15cm (6").

Peaches / Nectarines: Twice: to 10cm (4") when hazelnut size then to 20-25cm (8-10") when walnut size.

Apricots: unusual to have to thin apricots – 5-8cm (2-3") when hazelnut size.

Another recommendation for the final spacing of apples is 120 apples spread along a branch. To make use of this information we need two vital pieces of information: 'What is the variety?' and 'How long is the branch?'. Maybe for the average variety on a full sized tree this is useful but it still requires being able to count up to 120 which is not as easy as you may think when branches are waving about, leaves hide half the fruit and your 'phone has gone off three times already.

There are chemicals available to spray on and do the thinning for you. This is about as sensible as bungee jumping with liquorice rope. It is random and inexact and removes the opportunity to examine the fruit, as well as expensive and almost as time-consuming to carry out. So there.

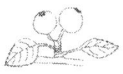

STORAGE OF FRESH FRUIT

Fresh Storage

Unlike the majority of fruits in this book, apples and, to a lesser extent, pears can be stored fresh. Clearly this is nothing new – it makes sense that if something can be made to last in its original state then it saves a lot of trouble, avoiding the need for drying, bottling and so on. Commercial storage is now carried out with such a degree of success that we have the dubious pleasure of being able to eat apples that were picked over 12 months ago. All we are looking to do at home is keep them edible for less than half that.

No problem, eh?

To stand the remotest chance of being fruitful (sorry, that had to happen at some point) with our storage, we have to deal with sleep, hormones and security, just like any self-respecting adolescent. Let us fumble our way through each of these factors in turn to establish the ideal storage space.

Sleep

This isn't really sleep (or even dormancy). It is just a little apple sitting, respiring at a low rate and minding its own business. To make an apple respire at a low rate the following would be ideal: low temperature (but not freezing), low oxygen and high carbon dioxide. Achieving, say, 5°C is not that difficult for us but changing gas composition? Commercially this can be done by pumping into a sealed room whatever gases are required e.g. nitrogen gas N_2 or carbon dioxide CO_2 to displace the oxygen O_2. It is important not to go too low with the oxygen: 6% is normally the lowest (ambient is 21%) otherwise things start to get a little frisky and alcohol production in the fruit can start. Which is anaerobic respiration, for those of you still concentrating. There isn't much chance of that happening with our domestic storage, not unless it was deliberate and storage of our apples is in a liquid form in a cider barrel.

Hormones

The gas ethylene, given off by over-ripe fruit, is known as 'the ripening gas' and it is the reason why a spotty banana might be put in a bag with some under-ripe fruit to speed up their palatability. With apples in store, as long as you don't mistakenly leave some blackening bananas in with them, ethylene is not a major problem: ripe apples would be removed as required. However, it is recommended that early ripening fruit is not stored next to long term storage fruit for that reason.

Security

We need to have our fruit in a rodent-proof container. Very small mesh chicken wire may help here.

Other factors to consider:

Ripeness of Fruit

The recommendation is to store fruit that is slightly under-ripe, so that they can slowly ripen in store. This is definitely the case, and is easy, with late season apples. They are picked in October and won't be ready to eat, potentially, for several weeks. Earlies aren't storable, which leaves the mid-season apples and pears as being the hardest to judge: how do you know when, for example, apple 'Egremont Russet' (a mid-season apple, theoretically ripe around October and November) is slightly under-ripe and so ready for storing? The season can fluctuate by three weeks, year on year. The answer is not terribly scientific: wing it. You know when they should be ripe so start looking before this time, even earlier if you were aware from other plants that it is an 'advanced' season. As soon as you get a ripe specimen then the lot should come off. Incidentally, mid-season apples only last a month or two in domestic storage.

Moisture

There is a rather interesting 'fact' that may be useful here: if an apple loses 5% of its moisture content, it will be wrinkled. Now you know why we spend so much money on moisturisers. How can we prevent water loss? The most obvious answer might be not to have them in a dry place. In other words, maintain a good level of humidity around them. Too great a humidity and there may be issues of rotting.

Rotting

Lots of things apart from us want to eat our fruit, not least micro-organisms. If the conditions are good for fungi, as with the aforementioned high humidity, then they will be encouraged to have a go. Inevitably some will get a hold, but we can minimise the ease with which they enter a fruit by only selecting the soundest, unblemished specimens. If the skin is broken in any way such as a tiny bird-peck, a bruise or some spotty disease then we are asking for it. The problem then is not whether it will rot – it isn't even when it will rot – but how many other fruit will it infect.

So, apart from selecting only unmarked fruit, there are another couple of defence suggestions: spacing the fruit apart as on the slatted racks of a traditional fruit house is the first. The issue there is the extra space required – it is bad enough having them spread out in a single layer without having gaps in between as well. Normally we'll have them piled up in a crate or cardboard box and, though this may be unavoidable, it is far from ideal.

The second possibility is putting a barrier between adjacent specimens, otherwise known as wrapping in paper. This gives a small breathing space between a fruit going rotten and its neighbours going the same way. Whatever is done, they must be checked regularly and any rotters duly culled. The full box or crate method is especially wearisome when it comes to checking, since they have to be partially removed to be able to inspect them all.

Practical Solutions

1) **The fridge**. Put up to three kilogrammes of apples in a plastic bag. We have all of the above requirements satisfied, even the gases: as the apples respire in the bag, oxygen is used up and carbon dioxide is increased, so gradually limiting further respiration. Humidity is good, possibly getting a little high, so regular checking for rotting is especially necessary. The single biggest problem with fridge storage is the fridge – its size. Most of us have problems squeezing in everything as it is, let alone a couple of dozen 3kg bags of apples.

2) **In the cellar**. What a great place. On a hot spring day, just pop down to the cool of the cellar and sit amongst bottles of cherries, a collection of fine vintages, some boxes of root vegetables and, of course, all of the apples on racks, filling the space with a wonderful scent. At this point you ask, 'In what era are you living, you moron?'. Most of us simply don't have one – shame really – though I have often thought about excavating a hole in the lounge floor.

3) **The shed / garage / outhouse**. This is where desperation is setting in. The apple houses of years ago were small, bespoke buildings: cool and highly insulated. They were often thatched, with thick walls and no windows, and with lots of racks. Our problems include, therefore, temperature fluctuation – with mild winters evident, we may have temperatures regularly in double figures in December or January in a shed. Also, security / protection – mice and rats love a shed at the best of times. Provide a supply of fresh fruit and they'll be in rodent heaven. If I were a rat – the similarity has been remarked upon – I'd love to spend the winter in a (relatively) warm wooden shed or garage particularly if there were several boxes of 'Sturmer Pippin' provided for regular snacks. Depending on the structure we may try insulating it and putting the fruit in mouse-proof boxes. Remember mice can squeeze through a gap the size of their own anal sphincter. Actually, I made that up, though they do get through the minutest of apertures.

Other possibilities include a dead fridge or freezer parked in a shady place to provide a steady protected environment. It can be camouflaged to stop it adding to the overall junk yard appearance of the allotment. An attic or unheated room could be useful in that it is likely to be mouse-free but, even though it feels perishing every time you go in there, the temperature will be higher than desirable. More positively, that temperature will probably fluctuate less in an unheated room than a shed or garage.

PROPAGATION

Propagation of fruit is either by cuttings or grafting; cuttings for soft fruit bushes and grafting for fruit trees. There are some exceptions mentioned below.
Any variations from the standard procedures given are discussed under individual fruits.

Cuttings

These can be taken at a number of times in the year but the easiest and often most successful is the hardwood cutting. A definition of a hardwood cutting is a shoot of current season's growth which has become woody. The only time of year when this is satisfied is the autumn and a hardwood cutting is 'struck' when the leaves have dropped off – November is perhaps the best month. Mulberry *Morus nigra* is an exception for a tree, in that it is propagated by cuttings (not grafting). Again, hardwood cuttings are recommended, taken with a heel.

Basic procedure

A piece of stem as described above is prepared. The length can vary between 20 and 35cm (8-14") and a cut is made just below a bud at the base and just above a bud at the top. The number of buds removed depends on the fruit but it is usual to rub off all except the top four or so. There is a really rather fascinating discussion about this under 'Gooseberries'. Mainly because they contain fungicides, I would recommend against using rooting hormone powder, but also most fruit cuttings produce roots exceptionally easily without it.

The cuttings are inserted in a gritty compost in a pot which is then placed in a cold frame or greenhouse. Alternatively, the low-tech, low-input option is to line them out to half their depth in a narrow slot in well-prepared soil. Coarse sand can be trickled into the bottom of the slot before spacing out the cuttings at about 15cm / 6" apart. This can be done in any decent bit of ground but it is best to choose a sheltered spot, maybe even a cold frame again.
Lifting and transplanting is done in almost exactly a year's time.

Division

In the fruit world, this is exclusively reserved for raspberries and even then isn't your typical herbaceous perennial plant division. The plants naturally sucker in that new canes arise from the root system. When the row of raspberry plants is relatively new, meaning vigorous and disease-free, canes can be separated from the parents using a spade for re-use. Choose a sucker that has wandered away

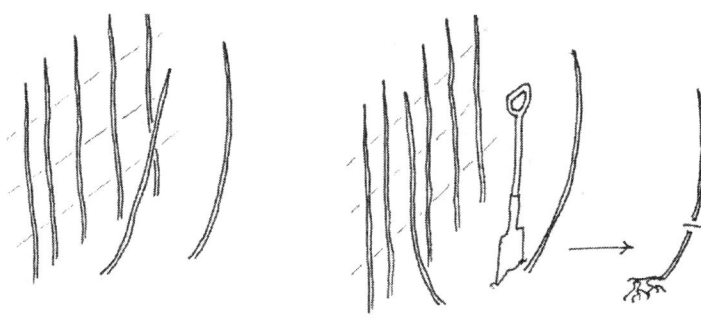

DEALING WITH WAYWARD RASPBERRY CANES: TYING IN OR CUTTING OUT

from the row – it is too far away to include – and teach it a lesson by cutting down through the connecting root system. This is best done in the autumn once the leaves have come off to lessen the shock to both remaining plants and the sucker. Lift it carefully and transplant to extend the row or start a new one.

Grafting

One bit of plant is stuck on to a different plant. Well, that's that sorted out. Actually, there are so many variations that we could devote this entire book to the subject: what part of the plants is used, when it is done, what actual cuts are made and so on.

The principle is usually to use one plant as the root system (the rootstock) and attach a piece from the chosen variety known as the scion – a section of young stem – or a bud. The 'root system' could be an existing tree and more than one scion could be attached to it.

For more on the choice of rootstocks see individual fruits and a summary at the end of this chapter.

Whip-and-Tongue Grafting

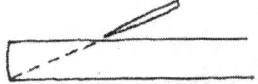

This is one of the best grafts to use when the scion is the same diameter as the rootstock. It has an excellent lock to hold the two pieces together and there should be a complete connection between the dividing tissue in both pieces – the cambium. The cambium is found just underneath the bark.

The scion can be prepared so that it is relatively short in length, perhaps 15cm / 6", to avoid the whole thing being top heavy. A section to work on at the base of the scion can be chosen away from

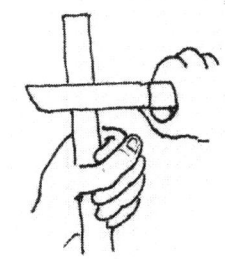

THE FIRST CUT

buds which might distort the cut. The rootstock is cut likewise to a distance of about 15cm / 6" above the roots / soil line.

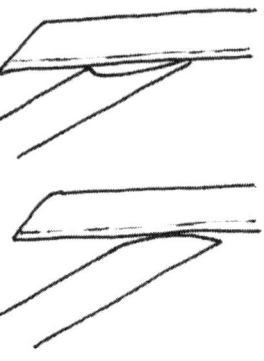

Preparation is the same for both pieces. With a very sharp knife a slice is made that is flat, an elongated oval shape and is about 1.5cm / ½" depending on the diameter. Check the 'flatness'. Incidentally, the action used is one where the blade moves away from the body in a sweep. It is advisable not to carry out this bit whilst standing in a bus queue or at a football match.

THE FLATNESS TEST

The next cut, the tongue, is the tricky part. It is started with the edge of the blade positioned flat on the cut surface to which it is at right angles (see picture), The thumb of the knife-holding hand is pushed into the side of the scion (or rootstock) and this is the most important feature: the thumb braces the knife and will stop it slipping. If this is done correctly, it is impossible to create a flesh wound. The blade is then gently rocked with little pressure – not with a sawing action. As this

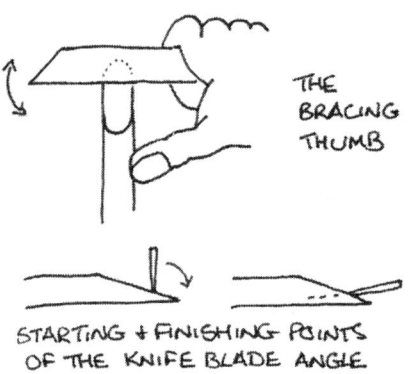

STARTING + FINISHING POINTS OF THE KNIFE BLADE ANGLE

is done the blade bites into the cut surface a little allowing the knife to be gradually lowered towards the horizontal, still rocking. The blade should ease into the piece and not run down the grain. If it suddenly moves, too much pressure was being applied. This cut needs to be no more than 0.5-1cm / ¼".

The scion and rootstock can now be fitted together. Because no wood has actually been removed, it is not a woodworking joint. It is possible that, because the pieces are simply pushing each other apart, there may be a gap visible through the graft – don't worry.

The final stage is to prevent water loss and aid with support by binding it. This is normally done with special clear plastic non-biodegradable grafting tape or special stretchy biodegradable wax tape. In the absence of these we could try using unspecial, inferior slightly stretchy strip of

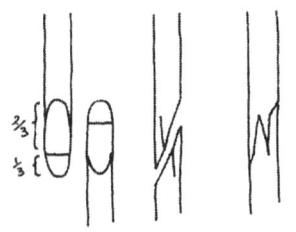

WHIP AND TONGUE GRAFTING (SCION AND ROOTSTOCK ARE THE SAME DIAMETER)

plastic bag. Start below the graft and work upwards pulling quite tightly – too tight and all three will snap. Go above the graft and then come back down again, tying off with a simple loop.

Side Veneer Grafting

This is when the scion is narrower than the rootstock. The scion is prepared as with whip-and-tongue, cutting a little ledge at the upper end of the 'oval'. The rootstock has a shallow slice off the side – it needs to be slightly wider than the scion cut: you should be able to see a fine green-white line around the edge.

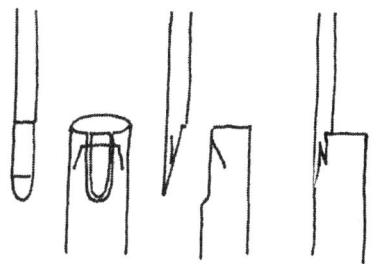

SIDE VENEER GRAFTING
(SCION IS NARROWER THAN THE ROOTSTOCK)

The tongue on the rootstock is quite tough to make, so it requires patience. The positive side of this is that, when fitted together, the pieces hold exceptionally tightly. Taping should include covering the top cut surface of the rootstock.

Grafting onto an existing tree

A modestly-sized tree can be converted to a different variety or multiple varieties which makes it exceptionally exciting. Grafting small scions onto the very ends of branches by whip-and-tongue is possible but is rarely successful in the long term due to pruning issues, so the answer might be to cut through branches closer to the trunk.

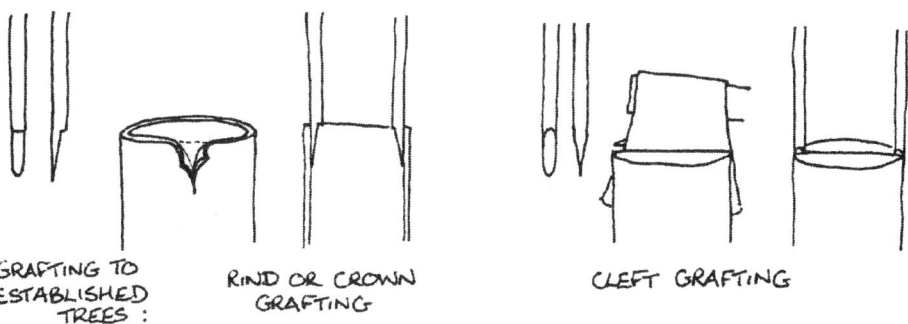

GRAFTING TO ESTABLISHED TREES :

RIND OR CROWN GRAFTING

CLEFT GRAFTING

Scions prepared as for the side veneer but without the tongue can be fitted behind the bark which has been locally peeled back, or by splitting the branch and wedging wedge-shaped scions at the very edges. Scions from different varieties can be used, of course. Taping is still necessary and quite fiddly.

Budding

This is a form of grafting but carried out in the summer – July into the beginning of August.

Chip budding consists of removing a small section from a piece of new growth from the chosen variety that has a single bud and the leaf stalk (petiole) left. It is slotted into similar shaped cut made into the rootstock and taped up around the bud.

T-budding is not quite as successful and is actually trickier to carry out so I'm not sure why I've included it. I suppose you'd only ask if I didn't. This time the slice from the new growth is very fine, in fact if there is still any wood fitted at the back it is popped out so that you are left with a thin piece of bark plus associated layers including cambium. It is fitted behind a T-shaped cut in the rootstock, the top part trimmed off and taped up.

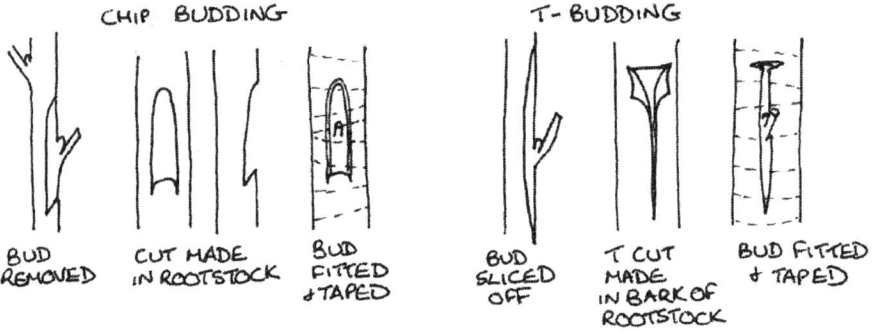

If a bud has successfully fused you'll know about it because the bit of petiole will drop off – three weeks? Remove the tape. In the February of the following year the rootstock above the bud is removed at the bud.

If a tree has a characteristic kink near the base it has either been budded or side-veneer grafted.

Layering

In terms of vegetative reproduction, layering is perhaps the most natural. Low branches can, all by themselves, touch the ground, perhaps accumulate a bit of leaf litter and produce roots. Redcurrants, for example, can happily wander around a garden by doing just that. Gooseberries are often pruned to upward facing buds to discourage them from doing it. Because of the rootstock requirement, fruit trees aren't layered. There are two exceptions: possibly mulberries and definitely figs. The procedure is as follows:

A WOUNDED, WEIGHTED DOWN, STAKED, LOW BRANCH   SUMMER GROWTH   BRANCH DETACHED, NEXT WINTER. NEW PLANT TRANSPLANTED

A pliable stem towards the edge of a plant is bent down to the ground and the youngest part, usually at the end of the stem, is buried. Be careful with some plants like the currants that the whole branch doesn't break as it is lowered. The soil should have been well prepared (loosened, weeded, etc.) and a shallow depression made. The shoot is bent into this and covered over; sometimes a wound is made on the underside to help stimulate roots, most of the time this is not necessary with fruit bushes; it's perhaps worth doing with figs.

It is quite likely that the plant will be deeply affronted by this treatment and will want to spring back out of the hole, throwing soil in your face. Anticipate this rebellion by placing a stone over the buried section.

The tip of this young shoot should emerge from the hole and can be staked upright with a short stick. With cane fruit such as blackberries and hybrid berries it is the tip that is buried completely (see 'Blackberries'). If the layering has been done in, say, spring it should have produced roots by the autumn when the section of the stem between the parent and the new plant can be severed and the latter carefully lifted and transplanted.

Seeds

Most of the plants in this book can be grown from seed, after all that is how new varieties are produced. It is great fun sowing pips and seeing what turns up. In practice, if we want a particular variety with particular desirable properties then the variability generated by seed-sowing is not the way forward, and we resort to vegetative propagation to get an exact copy, a clone. Annual fruit plants such as melons and cape gooseberries are started from seed every year: see 'Other Fruits'.

Rootstocks, a summary

Rootstocks are a way of introducing certain characteristics, not least a way of regulating of the size of the resulting tree. Below is a summary of the current rootstocks available (via specialist nurseries) to most of us: trees grown as free-standing open centre specimens. The actual sizes depend on the location and on the variety being attached.

Apple Rootstocks (all are *Malus domestica* varieties)

M27 (1.2-1.8m/4-6')	can be used to grow a tree in a container, is allowed on allotments and can be used to grow a stepover tree.
M9 (1.8-2.4m/6-8')	the world's most used apple rootstock, trained as a short-term spindle tree.
M26 (2.4-3.5m/8-12')	the best rootstock for domestic cordons and espaliers.
MM106 (4.5-5m/15-18')	a great-sized, climbable, free-standing tree, also used for larger espaliers.
MM111 or M25	(both above 6m/20') for that old, traditional orchard.

Apricot Rootstocks (a mixture of *Prunus* species)

'Wavit' (3m/10')	
'Torinel' (4m/14')	good disease resistance and copes with wet soils
'Apricor' (4m/14')	an apricot seedling so compatibility is excellent.
'St. Julien A' (5m/16')	

Cherry Rootstocks

'Gisela 5' (3m/10')	needs long term staking (or against a wall) and good feeding and watering.
'Krymsk 6' (3.5m/12')	not readily available
'Gisela 6' (4m/14')	" " "
'Krymsk 5'(4.5m/15')	" " "
'Colt'(3.5-5m/12-18')	
'F12.1'(over 6m/20')	All rootstocks here are more tolerant of poor soils than 'Gisela 5'.

Damson Rootstock
'Pixy' (2-2.5m/6-8')

Medlar Rootstocks
Quince 'C' (2.5-3m/8-10')
Quince 'A' (3-4m/10-14')
BA29 (3-4m+/10-14'+)

Peach, Nectarine Rootstocks
'VVA-1' (a.k.a. 'Krymsk 1') (2.5m/8') not yet fully tested
'Montclare' (3m/10')
'Wavit'(3m/10')   plum rootstock also suitable for peaches
'Torinel' (4m/14')   better disease resistance and tolerance of wet soils
'St. Julien A' (5m/16')

Pear Rootstocks (various species)
Quince 'C' (2.5-3m/8-10')
Quince 'A' (3-4m/10-14')
BA29 (3-4m+/10-14'+)
'Pyrodwarf' (4-4.5m/13-15')
Hawthorn (over 6m/20')

Plum Rootstocks
'VVA-1' (2.5m/8')   not yet fully tested
'Pixy' (2.5-3m/8-10')
'Plumina' (2.5-3m/8-10') as 'Pixy' but with larger fruit
'Wavit'(3-3.5m/10-12')
'St. Julien A' (4-5m/14-17')

Quince Rootstocks
Quince 'C' (2.5-3m/8-10')
Quince 'A' (3-4m/10-14')

Features of Rootstocks

Generally speaking, the more dwarfing a rootstock, the quicker it is to start cropping. The fruit is usually high quality especially for the first few years, hence the modern orchard consisting of dwarf, closely spaced trees lasting perhaps only 10 to 15 years.

Very dwarf trees also need permanent staking: their root systems are very weak which is how they restrict the growth of the tree. When in full leaf and given a bit of a shove in strong wind and rain, they will fall over unless they are staked or held on wires. The latter is the commercial approach.

Perhaps the biggest reasons for using very dwarf trees are ease of picking and protection.

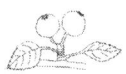

WEEDING

Fruit plants are, in the main, substantial things and should be able to take care of themselves. Just be aware that, even when they are established and cropping, excessive weed growth around the plant can reduce the yield in terms of quantity and quality.

In the establishment phase, it is important to let a fruit plant develop unhindered. It has been shown (with native trees) that when a sapling has strong grass growth around it from the moment it is planted, it can be very slow to develop and in some cases be killed. The tree gets its water and nutrients in two ways: directly from the soil into the root system or indirectly from the soil via a network of fungal strands (mycorrhizal fungi) that are plugged into the tree's roots.

The grass, in a desperate attempt not to get shaded out by the tree, takes as much water and nutrient as it can – direct competition. It also releases chemicals (allelopathy) that suppresses the association between the tree and the fungus to reduce the uptake via that route. Pretty dashed clever, I'd say, but it emphasises the need to keep plants weed-free, particularly for those first few years.

As mentioned, it is still worthwhile later on, especially for the smaller specimens such as soft fruit and very dwarf trees. It can be less critical for the stronger growing fruit trees. In fact, an apple tree on a vigorous rootstock like M25 or MM111 is quite often planted in grassland, being kept weed-free for those first three years, of course. Commercial 'orchards' that are grown nowadays consist of much smaller trees and these are, unless organic, kept constantly weed-free with herbicided strips.

Weeds are one thing, mixed planting is another; fruit trees, bushes, herbs and flowers can all be mixed up in a wonderful, self-protecting beautiful melange. To prevent excessive competition between adjacent plants, however, requires careful planning and spacing.

PESTS, DISEASES AND PREDATORS

Predators
Acorid bugs – *Anthocoris nemorum* feeds on aphids and spider mites.
Birds – a wide range but especially blue tits, *Parus caeruleus* which will eat almost anything they can find.
Ground beetles e.g. Violet ground beetle – *Carabus violaceus*, the adult predates slugs.
Hoverflies – e.g. *Syrphus balteatus* against woolly aphis and *Syphus ribesii* feeds on other aphids. The larvae in both species are the predators.
Lacewings – e.g. *Chrysopa* species, the larvae eat aphids.
Ladybirds – e.g. 7-spot ladybird *Coccinella 7-punctata* both adults and larvae eat a range of pests including aphids.
Rove beetles – e.g. Devil's coach horse – *Staphylinus olens* predates slugs and invertebrates.

Pests
Many of the following pests* have part of their lifecycle in the soil. Usually as a way of surviving the winter, these creatures have larvae which find their way to the soil to pupate – the pupa (or cocoon or chrysalis) has a hard, resistant coat giving it more protection.
Aphids° here are an exception, staying well away from the soil.

Apple grass aphid – *Rhopalosiphum insertum* °
Apple sawfly – *Hoplocampa testudinea* *
Big bud mite or **Blackcurrant gall mite** – *Cercidophyopsis ribis*
Blackcurrant leaf midge – *Dasineura tetensi* *
Cherry blackfly – *Myzus cerasi* °
Codling moth – *Cydia pomonella* *
Currant blister aphid – *Cryptomyzus ribis* °
Currant clearwing moth – *Synanthedon tipuliformis*
Gooseberry sawfly (common) – *Nematus ribesii* *
Leaf-curling plum aphid – *Brachycaudus helichrysi* °
Pear leaf blister mite – *Eriophyes pyri*
Pear midge – *Contarinia pyrivora* *
Plum moth – *Cydia funebrana* *
Plum sawfly – *Hoplocampa flava* *
Raspberry beetle – *Byturus tomentosus**
Red berry mite – *Acalitus essigi*

Red spider mite – *Panonychus ulmi*
Rosy apple aphid – *Dysaphis plantaginea* °
Slugworm – *Caliroa cerasi* *
Vine weevil – *Otiorhynchus sulcatus* *
Winter moth – *Operophtera brumata* *
Woolly aphis – *Eriosoma lanigerum* °

Diseases

The majority of the diseases below either use rain as a method of moving / spreading or use it as an aid to spore germination and infection. Therefore, factors that increase exposure to rain and increase the incidence of wet leaves need to be considered – a wetness protection programme? This includes location in terms of part of the country and the location within a garden, as well as maintenance – pruning, spacing etc. One of the main prevention methods is to select resistant varieties.

American gooseberry mildew – *Sphaerotheca mors-uvae*
Apple powdery mildew – *Podosphaera leucotricha*
Apple and Pear canker – *Nectria galligena*
Apple scab – *Venturia inequalis*
Bacterial canker and shot-hole – *Pseudomonas syringae var. mors-prunorum*
Blossom wilt (apple) – *Sclerotinia laxa f. laxa*
Blossom wilt and **Brown rot** (*Prunus*, pear) – *Sclerotinia laxa*
Blueberry rust – *Pucciniastrum vaccinii*
Brown rot (apples) – *Sclerotinia fructigena*
Cane Spot – *Elsinoe veneta*
Coral spot – *Nectria cinnabarina*
Currant leaf spot – *Drepanopezizsa ribis* (syn. *Pseudopeziza ribis*)
Grey mould – *Botrytis cinerea*
Fireblight – *Erwinia amylovora*
Pear rust – *Gymnosporangium fuscum*
Pear scab – *Venturia pirina*
Plum rust – *Transzschelia pruni-spinosae*
Pocket plum – *Taphrina pruni*
Quince leaf blight – *Diplocarpon mespili*
Quince powdery mildew – *Podosphaera leucotricha*
Raspberry cane spot – *Elsinoe veneta*
Silver leaf – *Chondrostereum purpureum*
Strawberry leaf spot – *Mycosphaerella fragariae*
Strawberry red core – *Phytophthera fragariae*

There are pests and diseases not covered under individual fruits because of their universality. For example, honey fungus *Armillaria mellea* is a soil-dwelling fungus which can attack any of the plants in this book, and plenty of others not in it. Similarly, larger universal pests such as birds and mammals, including bears and piglets, have not been included.

HUNNY FUNGUS

A universal pest perhaps worth a separate mention is a new arrival, *Drosophila suzukii* or the spotted-wing fruit fly. Unlike other fruit flies, it lays its eggs in ripening fruit as opposed to overripe / decaying fruit. It seems to particularly go for cherries and soft fruit but nothing is immune to its attention apparently. Try hanging up a jam jar containing a squirt of washing up liquid mixed with an inch of apple cider vinegar. Punch about six 3mm holes in the lid and see if that traps them before they can do their worst.

In an edition of the RHS The Fruit Garden Displayed from the 1960s there is a spraying programme for top fruit. There are over 14 sprays recommended for apples alone against the pests and diseases listed above. Remember this is for us, the amateurs; commercial (conventional) orchards were sprayed over 20 times a year – and still are. Interestingly, not one of the chemicals recommended is still in use. They have been banned because of their effect on us and the environment or they are no good. And that is after they have been 'rigorously' tested before being sold to us.

With that kind of track record, why should we ever listen to, let alone trust, companies manufacturing chemicals for profit and, by extension, their genetically modified plants?

GLOSSARY

Achene – a simple single-seeded fruit. The 'pips' found on the surface of a strawberry are achenes.

Biennial cropping – the plant produces crops only every other year. The word 'biennial' is also used to refer to plants which have a lifecycle spread over two years.

Berry – a kind of true fruit consisting of an outer skin encasing flesh and multiple seeds e.g. redcurrants.

Brix – a unit of measurement of sweetness. One degree of Brix (1°Bx) is one gramme of sucrose per 100 grammes of solution

Cambium – a layer of dividing cells found just underneath the bark.

Carpel or **Pistil** – the female part of a flower consisting of a sticky stigma at the top attached to the ovary by a short stalk called a style.

Cultivar – a variation within a species of fruit that has arisen in a garden or nursery, usually deliberately (by breeding) but not always, such as Apple 'Bramley's Seedling'. Strictly speaking, we should be using this term instead of 'variety'.

Dioecious – plants that have male and female flowers on separate plants. See 'kiwi'. Most plants are bisexual.

Drupe – a true fruit typified by a thin outer skin, a fleshy middle part and a single seed encased in a hard woody shell. Stone fruit including plums and cherries.

Drupelet – as for drupe but smaller and joined together with several others to make up a compound fruit e.g. raspberry.

Farage – the unpleasant liquid at the bottom of a compost bucket.

Festooning – bending a branch towards the horizontal and making it stay there to improve the fruiting.

Maiden – a one-year old tree. It has no branches (yet). A feathered maiden is a year older and has side shoots / branches, usually lower on the stem.

Mulch – a covering of the soil, usually consisting of organic matter but could include cardboard, plastic, etc.

Pectin – a substance found in the walls of plant cells, important for the setting of jam and plant cells.

Nut – a single-seeded fruit with a woody outer coat. The seed is the only one remaining from multiple carpels.

Ovary – the structure at the base of the carpel that houses one or more ovules which in turn house the female sex cell or egg. After fertilisation the ovules develop into seeds and the ovary develops into the fruit.

Parthenocarpy – the production of fruit without fertilisation.

Pedicel – the stalk bearing a flower (and ultimately the fruit).

Petiole – the stalk of a leaf.

Pistil or **Carpel** – the female part of a flower consisting of a sticky stigma at the top attached to the ovary by a short stalk called a style.

Pome – a type of false fruit where the majority has developed, not from the ovary, but from the top of the flower stalk called the receptacle. Apples, pears, etcetera.

Primocane – a type of cane fruit that produces fruit on growth produced in the same year, such as autumn raspberries.

Receptacle – the top of the flower stalk (pedicel) which can, with some false fruits, develop into the bulk of the fruit such as a strawberry.

Russet / russetting – rough, brown or (optimistically) bronze patches to the skin of fruits such as apples and pears. Some varieties have a skin entirely russetted, such as Apple 'Egremont Russet' and, as such, some people hate them.

Sclerenchyma – strengthening tissue in plants, also making up the 'stones' of fruits.

Sport – a mutation, usually in the tip (terminal bud) of a shoot, that gives rise to a variation in some form. For example, a sport arising on Apple 'Cox's Orange Pippin' was one which had dark red fruit compared to the rest of the tree. It was propagated (by grafting) and is now available called 'Crimson Cox'.

Spur bearer – a plant that produces fruit on short stubby wrinkly bits on older wood.

Stigma – the landing pad for pollen found at the top of a carpel (the female part in a flower). It is sticky to trap the pollen.

Strig – short, finely-branching fruiting stems which bear particular currants.

Sucker – a shoot that develops from below ground, usually from the root system.

Syconium – the inverted flower of a fig.

Tip bearer – a tree that produces fruit at the end of new growth. Compare to spur bearer.

Triploid – a plant with three sets of chromosomes per cell as opposed to the usual two (diploid). A triploid plant will usually show increased vigour and larger fruit but there may be issues with pollination: they sometimes don't produce viable pollen.

Variety – a naturally-occurring variation within a species. Since most varieties that we talk about are not naturally occurring we should really be referring to 'Cultivars' instead.

BIBLIOGRAHY

Beeton's Shilling Gardening Book, 1873, Ward, Lock & Co.

Brickell, Christopher and Joyce, David
RHS Pruning and Training, 2011, Dorling Kindersley

Buczaki, Stefan and Harris, Keith
Collins Shorter Guide to the Pests, Diseases and Disorders of Garden Plants, 1983, Collins

Crawford, Martin,
Creating a Forest Garden, 2010, Green Books

Deakin, Roger,
Wildwood, 2007, Hamish Hamilton

Diacono, Mark
Fruit – River Cottage Handbook No. 9, 2012, Bloomsbury

Glenny, George
The Culture of Fruits and Vegetables, 1878, Houlston and Sons

Flowerdew, Bob,
Complete Fruit Book, 1995, Kyle Cathie Ltd

Goulson, Dave,
A Sting in the Tale, 2013, Jonathan Cape

Goulson, Dave,
A Buzz in the Meadow, 2015, Jonathan Cape

Greenwood, Pippa and Halstead, Andrew,
Pests and Diseases, 2009, Dorling Kindersley

Hills, Lawrence D.
Grow Your Own Fruit and Vegetables, 1979, Faber and Faber

MAFF Gooseberries, 1979, Leaflet 215

MAFF The Pollination of Apples and Pears, 1980, Leaflet 377

MAFF Redcurrants, 1982, Leaflet 521

McFarlane, Robert,
Landmarks, 2015, Hamish Hamilton

Morgan, Joan and Alison Richards
The Book of Apples, 1993, Ebury Press

Readman, Joanna,
Fruity Stories, 1996, Boxtree

RHS, Encyclopaedia of Gardening, 1992, Dorling Kindersley

RHS, The Fruit Garden Displayed, 1965, RHS

Roberts, Jonathan,
Cabbages and Kings, 2001, Harper Collins

Trehane, Jennifer
Blueberries etc. for Everyone, 2010, Jentree Productions

Vaughan, J.G. and Geissler, C.A.
The New Oxford Book of Food Plants 2nd Ed. 2009, Oxford University Press

Westwood, Melvin,
Temperate-Zone Pomology, 1995, Timber Press

Witham Fogg, H.G.,
Fruit Growing, 1963, John Gifford Ltd.

Orange Pippin website

The Guardian articles

INDEX

(not including references found in the 'Essentials' of each fruit)

Achene 82, 177, **266**
Acid soil 63, **65**
Acorid bug 31, 73, 144, 263
Actinidia deliciosa, see 'Kiwis'
Alpine strawberries 195
American gooseberry mildew **60**, **94**, 264
Aminopyralid 213
Aphids **263-263**
    On apples 29,30
    On blackberries 50, 51
    On blackcurrants 57,58
    On cherries 73
    On peaches 127
    On plums 144
    On raspberries 160, 162
Apples **15**, 193, 195, 222, 229, 242-245, 248-252, 265, 267, 268
    Blossom 21, 24, 33, 243, 245
    Choice 15
    Culinary 23-24
    Flowering groups 242
    Games 37
    Harvest 26-27
    Histories 35
    Identifying 26
    Juice 36
    Of love 151
    Pie 147
    Pressing 36
    Problems 28
    Pruning 24
    Ripeness 251
    Ripening times 21
    Root pruning 236
    Rootstocks 260
    Spraying 265
    Storage 250
    Thinning 248
    Varieties 15
    Wassailing 37
    Weather, effect of 17
Apple 'Adam's Pearmain' **22**
Apple 'Annie Elizabeth' **23**
Apple 'Ashmead's Kernal' **22**, 243
Apple 'Beauty of Bath' **20**
Apple 'Braeburn' **17**, 19
Apple 'Bramley's Seedling' **23**, 24, 243, 245, 266
Apple 'Charles Ross' **21**
Apple 'Christmas Pippin' **21**
Apple 'Court Pendu Plat' **23**
Apple 'Cox's Orange Pippin' 8, 17-18, 20, 22, 26, 238, 242, 244, 268
Apple 'Crimson Cox' 268
Apple 'D'Arcy Spice' **21**
Apple 'Discovery' **20**, 127, 352
Apple 'Egremont Russet' **21**, 243, 251, 268
Apple 'Falstaff' **21**, 243
Apple 'Gala' 19
Apple 'Golden Delicious' 16, 19, 137, 140
Apple 'Granny Smith' 16, 19
Apple 'Grenadier' **23**
Apple 'Howgate Wonder' **24**
Apple 'John Standish' **22**
Apple 'Jupiter' **22**, 25, 245
Apple 'Lane's Prince Albert' **24**
Apple 'Laxton's Superb' **20**, 22
Apple 'Lord Lambourne' **21**
Apple 'Newton Wonder' **24**, 25, 243
Apple 'Pink Lady' 18, **19**
Apple 'Pitmaston Pine Apple' 18, **22**
Apple 'Ribston Pippin' 16, 20
Apple 'Rosemary Russet' **22**

Apple 'Saint Edmund's Pippin' **21**
Apple 'Sturmer Pippin' **23**, 252
Apple 'Tom Putt' **23**
Apple 'Tydeman's Late Orange' **22**
Apple 'Winston' 20, **22**, 243
Apple 'Winter Gem' **23**
Apple canker 19, 20, 21, 22, 23, 24, 29, **33-34**, 137
Apple sawfly **32**, 263
Apple scab 19, 21, 24, **34-35**, 254
Apricor 40, **260**
Apricots **39**, 193, 249
    Pruning 224, 220
    Rootstocks 260
    Thinning 249
Apricot crosses **41**
Aprium 41
Aronia xprunifolia, see 'Chokeberries'
Averuncator **203**
Bacterial canker 44, **74**, 127, 143, 145, 264
Bark-ringing **236-237**
Biennial bearing / cropping 18, 21, 22, 24, **25**, **245**, 248, 266
Big bud mite 52, **58**, 263
Birds, as predators 30, 32, 144, 145, 160, 161, 263
Bitter pit **28**
Blackberries **45**, 106, 141, 160, 259
Blackcurrant gall mite 52, **58**
Blackcurrant leaf midge **58**, 263
Blackthorn (see also 'sloes') **77**, 140
Bletting 116
Blossom wilt **33**, 44, 142, 264
Blueberries **63-68,** 148, 214
Blueberry pruning **64, 66**
Blueberry rust **68**, 264
Botrytis 264
    On blueberries 68
    On grapes 102-103

    On raspberries 162
Boysenberry 106
Bracken compost 160
Breba crop **182-84**
Brix 46, 61, 105, 266
Brown rot 33, 43, 44, 126, 142, 149, 264
Brutting 189
Budding **258**
    Chip 258
    T bud 258
Bullaces 78
Bumble bees 239, 241
Bumblekites 47
Cane spot **50**, 108, 264
Cantaloup melon **189**
Cape gooseberry **187**
Capsid bug 51 113
Cardboard 31, 159, 183, 210
Cherries **69**, 193, 224, 229, 230, 243, 248, 252
    Harvesting 71
    Pollination 243, 244
    Pruning 229
    Rootstocks 260
Cherry 'Morello' 69, 242
Cherry blackfly **73**, 263
Cherry plum 77-79, 140
Chicken pellets **216**
Chokeberries **187-188**
Chuckleberry 61
Climbing trees 219, **233-234**
Cobnuts **188**
Codling moth **30-31**, 263
Cold periods 10
    Apples 15
    Apricots 42
    Kiwis 113
    Quinces 148
Colt 70, 260

Comfrey 52, 88, 153, 164, 176, 183, 195-196
Compost and composting 10, 15. 63-70, **88**, 90, 94, 96, 102, 105-106, 115, 119, 124, 131, 136, 139, 153, 160, 172-175, 181-185, 198, , **212-215**, 234. 254
Compost tea 94
Compost toilet 215
Compost, for potting and propagation 181-182, 198, 203
Compound fruit 120, 141, 154, 240, 266
Container-grown trees 208
Coral spot **60**, 168, 264
Cordons 10, 15, 91, 131, 219, **222-224, 228-229**, 260
Corylus avellana, see 'Hazelnuts'
Cucumis melo, see 'Melons'
Cultivar **7-8**, 18, 46-47, 266, 268
Cuttings **254**
    Blackcurrants 53
    Blueberries 64
    Figs 81
    Gooseberries 89
    Grapes 97
    Hazelnuts 189
    Mulberries 120
Currant and gooseberry leaf spot 52, 94, 264
Currant clearwing moth **59**, 263
Cydonia oblonga, see 'Quinces'
Damson rootstocks 260
Damsons **77-80**, 141, 143
Dioecious 111, 266
Disposal of prunings **234-235**
Division 169, **254-255**
Dried blood 216
Drupe 41, 51, 71, 125, 140, 141, 191, 240, 266

Drupelet 51, 120, 141, 154, §57, 161, 240, 266
Duke cherries 270
Dwarf pyramids, regulatory pruning 219 **231**
Elderberries **188**
Ericaceous compost 65-66
Ericaceous plants 63
Family Tree 242
Family 7, 87, 136, 242
Fan trees 229
    Cherries 70
    Figs 81
    Formative pruning 224
    Regulatory pruning 225
Feeding 9, **211-218**
Fertilisers, animal **216-217**
Festooning 131, 219, **235-236**, 237
Figs **81**, 193, 196, 258, 259
    Dried 85
    Planting 83
    Pollination 86
    Pruning 83, 84
Ficus carica, see 'Figs'
Filberts 188
Fish, blood and bone **212**, 216
Flowering groups 238, **242-244**
Forest gardens 6, 93, 166, 188, 193, **194-196**, 218, 269
Fragaria xananassa, see 'Strawberries'
Frost and frost damage 10, 40, 42, 44, 53, 61, 96, 103, 128, 132, 191, 245-246
Frost pockets 44, 96, 209
Fruit gardens 47, **193**, 265, 270
Genus 7. 78. 82, 103, 141, 142, 177
Gisela 69, 70, 73, 260
Glassiness 28

273

Gooseberries **88**, 193, 194, 197, 254, 258
    Propagation 89
    Pruning 91, 92
Gooseberry sawfly **93**, 263
Grafting **255**
    Cleft 257
    Rind / crown 257
    Side veneer 257
    Whip and tongue 255
Grapes 12, **96**, 193
    Propagation 97
    Pruning 96-99
    Weather 101
Grey mould 264
    On blueberries 68
    On grapes 102
    On raspberries 162
Gribble 27, 36
Gromore 212, 217
Growing systems **193**
Harvesting 11
    Apples 26
    Blackberries 46
    Blackcurrants 53
    Cherries 70
    Tayberries 107
    Medlars 115
    Redcurrants 164
    Rhubarb 169
    Hazelnuts 189
Hazelnuts **188-189**
Hedges, fruit 77, 78, **194-195**
Hippophae rhamnoides, see 'Sea Buckthorn'
Honey bees 239
Honeydew melon 189
Hybrid berries **105-108**, 160, 259
Hybrid currants **60**, 106
Incompatibility 70, 133, 238, **243-244**

Incompatibility groups 70, 133, 238, 243
Japanese wineberry 107
Johnny Appleseed 35
Jostaberry 60-61
Juglans nigra, see 'Walnuts'
Kiwis 12, **109**, 193, 197, 240, 266
    Pruning 109
    Weather 113
Knives 33, 137, 151-152, **204**, 205, 234, 236
Layering **258**
    Figs 81
    Gooseberries 89
    Redcurrants 165
    Hazelnuts 189
Loganberry **106**, 108
Long arm pruner **203**
Loppers 860, 166, **203-204**, 205, 234
Maintenance pruning, see 'Pruning, regulatory'
Malus domestica, see 'Apples'
Manure 52, 63, 88, 115, 153, 169, 173, 210, 212, 213, 2216, 217
Marmalade 150
Medlar jelly **117-118**
Medlars **115-118**
Melons **189-190**, 259
Membrillo 150
Mespilus germanica, see 'Medlars'
Montclare 123, 261
Morus nigra, see 'Mulberries'
Mulberries **119-122**, 254
Mulches and mulching 28, 34, 35, 49, 53, 53, 63, 64, 70, 74, 77, 89, 96, 203, 206, 109, 115, 119, 124, 131, 139, 149, 153, 159, 160, 164, 169, 176, 177, 181, 196, **209-210**, 215
Mycorrhizal fungi 206, 211-21, 262
National Collections 15, 140, 150

Nectarines **123**
    Dwarf 129
    Rootstock 261
    Thinning 125, 249
Nematodes 68, 184
Neochlorogenic acid 140
Nettles 73, 144, 214
Noble rot 103
Nutrients, for plants 9-11, 87, 131, 139, 160, 173, 171, 182, **211-218**, 235, 240, 262
Nutrition, for us – for nutrition of plants see 'Feeding' 9, 10, **211**
Orchards 19, 26-27, 34, 37, 40, 43, 70, 134-137, 148, 151, 189, 183-184, 239, 241, 260-262
Oxalic acid 170-172
Parthenocarpy 181. 86. 267
Peach leaf curl 123, **125-129**
Peach potato aphid 127
Peaches **123**, 249
    Dwarf 123, 129
    Pruning 125, 229-230
    Rootstocks 261
    Thinning 125
    Weather 128
Pears **130.** 263, 268
    Pollination 131,132, 238
    Pruning 131, 146
    Ripening 135
    Rootstocks 135, 251
    Storage 134
    Thinning 249
Pear 'Conference' 130-131, 133-134. 242
Pear canker **137**, 264
Pear leaf blister mite **136**, 263
Pear rust **136**, 264
Pear scab **136**, 264
Peat 65-66
Pectin 164, 168, 267

pH 9, 63, 65, 109, 153, 159, 214
Pheromone trap 31, 144
Physalis peruviana, see 'Cape gooseberries'
Pine needles 65, 160
Pippin 26
Pixy 77, 139, 221, 260-261
Planting **206**
    Blackberries 49
    Blackcurrants 54
    Figs 83
    Raspberries 154
    Rhubarb 172
    Strawberries 179, 181
Plum 'Victoria' 138-139, 142-143, 242, 247
Plums 42, 74, **138**, 193, 243, 249
    Pollination 139
    Pruning 141, 221, 224, 229
    Rootstocks 261
    Storage 142
    Thinning 142, 247, 249
Plum moth **144**, 263
Plum rust **142-143**, 264
Plum sawfly **144-145**, 263
Plumcot 42
Pocket plum **143**, 264
Pome 16, 116, 132, 149, 247
Pollination **8. 238**, 268, 270
    Botany of 239
    Figs 81
    Hazelnuts 188
    Kiwis 109
    Pears 13, 132
Powdery mildew 264
    On apples 19, **34**, 244
    On grapes 103
    On quince **149**, 264
    On strawberries 176, **185**
Primocane 45, 47-48, 267
Procyanin 140

Propagation 8, **254**
    Blackberries 46, 50
    Blackcurrants 53
    Gooseberries 89
    Grapes 97, 101
    Mulberries 120
    Strawberries 177, 180
Pruning 10, **219**
    Apples 24-25
    Apricots 40
    Blackberries 48
    Blackcurrants 54
    Blueberries 66
    Cherries 70, 72
    Figs 83-85
    Gooseberries 91-93
    Grapes 97-99
    Hybrid berries 207
    Kiwis 111, 112
    Peaches 125
    Plums 141-143
    Raspberries 158-159
    Redcurrants 166-167
Pruning, formative 40, 66, 88, 91, 112, 141, 147, **219-225**. 232, 248
    Cordons 222
    Espaliers 223
    Fan trees 224
    Gooseberries 88, 91
    Open centre bush trees 220
    Plums 139, 141
Pruning, regulatory **225-231**
    Cordons and espaliers 228
    Dwarf pyramids 231
    Established fans 229
    Gooseberries 92, 95
    Redcurrants 166
Pruning saws **199-200**, 205, 233
Pruning, saws **199-200**, 225
Pruning, reasons for **219**
Pruning, with saws 199

Pruning, with secateurs 200-201
Prunings 55, 183, 203, 234-235
Prunus armenica, see 'Apricots'
Prunus avium, see 'Cherries, sweet'
Prunus cerasifera see 'Cherry plum'
Prunus cerasus, see 'Cherries, sour'
Prunus domestica, see 'Plums'
Prunus insititia see 'Damsons and Bullace'
Prunus persica, see 'Peaches and nectarines'
Prunus spinosa see 'Blackthorn'
Pyrethrum 127
Pyrus communis, see 'Pears'
Quercetin 140
Quince A 115, 131, 135, 147
Quince C 115, 131, 135, 147, 221
Quince jelly 149
Quince leaf blight **148-149**, 244
Quince powdery mildew **149**, 264
Quinces **147**,
Rapeseed oil 104, 127
Raspberries 12, 48, 50, 106, 108, **153-163**, 196, 214, 231, 254
    Picking 156
    Planting 154
    Propagation 154
    Pruning 158-159
    Thinning canes 156
    Training 155
    Weeding 159
Raspberry 'Glen Coe' **163**
Raspberry beetle 106, 157, **160-161**, 263
Raspberry cane spot **108**, 264
Receptacle 16, 86, 177, 267
Red berry mite **51**, 263
Red spider mite **31**, 113, 264

Redcurrants 58, **164-168**, 193, 197, 258, 270
    Picking 165
    Pruning 166-167
Redcurrant jelly 268
Resistance 18-24, 34, 39, 40m 45, 52, 58-60, 77, 88, 96, 123. 129, 138, 149, 153, 162, 163, 176, 243, 260
Reversion virus 52-53, 58
Rheum xhybridus, see 'Rhubarb'
Rhubarb **169-175**, 193
    Feeding 173
    Forcing 174
    Harvesting 173
    Planting 172
Rhubarb spray 127
Rhubarb triangle 170
Ribes grossularia / uva-crispa, see 'Gooseberries'
Ribes nigrum, see 'Blackcurrants'
Ribes rubrum / sativum, see 'Redcurrants'
Rock dust **216**
Root-pruning **236-237**
Rootstocks 8, 11, 15, 40, 69-70, 77, 101, 115, 123, 131, **135**, 137, 139, 147, 194-195, 220
Rosaceae 7, 15, 39, 45, 69, 77, 105, 115, 123, 130, 136, 147, 149, 153, 176
Rubus fruticosus, see 'Blackberries'
Rubus idaeus, see 'Raspberries'
Sambucus nigra, see 'Elderberries'
Saws **199-200**, 204-205
Scaldheads 47
Sclerenchyma 137, 146, 268
Sea buckthorn **190-191**
Seaweed 37, 63, 81, 96, 104, 147, 159, **212-213**, 215, 217

Seeds and sowing 259, 267
    Cape gooseberry 187
    Melons 189
Secateurs 67, 97, 158, 166, 183, **200-203**, 205, 222, 225, 231, 234
Sewage, as fertiliser 216
Shanking 104
Shield bug 51, 157, **161-162**
Silver leaf 264
    On apricots 44
    On cherries 73
    On peaches 127
    On plums **143**, 145
Sloe gin 79-80
Sloes (see also 'blackthorn') 78-80
Slugs 113, 122, 175, 182-183, 234, 263
Slugworm **74-75**, 136, 264
Snails 113, 122, 166, 175
Spindlebush 15
Splitting **28, 74**
Spur pruning, redcurrants 164, 166, gooseberries 91, **92**, 95
Squirrels 118, 188, 192
St. Julien A 40, 123, 139, 240-241
Stakes and staking 69, 78, 208, 260-261
Stink bug **51**, 157
Stony pit virus **137**
Strawberries 11, 12, 65, **176-186**
    Containers 181-182
    Cropping plan 179-181
    Forcing 183
    Maintenance 182
    Propagation 180
Strawberry leaf spot 185, 264
Strawberry powdery mildew 176, 185, 264
Strawberry red core 185, 264
Strig 56-57, 61, 165-166, 268

Suckers 48, 53-54, 90, 127, 135, 147, 149, 154-155, 189, 239, 269
Syconium 82, 86, 268
Tar oil winter wash 31, 73
Tayberries 105-108, 197
Thinning fruit **247-249**
    Apples 28
    Peaches 125
    Plums 142
    Spacings 249
Ties and tying 113, 156, **209**, 257
Tomatillo 187
Tools **198**
Torinel 40, 123, 260-261
Triploid 22, 24, 236, **245**, 268
Tummelberry 106
Urine 52, 63, **88**, 131, 183, 196, 214-215
Vaccinium corymbosum, see 'Blueberries'
Variety **7**, 47, 238, 242, 244, 245. 257, **268**
    Apple 18
    Gooseberry 88
    Quince 137
    Raspberry 153
    Rhubarb 169
Veitchberry 106
Vine weevil **67-68**, 176, **184-185**, 254
Viruses
    On apples 35
    On blackberries 51
    On raspberries 161
    On rhubarb 172
    On strawberries 185
Vitamin C 12, 52-53, 61-62, 82, 89, 106, 109, 110, 140, 149, 154, 165, 176, 177, 187, 190
Vitis vinifera, see 'Grapes'
VVA-1 123, 139, 261
Walnut blight 192

Walnuts 191
Wasps 86-87, 97, **102, 127,** 239
Wasps, parasitic 29
Water core 28
Wavit 40, 123, 139, 260, 261
Weeds and weeding 11, 37, 41, 46, 53, 64, 29, 89, 97. 110, 115, 120, 124, 132, 140, 147, 148, 154, 157, **159**, 165, 169, 172, 177, 185, 209, 210, 212, 213, 216, 217, 241, 259, **262**
Winter moth **32**, 264
Wood ash 49, 52, 81, 153, 214, 235
Woolly aphis **29-30**, 263, 264
Wormeries and wormery liquid 213, 214

ACKNOWLEDGEMENTS AND MANY THANKS

To Peter Andrews at eco-logic books for his vital help and advice.

To Steve Palmer of i-sight design for all of his hard work formatting the text.

To Mike Manson for the use of his cover photograph.

To the memory of my grandparents and parents for introducing me (intentionally or not) to the world of horticulture.

To friends, relations, colleagues and students for their enthusiasm and constant stimulation.

And to Melanie, with my love.

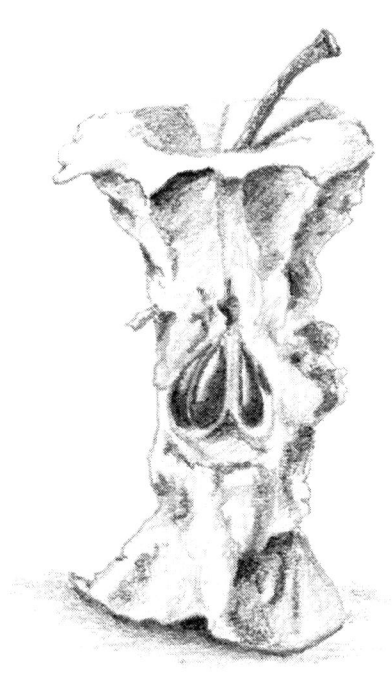